EPIC
SURF BREAKS
of the
WORLD

Explore the planet's most thrilling waves

Easy   Epic   Gnarly

CONTENTS

Clockwise from top: © Ted Grambeau; © All Canada Photos | Alamy Stock Photo; © Alan van Gysen (2)

INTRODUCTION

The first time a surfer packs up their board and sets off in search of a new wave is probably the day they realise their favourite break has become too crowded. This was how surf travel started, with adventurous wavehounds scouring the globe for virgin swell, guarding hand-marked nautical maps and saying nothing to anyone. Indeed, surfers have always had a special knack for describing waves, conditions, even the landscape, all without revealing the location (or even the continent) that they're talking about. But secrets never last – especially surf secrets.

Many would even say that when it comes to surfing, we live in a post-exploration era in which even the most remote, difficult-to-get-to breaks hold at least whispers of others having visited before you. And while some surfers mourn this loss of discovery, many more are celebrating the very compelling upside: more waves.

The truth is, surfing is more democratic than ever. There may be less in the way of surf discovery, but we are in a golden era for surf travel. Thanks to decades of surf exploration, such mythical unicorns as Cloudbreak, Thurso and Skeleton Bay are no longer just rumours. These are breaks where one single ride can be the crowning achievement of your surfing life – and today, they are accessible to anyone who has accumulated enough experience to take them on. We also now know that when time is precious, we can head to places like the Maldives or the Mentawai Islands: virtual amusement parks where perfectly curling turquoise tubes, seemingly created by Walt Disney himself, arrive with wave-pool frequency.

For the modern-day surf traveller, it is perhaps less about discovery than about seeking out that one transcendent ride, whatever your experience level. With a higher wave-count and access to a greater variety of breaks, surfers can now test themselves as never before: working to link up all of a wave's sections; to sit deeper in the tube, for longer; to ratchet upward in swell size until you catch – or get held down by – a wave so big you'll talk about it for the rest of your life.

This is precisely why even the world's most crowded breaks are still worthy surf goals. These are waves so perfect that they transcend the crowds – like the A-frame at Jeffreys Bay, or Malibu's right-hand point break, or the equally hypnotic left at Raglan. These are places where you might be lucky to snake a single wave, but where there's a decent chance that it will be the best wave of your life.

This book includes 200 of the greatest surf breaks in the world – all places where surfers regularly find that magical moment. The 50 featured breaks are the waves that have become seared into the imagination of more surfers than any others, as seen through the eyes of everyone from a Pulitzer prize-winning author to one of the world's best big-wave surfers. Many stories are told by people who have devoted their lives to searching for waves; all are vivid first-hand accounts that capture the essence of these iconic spots.

Surfing has been a part of Lonely Planet's DNA for decades, and most surfers embody the same spirit of exploration and curiosity that is at the heart of every guidebook we produce. Some Lonely Planet writers never embark on a research trip without their surfboard; many travelling surfers never leave home without their heavily annotated, dog-eared Lonely Planet guide. This book is a celebration of the fact that there has never been a better time to set off with your board-bag in search of the best wave of your life.

HOW TO USE THIS BOOK

On the following pages, we've sliced the planet up into five distinct surf regions. Within each of these regional chapters you'll find a curated collection of stories about the most famous and fascinating surf breaks in this part of the world. Alongside these stories, there's information about three additional surf spots that share some of the same characteristics as the featured break.

Each story also includes practical information about getting to the wave and making the most of your trip, as well as some intel on ideal conditions. However, surf forecasting is a pretty exact science these days, and this info is only meant as a jumping off point for a deeper dive into resources like Surfline, Magic Seaweed or, better yet, local knowledge.

At the front of the book, you'll find a colour-coded key designating difficulty levels. This will perhaps start even more arguments than the list of waves itself. Surfing is hard – like, really hard – and to call any wave easy is an oversimplification. Instead, think of an 'Easy' wave as anything from a great spot to learn, to a surf break so consistent that the ocean's unpredictability is less of a factor. 'Epic' waves are both notorious and intimidating – even for an expert – but are achievable for any truly dedicated surfer. 'Gnarly' waves are a different beast altogether: these are extremely consequential breaks that should only ever be attempted by experts, pros or Aquaman.

Clockwise from top: the endless lefts of Raglan, New Zealand; spectators crowd onto the beaches during the Oi Rio Pro competition at Saquarema, Brazil; Peruvian pro Cristobal De Col checks his boards in the Mentawai Islands

Previous spread: the legendary Mick Fanning defies gravity in Lofoten, Norway. Opening spread, clockwise from top: Australian pro Kipp Caddy at Shipstern Bluff; a sunset shortboard session at Canada's Long Beach; super-remote Skeleton Bay, Namibia; hiking to the wave in Equatorial Guinea

SKELETON BAY

The sandbars that create the perfect barrels of Skeleton Bay are in constant flux –
Will Bendix travelled to Namibia to experience the waves before they change.

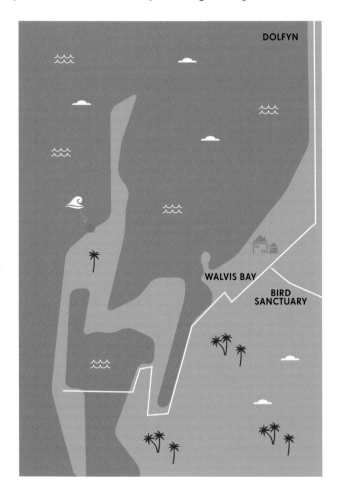

B y now I've become used to the sight of bright-pink flamingos filling the sky. The hordes of seals at the bottom of the point that seemed so hostile in the morning now feel like old friends. Even the occasional predatory jackal that stalks them along the waterline doesn't elicit much more than a sideways glance. Board under arm, I prepare to make the long trek back up the Skeleton Bay sandspit for the umpteenth time that day.

To my left lies one of the oldest deserts in the world, a vast expanse of open space mirrored by the briny Atlantic Ocean to my right. I listen to the sounds of rushing water and sand squelching underfoot that have become the familiar soundtrack to my maiden Namibian expedition. No matter how many times I trudge up the spit, though, I'm still astounded by these flawless waves that pour endlessly towards me.

There are a few other surfers scattered along the mile-long (1.6km) stretch, walking alone or in small clusters, but all headed in the same direction. We instinctively pause as a goofy-footer takes off in front of us, disappears underneath the curling lip, and is belched out of the tube 1000ft down the point before disappearing from sight again. Too tired to hoot or cheer, I put my head down and just continue walking, bracing myself against the relentless southerly wind. This very same wind brought Skeleton Bay into existence not too long ago. Ironically, it may destroy it in the future.

I'd arrived before sunrise that morning, among the first in a convoy of 4wds to make its way onto the sandy peninsula. Heavy fog made it impossible to see the surf, but I could certainly hear it: a steady boom and rumble that shook the beach incessantly. Located on the outskirts of Walvis Bay, Skeleton Bay's proximity to

"I hopped in my truck and followed a set as it peeled into the bay. When it ended, the odometer had clocked up 1.16 miles"

Namibia's largest port town is deceptive when viewed on a map, as there is no direct route to get there. Instead, you have to drive south into the desert then cut west towards the coast, leaving the thin vein of tar behind to navigate your way through a maze of crimson-coloured saltpans, before finally looping back along the shoreline.

The wave itself only awakens when powerful storms track upwards from Antarctica and spray swell towards the west coast of Africa. The phenomenon is rare and short-lived but, ever since it was first revealed in 2009, Skeleton Bay has become a holy grail of tube riding, attracting surfers from all over the world to this corner of the Namib Desert.

When the sun finally broke through the mist it vindicated the thousands of miles my companions and I had travelled to get there. A dark band of water gathered momentum, then cracked like a whip as it hit the top of the point and broke just shy of the shore. The following three waves were carbon copies of the first, each growing in size as they rifled down the sandspit at breakneck speed.

It was impossible to take in the full breadth of the spectacle from where we stood, so I actually hopped into my truck and followed one of the sets as it peeled into the bay. When it finally ended, the odometer counter had clocked up 1.16 miles (1.9km).

Looking back up the point, it all appeared surreal – the proximity to shore, the sheer length of ride, the intensity with which the waves grind into the desert. The landscape disorients you

further: an endless canvas of caramel-coloured sand waiting to swallow the chassis of Land Rovers and bury the bones of ships long run aground. But unlike the barren wilderness that surrounds it, Skeleton Bay is an infant in geological terms. 50 years ago, it didn't even exist.

According to a study published in 2003, the sandspit has changed drastically in shape and size in recent times, thanks to a slight counterclockwise shift in the prevailing wind direction since the 1970s. This resulted in sand being deposited from a new angle at a bump along the spit. As the bump grew out into the Atlantic Ocean and became more pronounced, the predominant southwesterly swells that sweep up the coast started to carve a deeper bay on the leeward side of the bump, coaxing swells to wrap further and further down the sandspit. The end result was the birth of one of the most spectacular waves in the world, like a mirage blooming in the desert. Details are vague as to who was first to surf here in earnest, but it wasn't until a magazine exposé in 2009 that Skeleton Bay's full potential was revealed. Surfers began gravitating towards its frigid tubes soon after.

The problem with mirages is that they appear perfect from a distance. Up close, it's a different story. My first attempt at catching one of these 'perfect' waves sees me cartwheeling over the falls. The second attempt is much the same: I struggle to match the speed as the swells move from deep water onto the shallow sandbank. The trick, I soon discover, is to find an 'in', a slower

BONEYARD

Author John Henry March is credited with officially coining the Skeleton Coast name, which he used as the title of his 1944 book about a shipwreck here. The name was inspired by the masses of whale and seal bones that litter the shoreline, intermingled with the jagged carcasses of wrecked ships.

From left: Hawaiian pro Koa Smith hangs in the Skeleton Bay green room; 4WD required; all-day sessions here feel like marathons. Previous page: spectacular Skeleton Bay defines remote

section where the wave momentarily backs off and gives you a chance to find your feet. After that, all you can really do is set your line and hold on for the ride of your life – or a merciless flogging.

Trying to paddle back up the point is futile. A relentless current sweeps you northwards as if on a conveyor belt. The most sensible approach is to ride a series of waves down the point (or one, if you're really lucky), then get out, walk back up to the top of the point, fling yourself into the briny ocean, and repeat the process. This is exactly what we do all day long, again and again, until the routine takes on the hypnotic effect of repeating a mantra.

The same study that traced the genesis of Skeleton Bay predicted that accelerated erosion could break up the sandspit in the future, as wave action cuts deeper and deeper into the bay. Signs of this appear late in the afternoon when the high tide pushes rivers of water up onto the sand flats, where they stretch towards the lagoon that lies on the other side of the spit. It's a strange contradiction, this wave that is simultaneously growing and eating itself.

The horizon is bloodshot by the time the swell eventually dies out. Most of us stand around in small groups, exhausted but elated, trying to fathom what we've just experienced. A Hawaiian pro likens it to running an adrenaline-filled marathon, while a videographer complains that it's impossible to film the wave properly due to its sheer length. In amongst the vehicles lies a pile of broken boards. They are the only tangible evidence left that, sometimes, mirages are real.

ORIENTATION

Type of wave // Endless sand-bottom left points.
Best conditions // Skeleton Bay works through all tides in the Southern Hemisphere winter, from June to September.
Nearest town // Walvis Bay.
Getting there // Walvis Bay is a 4-hour drive west of the Namibian capital Windoek, but it also has a small but well serviced international airport. From there it's a 20-minute drive to the wave (a 4x4 is essential).
Where to stay // Loubser's B&B is a firm favourite with surfers among the many guesthouses, B&Bs and Airbnbs.
Things to know // Water temps hover around 58°F (14°C), and the wind chill will cut through the most well insulated walrus. A good 4/3mm wetsuit is mandatory. A hoodie and booties won't go amiss either. A slightly thicker board will paddle harder and get you into a wave as early as possible.

Opposite from top: leaning into Namibia's Cape Cross wave; aprés-surf in Mozambique

MORE LIKE THIS
SKELETON BAY-STYLE WAVES

CAPE CROSS, NAMIBIA

Before Skeleton Bay stole the limelight, Namibia's best-known wave was Cape Cross, two hours' drive north of Walvis Bay. Like Skeleton Bay, it's an exceptionally long lefthander; but it's a far mellower prospect and is suitable for surfers of all abilities. Don't expect to be surfing alone, however: the wave lies inside the Cape Cross seal reserve, where thousands of the flippered beasts can be found hanging out in the waves on the tip of the peninsula. If that's a daunting prospect, the bottom of the peninsula is relatively seal-free, and sees the best part of the wave. Cape Cross is far more consistent than Skeleton Bay and only requires a medium swell to break. It prefers a low tide. Check beforehand about access, though – you may have to pay a fee to enter the seal reserve; and entering the water during mating season, when male seals are known to get feisty, is prohibited.

Nearest town // Walvis Bay

THE AFRICAN KIRRA, MOZAMBIQUE

Situated on the opposite side of the continent in Mozambique, the African Kirra is probably the closest wave to match Skeleton Bay. It's another sandspit that produces tubes close to an endlessly curling shoreline. Instead of a frigid lefthander, it's a warm, tropical right – but the nature of the wave is much the same: it grows in size and intensity as it peels down the line, and has all the potential to give you the ride of your life. The catch is that it's fickle – like, really fickle. It only comes to life during large easterly swells produced by the unpredictable tropical cyclones that bounce around the Mozambique Channel between December and March. It's located in the province of Inhambane; the best bet is to base yourself in the small beachside town of Tofo, which hosts a very good (and far more consistent) point break, then head north to check out the Kirra when the elements align.

Nearest town // Tofo

PUERTECILLO, CHILE

Lying 100 miles (160km) southwest of the capital Santiago, Puertecillo was one of Chile's best-kept secrets for decades, thanks to its harsh geography and the terrible roads to get there. The dredging lefthander requires a huge swell to wrap into the protected bay before it starts working – but when this happens, it produces clean, sand-bottom tubes that run for long enough to rival the best spots in the world. Originally, the only way to stay at Puertecillo was to camp rough after acquiring permission from an owner of one of the ranches that surround the bay, but nowadays there are a few lodges catering to travellers in the area. The wave was threatened by a marina development in 2014, which saw local surfers rallying to protect the break.

Nearest town // Pichilemu

COTTON TREES

Nicholai Lidow stumbled upon this wave off Robertsport, Liberia, almost by accident. Since then, he has made a powerful documentary about the area, and even put down Liberian roots.

The Robertsport coastline looked promising on the map, a series of points wrapping around a cape and eventually reaching a lake mouth. But I had spent enough time looking for waves in West Africa to have low expectations. I had been disappointed before; in fact, I seemed to be constantly striking out.

It was 2005, my first trip to Liberia, and heavy rains had washed out the only road into the capital. I ditched my car next to a squad of UN peacekeepers, who were hauling dirt to make the route passable again. It was a long hike into town along the shore of Lake Piso. I skirted the edge of the jungle-swathed Cape Mount and passed the old settler homes built by so-called 'free Blacks' from the US, who joined the locals here in the 1830s.

I climbed the hill above town, passing the Baptist church and the ruins of a once-luxurious hotel. As the ocean came into view, I expected the familiar slow, shapeless swell. Instead, I saw long period lines – lines so perfect that the waves almost seemed to stand still: deep-blue barrels stacked one after another.

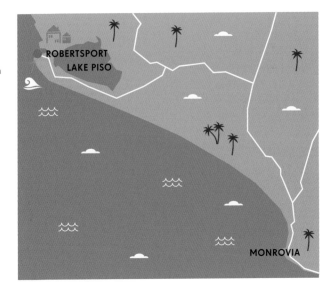

Funny thing is, I hadn't come to Liberia looking for surf, specifically, but I had lugged my 6'0" Stamps thruster all the way from Hermosa Beach, hoping to score during a year travelling around Africa. I had actually come to Liberia to meet up with some recently returned refugees, who I'd shared a house with in Ghana during a college internship. During that summer of 2003, as the war in Liberia reached its climax, I travelled around Ghana with the refugees while they tried to locate their families. When I graduated from college, the war in Liberia was over and my friends were trying to reconnect with a homeland they hadn't seen in more than a decade. When a job offer fell through at the last minute, I flew to Liberia. Not long after, I was living there.

From the top of the hill I stared in disbelief at the break I would later know to be Cotton Trees, named after the two giant trees that stand watch from the edge of the jungle. I couldn't wait to paddle out. When I did, I fount the takeoff was forgiving, with an outer boil that provided a chip shot before the wave ledged in shallow water. The bottom turn, however, required some nerve, and I decided to just ignore the exposed boulders. A long, rippable wall gave me a chance to catch my breath before a double-up section threw another tube at me.

Despite how journalists make it sound, Liberia is not 'war-torn'. Yes, there was a war. But it ended in 2003, and more than half of the current population wasn't even born back then. The sleepy town of Robertsport is about as far from a war zone as you can get. Ironically, the history of surfing in Robertsport is actually tied to the war – and can be traced to a man named Alfred Lomax.

In the dying days of the conflict, rebels sacked the town with the plan of using the lake mouth to receive arms shipments. The townspeople fled into the bush to avoid the rampage. Alfred, barely a teenager at the time, escaped down the beach, scampering across boulders and swimming across rivers to travel the 70 miles (112km) to the capital city, Monrovia. But the situation there was also desperate. Alfred raided the port with thousands of other starving people, looting whatever food was available. He scooped spilled rice off the ground with his hands and ate it raw. During his days of scouring the port, he spotted a bodyboard in an open shipping container, wrapped with a picture of a smiling kid sliding across a wave. He grabbed the bodyboard and kept it hidden, and when the war ended a few months later, he returned to Robertsport, board in hand, and taught himself how to 'slide'.

I met Alfred about a year after that, and by then he was already ripping. He took pity on me sleeping on the beach under a disused refugee tarpaulin (back then, there weren't any hotels or guesthouses), and invited me to stay in his family's home. He also showed me the waves beyond Cotton Trees. Fisherman's Point, near the centre of town, does an admirable interpretation of Skeleton Bay; on the smaller days, it produces Malibu-style walls peeling for over 3000ft (914m). Cassava Point (now known as Shipwrecks) holds up to triple-overhead.

PRE-WAR PIONEERS

Legendary surf explorers Kevin Naughton and Craig Peterson were probably the first people to surf Robertsport when they passed through in the 1970s. Their film, *The Far Shore*, shows them racing across perfect chest-high walls. They never name the spot, but the wave is Cotton Trees. One shot of the beach shows a luxury hotel and sunbathers. The hotel was looted and razed during the war; only the walls and foundation remain.

Clockwise from top left: Robertsport coastline; casualties of war; you'll find several decent breaks within walking distance of Cotton Trees. Previous page: Robertsport's local surf scene is on the rise

Almost all Liberia's beaches are pristine and secluded, places where sea turtles nest and red colobus monkeys saunter along the sand. There are some points near the Sierra Leone border that are still ripe for exploration.

But honestly, since my first visit to Robertsport I haven't had much motivation to look elsewhere. After a few months in Liberia I returned home and started telling people about Robertsport. My good friend Britton Caillouette, an aspiring filmmaker at the time, immediately saw the potential for a documentary. Next thing we knew, the Malloy Brothers were on board, and Dan Malloy and cinematographer Dave Homcy had joined the team. A week later, photographer Ted Grambeau signed on. We camped on the beach for a month and shot the film on old wind-up Bolex cameras because there was no electricity. The film we ended up making, *Sliding Liberia*, tells Alfred's story and the stories of others who survived the war and now see great potential for their country.

We left a few surfboards for the kids, and since then a handful of travelling surfers have added to the quiver. It's been 13 years since we released the film and now there's a committed group of locals who surf with increasing skill and style. For a while, the town seemed poised to take off as a surf destination. But Ebola struck in 2014 and the surf-travellers stopped coming. I, however, will never stop coming to Robertsport.

Nowadays, I run a solar business in Liberia. A few hundred houses in Robertsport get light from our systems, so I always have an excuse to visit. Most of the time I surf the waves alone, which is a joy. The locals, of course, hope that surfers will return, that the old hotel will reopen and bring new jobs and opportunities. And the truth is, for the first time in my life, I actually want nothing more than a crowded lineup.

"We camped on the beach for a month and shot the film on an old wind-up Bolex because there was no electricity"

ORIENTATION

Type of wave // Sand-bottom left-hand point break.
Best conditions // All tides, any time of year, but transitions between dry and rainy seasons (April–May and September–October) offer the best combo of swell and wind.
Nearest town // Robertsport.
Getting there // The capital, Monrovia, has an international airport; Robertsport is a 4-hour drive away.
Where to stay // Hippo Resort is a new development in Robertsport, just steps from the paddle-out for Cotton Trees. If the waves are flat, Hippo's can organise lake and fishing excursions (hippoliberia@yahoo.com). Nana Lodge offers colourful wooden cabins with great views.
Things to know // You'll need a visa to enter Liberia unless you're an ECOWAS (Economic Community of West African States) citizen.

Opposite: coastal life along the Cape Verde peninsula, Senegal

MORE LIKE THIS
WEST AFRICA'S BEST BREAKS

MAYUMBA, GABON

The southern coast of Gabon offers some sand-bottom point breaks that look eerily similar to Robertsport, with long, racing walls and clean tubes. The adventurous traveller will find empty waves, rough roads through pristine forests, and incredible wildlife. An estimated 30% of the world's population of leatherback turtles nest on the beach in front of the peeling waves, and humpback whales mate just outside the lineup. Elephants and buffalo have been known to patrol the beach, and gorillas and chimpanzees inhabit the surrounding forest. North of Mayumba is a left that peels for some 5000ft (1524m) near the village of Olendé. This wave was accidentally documented when a National Geographic expedition in the region emerged from the jungle to find hippos bodysurfing the waves. None of these spots is easy to reach, but Gabon offers perhaps the best combination of eco-adventure, wildlife spotting and wave hunting of anywhere in the world.

Nearest town // Mayumba

CAPE VERDE, SENEGAL

One of the most stylish and lively cities on the continent, Dakar also boasts some excellent waves. Rocky point breaks peel off either side of N'gor Island, which can be accessed by chartering a dugout canoe to cross the channel. If you're lucky, you may score the perfect tubes that dredge in front of Ouakam mosque. But those are just the name-brand spots. The peninsula boasts dozens of other reef and beach breaks. All of these spots were pioneered by Patina Ndiaye, who taught himself how to surf in the 1980s after seeing some tourists riding the waves. Like the old timers in California, Patina braved the chilly water with oilskins and thermal underwear until he could get his hands on a wetsuit. Most of Cape Verde's breaks are easily accessible, and with one of the largest swell windows in the world, it's always possible to find waves somewhere on the peninsula. The hardest part about surfing in this area is choosing a spot and paddling out with a bellyfull of *thiéboudienne* (fish stew) – and maybe a hangover from one of Dakar's music clubs.

Nearest town // Dakar

BURACO, ANGOLA

Like Liberia, Angola is best known for its war. But also like Liberia, the war here ended a long time ago, and travelling around the country is now fairly safe – if you take care to avoid the landmines. A few hours' drive from the capital, Luanda, is a sand-bottom left-hand beach break near the village of Buraco. The wave requires a fairly large swell to get interesting, but with enough energy in the water there are plenty of barrels and long walls to be had. If the swell is not enough for Buraco, you might find some tubes at Shipwrecks, just a short drive to the south. You'll need a 4x4 to navigate through deep sand and across the salt-mud of a nearby lagoon, and the challenges of reaching the waves are not limited to the road conditions: Luanda regularly tops the list of the most expensive city in the world in terms of living costs and accommodation. Fortunately, things get more affordable once you're out of town. And for those with the endurance to head further south, Angola offers a wealth of secret spots that rival the best waves on earth.

Nearest town // Buraco

JEFFREYS BAY

South Africa's trophy break serves up a uniquely long and fast ride. Andy Davis says just one perfect wave at 'J-Bay' will leave you more satisfied than an entire session elsewhere.

It was crowded. J-Bay during contest season is always crowded. The event had been called off for the day and it seemed everyone and their brother wanted one last wave before the sun set. The number of quality surfers in the lineup was making things even more difficult. I inserted myself amongst a group of older locals, some of whom I knew quite well. Kanoa Igarashi lurked on the outside and Owen Wright and Lakey Peterson sat further up the point on our inside. The waves were not perfect, but still a solid 4ft–5ft on the sets.

Pros tried to snag bombs, while still showing a bit of respect for the old bulls. As another set approached, the pack started positioning. Deon, a well-known local, broke and paddled purposefully and snagged it. But behind that was a bigger one. There was some jostling, the pros circled, the locals tried to assert themselves – but no one had yet claimed it. I turned as the wave slipped under Wright and Peterson, and I just sort of slid into it. Igarashi even looked on hungrily from the shoulder. This was it. Because in J-Bay, all you really need is one wave.

Like so many South African surfers, J-Bay was my first real surf trip. This little piece of magic up the coast had been ingrained in my consciousness through countless magazine articles and movie segments. I'd been expanding my universe in slowly increasing concentric circles around Cape Town, but it was time to pop the bubble and see for myself what everyone was talking about.

I manoeuvred my board on through the back door and on to the reclining front seat of my student ride, a navy Nissan Sentra 1400, gifted to me by a benevolent uncle. I set off, solo, towards Jeffreys Bay. The wave itself is set in an amphitheatre of aloe-covered dunes, hardly seeming to belong to South Africa. But just behind

the famous wave, you're back firmly in the Republic: functional face-brick homes, mostly inhabited by conservative, Christian Afrikaans families. Years of exposure to feral, pleasure-seeking surf nomads has left an indelible mark on the community. Not always in a good way.

Named after a Captain Jeffreys, who wrecked his ship on the beach here in the 1840s and took a liking to the place, Jeffreys Bay was once just a small township with a famous fish-and-chips stand. The area's surf potential was first surveyed by South African surfing pioneer John 'The Oom' Whitmore ('oom' is Afrikaans for uncle) in the late 1950s, during a business trip between Port

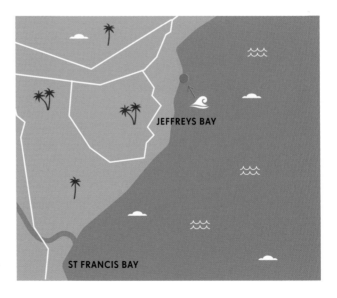

"Despite the fact that I'd surfed J-Bay my entire life, this particular wave felt like the only one that had ever mattered."

Elizabeth and Cape Town. However, Whitmore never had time to paddle out and claim the first ride himself. In 1961, Bruce Brown and his *Endless Summer* team lucked onto the perfect but more fickle Bruce's Beauties setup in nearby St Francis Bay, and they told a group of surfers in East London. When a crew of Cape Town surfers led by Gus Gobel and Brian McLarty went looking for Bruce's Beauties, they took a quick detour to hit up the legendary fish shop in Jeffreys Bay – they actually thought they were surfing Bruce's, when in fact they were discovering J-Bay.

Surfboard design innovations have made it possible to surf J-Bay from Boneyards at the top through Supertubes, Impossibles, Salad Bowls, Tubes, Point and, finally (if you can get that far), Albatross. If you do connect J-Bay from top to bottom, the ride will take over two minutes to complete and will be an absolute leg-shaker. Kelly Slater once said he had a 2½-minute ride there. Every name in surfing has moved through the place – Mickey Dora, Bunker Spreckels, Shaun Tomson, Tom Curren, Andy Irons, Steph Gilmore and, of course, Mick Fanning. It became the most famous surf break in the world when Fanning famously punched a great white shark here during a live televised contest in 2015.

Where J-Bay really sets itself apart from other historically significant breaks like Bells or Malibu is the way its centrepiece, Supertubes, provides the perfect canvas for technical advancements

in the sport. It's where performance continues to be redefined and it's the reason J-Bay has become such an important stop on the tour.

Indeed, there is no wave I've ridden that matches the pace of Supertubes. As it stood up on the reef that day during the tour, I whistled through its sections, incredulous I was making it. My turns felt incredible, even though they probably looked much less so from the stands. As I came out of another off-the-top crank, I saw it walling up down the line towards the section they call Impossibles. That section was wailing ahead so I pumped twice and took a safer highline to make sure I made it. I was through the section and out into Salad Bowls, already lining up the next turn in the bowl. I was smiling ear to ear, heart thumping in my chest. Despite the fact that I'd surfed J-Bay my entire life, this particular wave felt like the best I'd ever ridden, the only wave that had ever mattered.

Eventually, the canvas stretched enough for a few small, effortless cutbacks, depositing me at the bottom of the wall before I was finally shut down. But I couldn't ask anything more from this wave.

I turned left to see the marker pole on the beach for the tiny keyhole exit point. There are only a few small gullies along the whole stretch of razor-barnacled reef that allow a dignified exit. I dropped to my belly and rode the foam between the rocks, right up onto the sand. It was an entirely satisfying one-wave session. But a single wave in J-Bay fills the stoke tank to the brim.

Clockwise from top left: surfers from all over the world bring their A-game to J-Bay; Western Cape Province is rich with world-class waves; downtime diversions; the winding walkway to Supertubes. Previous page: Aussie CT pro Julian Wilson shows how it's done at Jeffreys Bay

SURF AND SAFARI

South Africa has a lot to offer when it comes to adventure. Within an hour's drive of J-Bay you can do one of the world's highest bungee jumps (708ft/216m) at the Bloukrans River Bridge in Tsitsikamma. Or take a safari: view wild elephants at the Addo Elephant National Park, see the big five at Shamwari Game Reserve, or camp and explore by 4x4 at Baviaanskloof Wilderness Area.

ORIENTATION

Type of wave // Right point break, over basalt lava rock.
Best conditions // Pushing mid-high tide.
Nearest town // Jeffreys Bay.
Getting there // There are regular flights to Port Elizabeth from Johannesburg, Cape Town and Durban. Jeffreys Bay is a seven-hour drive from Cape Town and 12 hours from Durban.
Where to stay // You can't do any better than African Perfection guesthouse, looking down on Supertubes.
Things to know // Take your regular shortboard and a step up in case it gets proper. Figuring out the keyhole exits is important, as barnacle-covered rocks will shred your feet and board. Aprés-surf – often alongside the world's best surfers – can be found at Nina's, just behind the break.

*Opposite: the right-hand point break
at Victoria Bay, just outside George,
is one of South Africa's best*

MORE LIKE THIS
J-BAY'S NEIGHBOURS

VICTORIA BAY

A little nook in the coastline between
the towns of George and Wilderness,
Vic Bay sits in a micro-bay cleft into the
hillside, with a picturesque little beach, a
campsite amongst the coastal milkwoods
and cute holiday houses running down
along the point. The southern headland
juts out into the ocean, creating a perfect
little right-hand point break that gathers
loads of swell and can hold up to 8–10ft.
Vic Bay is a popular stop for surfers in
need of a halfway wiggle while on the
road between Cape Town and J-Bay. It
can get crowded, so mind your manners
and be nice to the locals.
Nearest town // George

SEAL POINT

Seal Point is J-Bay's cousin, a long rock-
and-boulder shelf at the top of Cape St
Francis. The wave is less perfect than
the one at Jeffreys, but has a wider swell
window. About halfway down, it also
has a large rock, known as the Full Stop,
that tends to make things interesting
for both surfers and spectators. Seal's
beach, where the point wave ends, can
also deliver excellent A-frame peaks and
barrels. The area is truly blessed with
quality and abundance on the surf front.
There is a plethora of accommodation
on offer, from camping amongst the
windswept coastal scrub to established
Airbnbs.
Nearest town // Cape St Francis

LUBANZI BEACH

Lubanzi Beach might not hold South
Africa's best waves, but it has a good
claim to being one of the country's most
unspoiled and beautiful surf spots.
Located in the Eastern Cape Province,
about three hours further east than the
powerful right-handers of Nahoon Reef
near East London, this is an almost
forgotten part of the country that still runs
to ancient rhythms and without modern-
day influences. Named after the Lubanzi
Xhosa Village that is perched above it, the
beach has a variety of rip bowls that tend
to form in the nook of the rocky headlands
positioned at each end of the 2500ft-long
(800m) beach. You'll probably be sharing
the wave with more dolphins and whales
than surfers – and yes, great whites are
an issue in this part of the country. It's not
advisable to surf at dawn or dusk, or on
your own. However, this is a raw, beautiful
and dramatic beach that provides a rare
retreat from the 'real' world.
Nearest town // Coffee Bay

HILTON BEACH

*Tel Aviv's vibrant and welcoming Levant surf scene
helped Paul Evans make sense of a complex culture.*

'**O**ut here, the law of the desert rules', a local man tells me. 'The biggest and loudest survive, the meek and mild perish.' It's my first day in Israel and I'm at the Shuk Hapishpeshim street market in Jaffa, the southern part of the Tel Aviv–Yafo municipality. The man was trying to explain the chaotic approach to queuing here – and it sounded an awful lot like what I'd been told about Israeli lineup etiquette.

The following morning, I'm suiting up looking out at the waves off Hilton Beach. It's Saturday – Shabbat, as it's known here, a day of rest – so it's a busy scene in and out of the water. Volleyball games stretch out on the sand, boardwalk bars are serving up umbrella drinks and DJ beats, and throngs of surfers of all ages and abilities bob around in the Mediterranean Sea.

It's late January, and following a storm front that rattled through the previous day, the sunshine is warm and the water a pleasant 68°F (20°C). An eastern Mediterranean groundswell, born of a deceptively generous area of fetch between North Africa and the

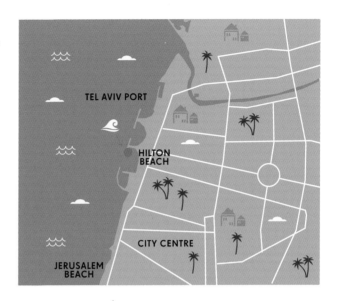

Greek islands, is on a collision course with the breakwater, built to protect the tourists who frolic on this coveted stretch of sand. Sets smash into the wall, sending spray high in the air, catching the bright morning sunshine. But a gap in the breakwater allows plenty of swell to continue shoreward, putting on a slight bend towards rocky sandbars. Waves stand up on an outside A-frame peak, before blue head-high peelers taper off in each direction towards the shallows.

It's crowded, but the locals are welcoming, stoked to share a slice of Israeli surf culture. I paddle out, aiming for what seems like a slightly less chaotic part of the lineup. It's a classic city-beach break, in which you just manoeuvre about trying to snaffle a bomb from the peak, highline a few sections, and try to avoid collisions.

Israel is surprisingly wave rich. About 30 minutes' drive north of this part of Tel Avivi is Netanya, site of the annual World Surf League event. Even further north, just shy of the Lebanese border, spots like Haifa and Nahariya offer punchier, hollower peaks. But Hilton is the epicentre of the Levant surf scene, with a thriving crew of surfers making a tight-knit but welcoming surf community. It is one of the most interesting slices of surf culture in the Middle East.

The Hilton seafront is home to surf schools, shops and local board-shapers. And there's plenty to do between sessions right on shore. In many ways, it feels like any southern European, Mediterranean spot: the colour of the water, the vegetation, the bleached-out afternoon light – it all feels very familiar. But a bit of barbed wire here, a very well-armed patrol there quickly remind you that despite the short flight in, you're a very long way from home indeed.

A few days later, I'm checking the waves at Hilton with a group of local surfers when a heavily armed border patrol vehicle pulls up. Looking us over, the driver immediately demands something in Hebrew of two of the group. They reply sharply and the patrol peels away. 'He asked them their names because they look Arab', explains one of my new friends. 'They can tell by the accent.'

To say Israel is a complicated place is an understatement, and its surf culture reflects this complexity. Surfing was in fact a very secular refuge of sorts. Indeed, it was conflict that gave rise to wave riding in these parts. American teenager Dorian 'Doc' Paskowitz arrived in 1956 to enlist in the Israeli army to fight in the Suez Crisis. Unimpressed, the enrolling officer turned him away. The story goes that a disgruntled Doc decided to let off steam by grabbing the board he'd brought from the US and paddling out at Frishman Beach, just south of Hilton. A pair of lifeguards saw him, and the Israeli stoke seed was sewn.

When some chunky southerlies blew in and ruined the swell, I decided to check out the adjoining historic city of Jaffa. The city's port has been in use for over 4000 years, and is said to have been established by Noah's son Japeth after the Great Flood. Just outside are a series of ominous whitewater-fringed rocks where, according to Greek mythology, Andromeda's naked body was sacrificed to a sea monster sent by Poseidon. But there's also surf here.

Jaffa's West Beach was in fact grooming a southwest windswell

SURFING FOR PEACE

When Doc Paskowitz visited Israel in 2005, he brought surfboards to donate to the fledgling Israeli/Arab surf community, and Surfing 4 Peace was born. In 2007, Doc and local Israeli Arthur Rashkovan made a defiant trip over the border into Gaza to deliver boards to Palestinian surfers, while also securing boards for the first ever female Palestinian surfers. S4P and Gaza Surf Relief's efforts are featured in the documentary *God Went Surfing With The Devil*.

Clockwise from top left: Hilton waves; Israeli surf culture; fun lefthanders in Jaffa. Previous page, from left: Tel Aviv from above; Hilton Beach

"As I checked the waves with a group of locals, a heavily armed border patrol vehicle pulled up"

into long, shapely left-hand walls with occasional hollow sections. I'd surfed in front of castles and temples before, but this Holy Land backdrop was something truly special.

After a day riding the waves, I was back in Tel Aviv before the sun set, ready to experience the city's legendary nightlife. But the swell was supposed to pick up in the morning, and the winds were forecast to be offshore so I made a pledge to proceed with caution. As well, hedonism here comes with a bit of an edge – some of the deadliest bomb attacks have taken place in the region's nightclubs.

A local surfer friend explained that it's best to keep it low-key, so we drank street beers near Hilton after dinner, then cut a few blocks along Ben Yehuda Street and ducked into a tiny yoghurt shop. But I was then ushered to a corner doorway where a security guard pulled back a curtain. Behind it, two more guys held a door open. I was standing on a gangway above a throbbing dancefloor. Several hours later, my night was winding down just as a few dawn patrollers were paddling out.

Of course, my need for surf was stronger than my need for sleep, and it was not long before I was back at the beach. The fresh 4ft swell was fizzing along shapely sandbars with renewed vigour, and the Tel Aviv skyline glistened in sunshine. As the biggest set of the morning stood up on the outside bar, the crowd jockeyed for position. But it rolled underneath them and headed in my direction. I spun and dropped in, surfing it all the way in, until my fins ground along Hilton's soft sand for the last time.

ORIENTATION

Type of wave // Beach break peaks with sand and rock bottom.

Best conditions // Winter groundswells in the 3ft–5ft range, but will work year-round on windswells.

Nearest town // Tel Aviv.

Getting there // Fly into Ben Gurion Airport, a short taxi ride away. Expect heavy security checks on both arrival and departure.

Where to stay // If the hotel that gives Hilton Beach its name blows your budget, there are plenty of Airbnbs, hostels and cheaper hotels a few blocks back.

Things to know // Like much of the Mediterranean, December to April is prime season for surf. Bring a small-wave shortboard, and a 3/2 full or springsuit for winter.

*Clockwise from top: surf's up near
Alexandria, Egypt; taking a stroll
along Alexandria's Corniche;
Turkey's rugged Alanya coastline*

MORE LIKE THIS
MEDITERRANEAN SURF HUBS

ALEXANDRIA, EGYPT

Alexandria has a burgeoning surf community (mostly made up of a handful of locals); the playful waves and highly photogenic backdrop of this ancient seat of civilisation were featured in Taylor Steele's 2006 film *Sipping Jetstreams*. Exposed to long-range winter swells from the west and north, regular northwest onshore winds create enough fetch to produce relatively consistent waves, even in the summer months. Just to the west of central Alexandria, Agami is the swell-puller, exposed to most of the activity in this part of the Mediterranean, while nearby Shatby is a more protected spot, best targeted during bigger, stormier conditions.

Nearest town // Alexandria

ALANYA, TURKEY

As in so much of the Mediterranean, the surf season in Alanya fires up after the summer-holiday tourists leave. December through April sees most consistent waves, and often brings more size (sometimes topping 6ft). Located about midway along the southern Anatolian coast, on what's known as the Turkish Riviera, Alanya has a series of wide beach breaks either side of a rocky peninsula headland. The region is open to most swell directions in the eastern Med, particularly from west and southwesterly wind belts. And when you've had your fill of Med shred, Turkey even has waves on its Black Sea coast, near the Bulgarian border.

Nearest town // Alanya

IKARIA, GREECE

Sitting pretty in the eastern Mediterranean, the Greek island of Ikaria is often referred to as the 'island of longevity'. On average, the locals here live 10 years longer than most Westerners, and many believe this is down to their connection with the sea – a source of food and of general well-being. Messakti is the epicentre of the island's burgeoning surf community, where a lone surfing school combines surf with activities like yoga or Brazilian jiu-jitsu. Sets here are generated by windswell and break on a sandy beach. Waves are a little inconsistent, but those with time will enjoy kicking back and waiting for the swell to arrive in this very laid-back corner of Greece, shrouded in legend and with steep valleys, rocky cliffs and dreamy coves.

Nearest town // Messakti Beach

ANCHOR POINT

Matt Pruett went to central Morocco's Taghazout point break to drown his sorrows in surf. But it was a little faith and friendship that changed him.

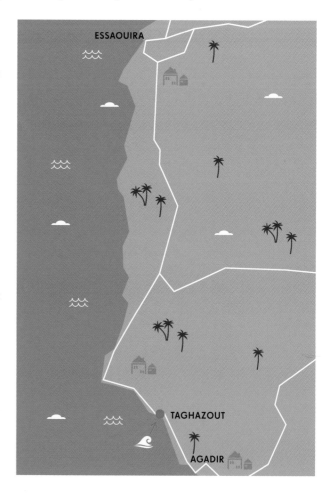

Simo points. 'Whenever you see whitewater breaking off that rock way out there, you know this wave will be... Please, one moment, my friend...' Then he stops, mid-conversation, closes his eyes, bows and starts whispering 'Allahu akbar... Allahu akbar...' It's a knee-jerk reaction to the Adhan (call to prayer) blasting out from a distant minaret. I give him his space and turn toward the North Atlantic, its emerald sets backlit by the fierce Moroccan sun. The cool Harmattan trade winds blow back what's left of my receding hairline. I can't smell anything – my sinuses are too clogged with dust, sand and detritus from the reef break we just surfed, somewhere on the fringe of Taghazout, my last session of a month-long surf bender in North Africa.

Behind me, everything is dying, dead or fossilised. The colour of the rock bleeds into the colour of the beach, which bleeds into the colour of the buildings. Toward the sea, birds are swooping, fish are jumping, killer whales are blowing plumes of spray. Three minutes pass. Then Simo picks right up where he left off: '... at least 6ft. It's good we surfed before the tide got too low.'

Over the past month, Simo and I have scored every known spot in this zone: Anchor Point, with its four spacious barrel sections interspersed by powerful horseshoe bowls; Killers Bay, its easily triangulated takeoff zone guaranteeing a clean line through the inside; Boilers, its feathery lips begging to be smashed; Drakula, Mysteries, the Slab – and even a few creepier ones like the urchin-coated deathtrap we'd visited the day before. Making our way up the cliff towards Simo's van – staying vigilant to avoid scorpions, cacti, camel dung and the odd rogue puff adder – I start feeling sad. By the time we reach the car park, I'm straight-up sulking.

I feel like a child who refuses to leave the park. And in that moment, it was hitting me especially hard that there was not really anything waiting for me back in the US, except for a recession. Specifically, the death-rattle of print media, my professional sphere for the better part of the last two decades. As a freelancer, I had come to feel untethered and confused, constantly asking myself 'what next?'. With no prospects on the horizon and little faith in myself, I sold all my possessions to fund one last surf trip. I vowed to clear out the cobwebs, eradicate the static, and put myself in a positive headspace. I packed no phone, laptop or camera – all things I associated with what I did for a living – instead bringing just a backpack and a quiver of surfboards.

As a surf destination, Morocco is well-worn territory. When American soldiers left their surfboards on the beaches in the 1950s, a latency period followed as spooked locals left these strange industrial wings alone. But as surfing expanded globally, and the bohemian European counterculture ventured down the West African coast, it was the Moroccans themselves who realized the potential of their swell-exposed coastline. In 1994, King Mohammed VI helped found the Rabat Surf Club, and even sponsored a Moroccan team to compete in the World Amateur Championships.

Since then, the local surf population has grown exponentially. Naturally, legions of surf schools, surf tours and surf camps (some operated by foreigners, but many by Berber or Arab entities) are posted up in and around Taghazout. With open exposure to nearly every conceivable wintertime northwest swell churning across the North Atlantic, central Morocco lights up whenever a massive low-pressure system parks itself off North America's Eastern Seaboard, delivering groomed power. Meanwhile, high pressure over Europe ensures predominantly offshore winds for the many right-hand points

GENTLE GIANTS

Two miles (3km) north of Taghazout, a popular right-hand point break called Killers is named for the pods of orca that pass by the bay during their annual migration. One oft-told local legend is that of a surfer who, after losing consciousness in the lineup, was lifted out of the water by one of these fearsome giants and carried shoreward, where he was then rescued. No fewer than a hundred people claimed to have witnessed the incident.

Clockwise from top left: Taghazout locals hit the beach at sunset; the area has waves for every ability; cool colours and camels along the Moroccan coast. Previous page: the dramatic Taghazout coastline is dotted with right-hand point breaks

tucked under Cape Ghir. Basically, if there's a big winter storm across the Atlantic, it will be pumping in Morocco a week later.

But in Morocco, there's just as much magic on land as at sea. It's a truly enchanting and somewhat mysterious place, where creativity and faith sort of meld into an otherwordly landscape. Prehistoric architecture, bustling bazaars and an evocative culture complement the cosy wintertime weather.

But now, the party's over. My credit card is nearly maxed out. My boards are shredded to pieces from the barnacle-encrusted rocks. And, frankly, my ageing carcass can't take any more abuse. Sitting in Simo's favourite cafe post-surf, enjoying one last feast of tagine and mint tea before heading to the airport, he senses my dread: 'My father once tell me', he says, '"we make plans. God laughs."' Have faith, my friend.'

Then Simo starts citing Kalimah, the first of the Five Pillars of Islam. My eyes glaze over until he finally says it: why don't I just stay – live here in Taghazout and work as a surf guide, like him. I could earn just enough to pay my bills back home and spend the rest of my adult life eating healthy food, breathing clean air, chauffeuring tourists around the coast and surfing my infidel brains out. Forget ambition or identity, my calling or my potential. I could trade it all for simply existing.

And I actually consider it. But then something happens. I don't know if somebody's dosed my tagine with cobra venom or hashish. Or if the sublimating Moroccan music – mostly *bendir* drum and *oud* lute – have cast some sort of spell on me. Maybe I've simply absorbed a bit of my friend's faith by osmosis; perhaps Simo's afternoon *salat* had subliminal powers. Whatever it is, a voice inside my head whispers: 'Go home, dig deep, stay the course.'

I embrace Simo, thanking him for his friendship and his guidance. I bequeath the remainder of my surf gear to him. I'm not three hours off the plane when a job offer comes in.

"In Taghazout, the colour of the rock bleeds into the colour of the beach and the colour of the buildings"

ORIENTATION

Type of wave // Right-hand point break.
Best conditions // Anchor Point only works on a low tide. A major winter storm off the US East Coast will cause Morocco's west- and northwest-facing breaks to fire.
Nearest town // Taghazout.
Getting there // Fly into Agadir-Al Massira Airport, which is about a 30-minute drive from Taghazout.
Where to stay // Several full-service surf resorts like Surf Maroc and Moroccan Surf Adventures operate out of Taghazout, and they typically employ the area's most experienced local surfers as guides.
Things to know // Morocco's coastline has the straightest exposure in the North Atlantic. Generally, the bigger a northwest swell, the more options. Water temps bottom out at 60°F (15°C) in the winter, so a 3/2mm fullsuit is all you'll ever need. Booties protect against rocks and urchins.

Opposite: the untapped coastline of the Western Sahara promises good swell and empty lineups

MORE LIKE THIS
EPIC DESERT POINT BREAKS

DAKHLA, WESTERN SAHARA

South of Morocco, the sparsely populated, still-disputed territory of the Western Sahara features an abundance of untapped, unnamed waves and, like Morocco, some truly world-class right-hand point breaks. Dakhla, on a sheltered peninsula, is one of the best. The Canary Islands do cause some swell blockage for Western Saharan waves. But for those thirsting (no pun intended) for a raw, off-the-grid experience, the Saharan coastline is a North African desert adventure like no other. An experienced guide is imperative, because the country can be dangerous. At most points there are no buildings, no running water, no people and no law. Just rocks and dust, carcasses, saltwater, and one road.
Nearest town // Dakhla

CHICAMA, PERU

Chicama's bleak, foggy desert ambience might have something to do with its failure to launch. The left-hand point break of Chicama, located in one of Peru's arid zones between Lima and Ecuador, was once hailed as the 'longest wave in the world'. And who knows, even in the age of Skeleton Bay, maybe it still is. There are certainly more thrilling, more powerful, more barrelling left-hand points in the country that divert most surfers from this obsolete classic. But when monster south-southwesterly swells from the Southern Hemisphere do their thing, Chicama is still as tantalisingly long as it's ever been – around 5000ft (1524m) from takeoff to jetty. And the wind pattern is primo. Limited accommodation and challenging access add a fun sense of adventure to the mix.
Nearest town // Puerto Chicama

SALINA CRUZ, MEXICO

Easily one of the most popular surfing destinations in the world, with guides and several full-service surf camps operating in and around southern Mexico's Bahías de Huatulco region, Salina Cruz is pretty much a sure thing between April and October – barring any despicable 'devil wind' patterns. Even maxed-out, XXL swell energy from the Southern Hemisphere receives a warm welcome at no less than a dozen divinely long, sand-bottomed, right-hand point breaks – some fast and hollow, others slow and mellow – all scattered within an hour's drive of each other. Steel yourself for 1500ft-long waves, long walks back up the point, dry desert air and the merciless Mexican sunshine.
Nearest town // Salina Cruz

FLAMEBALLS

An obscure wave off Madagascar is far more serious than its name implies.
But Andy Davis says that knowing how it got its name will keep you on your toes.

The whitewashed tomb of Zerado is adorned with his most prized possessions: an old boombox, his speargun and the wooden paddle he used to steer his pirogue on his daily fishing excursions. In this part of Madagascar, the Vezo tribe of semi-nomadic fisherfolk have strange burial customs. Every few years they ritualistically unearth the bones of their ancestors and take them for a tour of the village, ostensibly to show how things have changed, but also to commune with their departed loved ones and lobby them for blessings and guidance from the other world.

Southern Madagascar is alive with strange experiences and superstitions. And one of its finest experiences – sometimes so fickle that it can feel like a superstition itself – is to surf a wave known as Flameballs. Zerado's tomb is situated on the southern end of the Anakao village beach, facing out west toward the swells that march up the Mozambique Channel every winter and fold themselves over the reef beyond.

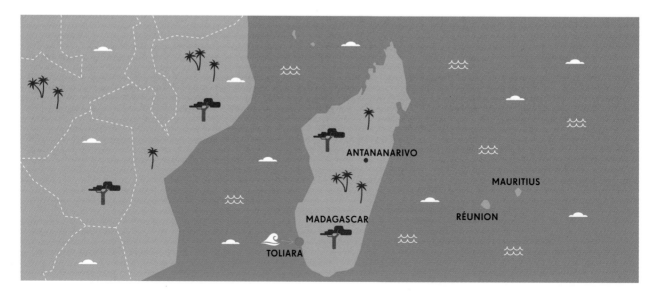

Flameballs is Madagascar's most celebrated wave. Although probably discovered and enjoyed by a few hardy Réunionnais yachties for years, I first laid eyes on it in an old copy of *Zigzag*, South Africa's biggest and oldest surf mag. It was an advert for the South African surf brand Island Style and it showed four waves stacked up, fluorescent blue, unfurling in metronomic perfection down the reef. A catamaran bobbed serenely in the channel. It was as if someone had finally reached into my mind and produced an image that matched my idea of paradise. I had to go.

A few years later, I finally did go. Even stayed a while. Armed with my high school French, I somehow wrangled myself work as a 'guide' at the small seasonal surf camp. I was hooked on how far away it felt from my familiar surf world in Durban: the charming Vezo, with their wooden beach shacks and pirogues; the smell of woodsmoke that wafted in with the morning offshore breeze; the coffee; the vanilla and fish cooked on a fire and eaten with your fingers, right on the deserted beach. And, of course, the heaving, tossing blue walls of Indian Ocean.

This hollow, shallow setup was in fact at least 1½ hours away from the most basic, rudimentary medical attention, so I always approached the arrival of a new swell with a mixture of apprehension and excitement. Injuries were clearly on people's minds here. During one trip, a Réunionnais surfer by the name of Julien kept mispronouncing the spot as 'Flame Bowls'. When I finally corrected him, he asked 'is it called that because it's so fast that you must surf it like your balls are on fire?' We laughed. The wave actually got its name when prolific surf lensman Lance Slabbert, Durban big-wave pioneer John Whittle, his brother Jamie and a guy by the name of Nick 'Flame' Robinson visited on an exploratory trip. Apparently during one of their first sessions, Flame's front foot slipped off his board mid-turn and he skewered the nose straight into his crotch, slicing open his scrotum.

Indeed, Flameballs is not an easy wave to surf, or to get to. It breaks off the back of a small uninhabited island called Nosy Ve, which lies about 2.5 miles (4km) from the mainland and is part of an extensive barrier reef system. Even from Durban, the journey requires a series of flights in planes that get progressively smaller, older and more rickety with each leg of the trip. A night in the dusty frontier town of Toliara is followed by an early morning ox-cart ride across the mudflats to meet the boat that would take us to the village of Anakao. To gee up the the *zebu* (Madagascan long-horned cattle) that pull the cart, a small Malagasy boy shouts and clicks and pops his lips absurdly, while alternating between whipping the animals with a stick or lifting their tails high up and sticking a finger in their anuses. Once the carts reached deeper water, a fast boat spluttered and grumbled to life, ready to whisk us into the blue.

On my first trip to Flameballs, I wanted to surf it the minute I arrived. I dumped my bags at the small beachfront lodgings in Anakao village and took the smaller, slower 'Surf Taxi' skiff another 45 minutes west to the break. The tide was pushing in and the afternoon southeast trade wind was stiffening. Conditions aligned.

WILDLIFE WATCH

Madagascar is full of unique fauna and flora. The spiny forest around Toliara is a sparse desert of prickly plants, full of endemic birds, snakes, lizards and chameleons. Look out for fat-tailed dwarf lemur, which are active at night – they make a sweet chirruping sound. The Indian Ocean also supports a rich array of marine life, including the musselcracker fish with its distinctive 'nose'. Out on the waves, you may spot humpback whales, dolphins, turtles and sharks.

Clockwise from top left: traditional Malagasy fishing pirogues ferry surfers to the breaks; turtle hatchlings race for the sea in nesting season; zebu provide the horsepower in this part of Madagascar. Previous page: South African pro Kyle Lane sits deep at Flameballs, Madagascar's most celebrated wave

"Each Flameballs wave feels all-consuming — a ride that requires my full attention and commitment"

ORIENTATION

Type of wave // Left-hand reef break over coral.
Best conditions // Pushing tide, mid-high.
Nearest town // Toliara.
Getting there // There are regular flights from regional centres Johannesburg, Mauritius and Réunion to Antananarivo. From there, take a regional flight to Toliara, then a ferry or an overnight pirogue (the latter are quicker and cheaper, if less convenient) to Anakao, which is still a 45-minute boat ride from Flameballs.
Where to stay // Safari Vezo Hotel has comfortable rooms right on the beach. Chez Emile is a budget option.
Things to know // Take a fun board and a step-up board. A shorty wetsuit or at least a neoprene top helps to cut the windchill. Factor in your commute by boat to ensure you're at the spot on the right tide and wind.

But the swell was actually small and it was impossible to generate enough speed to connect more than a section or two. It was a long way to come for this.

A few days later, however, I got to meet the real Flameballs. It was 4ft–6ft; at this size (or bigger), the whole wave stands up, then slows down just right, before launching you down the line. At the top of the reef, the takeoff spot, it sucks hard off the ledge, warps and then whips you in. The wave is long and has at least three distinct barrel sections, which was intimidating for me on my backhand, since I could see the water drawing off the reef. Trying to not look down, I propelled myself as far down the line as possible as the final section sucked off a big coral head – a warping shallow 'Surgeon's Table' – offering me the promise of a big, final backdoor pit.

For some reason, no matter how many times I surf here, each Flameballs wave feels like an all-consuming experience, a ride that requires my full attention and commitment. It's almost like time travel. When I've threaded my way through a particularly long ride, I often kick out, look back and marvel at the distance I've travelled. I find myself wondering 'how did I get here?' and, in some ways, it hardly feels like it happened at all. So I just have to paddle back up to the top for another one.

Flameballs

Opposite: for surfers, Réunion's barrels are worth the risk of the island's all-too-common shark encounters

MORE LIKE THIS
INDIAN OCEAN LEFTHANDERS

SAINT-LEU, RÉUNION

Saint-Leu on nearby Réunion Island is Flameballs' more urbane twin. Also a left-hand reef break, it picks up more swell, works through the tides and, arguably, has a more perfectly shaped reef. The wave does a strange U-bend about halfway down, grows a few feet and then slingshots you over a perfect ledge of fire coral. It breaks right on the northern edge of the small west-coast town of Saint-Leu. It's hard to miss, on your right, as you drive into town from the island's capital, Saint-Denis. The little snack bar under the casuarina trees on the shore is a perfect vantage point for watching the action; the baguettes and cold beers here are not bad either. The upside of the island's much publicised, but perhaps overhyped, 'shark crisis' is that Saint-Leu is now a lot less crowded than it used to be. But please be careful out there.

Nearest town // Saint-Leu

TAMARIN BAY, MAURITIUS

Tamarin Bay burst into surf history via 1970s surf film *The Forgotten Island of Santosha*, in which 'Santosha' was used as a *nom de guerre* designed to throw hungry surf explorers off the Mauritius surf trail. Maybe that set the precedent for Tamarin's long history of localism. The island's surfers covet Tamarin for good reason. The Saint-Leu of Mauritius, it is a perfect left. It can be a bit fickle and needs a solid groundswell to turn on, but when it does, the local surf community come down to enjoy the fast, long, walling lefts. Be respectful and you can still pick off some good rides on a crowded day. Tamarin itself is a sleepy little town, where life revolves around the beach. The Veranda Tamarin Hotel is a good place to plan your attack – a quirky Art Deco hotel, with a good restaurant and an adjoining surf shop and dive centre.

Nearest town // Tamarin

IFATY, MADAGASCAR

The pass on the barrier reef in front of the village of Ifaty, Madagascar, is where Jeremy Flores cut his teeth as a young man. It boasts a left and a right, on either side of the hole, where the lagoon ventilates itself on the incoming and outgoing tides. Both setups can offer ridiculously good waves, but surfers will definitely need a boat to get out there, and to ferry them back to shore, as the reef is about 2.5 miles (4km) from the mainland. Watch out for the rip current through the pass on the outgoing tide. And don't worry about crowds. Most of the time, surfers are happy for company in Madagascar, to spread the odds and to have a witness in case anyone gets barrelled. There are plenty of restaurant and bungalow operations along the Ifaty shoreline.

Nearest town // Ifaty

JOE'S POINT

*As an expat living in the United Arab Emirates, Jade Bremner decided
to beat the heat by joining a surf safari to the coast of Oman.*

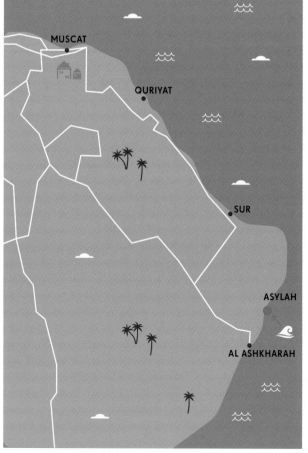

As night fell on the desert, it was eerily quiet, amplifying the crashing of the waves. As stars appeared in the hazy sky, we started a fire on the floor of our primitive camp. The leader of our crew, Carl de Villiers, pointed out a shovel, on hand in case nature called. A few campers set up raised camp beds; others put up traditional dome tents. We molded the sand into makeshift pillows and left our sleeping bags packed away because of the warm night air. Carl fired up a barbecue of locally caught fish – collected at a market en route – and offered up a fattoush salad and lavash flatbread. We were all starving after a day catching waves off the desolate eastern coast of Oman.

Joe's Point, at Asylah Beach, is about as off-grid as one can get in search of waves these days. But those who do make the journey will discover one of the most unique surf settings in the world. I first surfed Joe's Point as an expat living in the UAE, during a typically sweltering summer in which temperatures regularly nudged 125°F (55°C) and the water in the Arabian Gulf was easily hotter than a bath. So I signed up with a local company which offered relief in the form of surf trips on the Oman coast, about 400 miles (644km) away. Even though they couldn't guarantee swell, they could guarantee it would be much cooler.

'The waves look pretty promising', said Carl, a South African surfer who runs regular trips to Asylah Beach. Aside from Carl and a few outfits like his, the surfing scene in Oman is almost non-existent. Thus, all the breaks are usually empty. The surf community here consists entirely of a few expats who are either desperate for respite from the heat, or desperate for a surf fix after months away from their home break. Carl tells me that expats living in Oman and the UAE have actually been making

this pilgrimage for more than a decade, on a mission to one particular right-hand point that peels off a stony groyne that people call Joe's Point.

Our safari was made up of around 30 people between the ages of 20 and 50, from various Western backgrounds and nationalities (including a dozen women). There was a teacher, a fashion buyer and a pilot on the trip, each part of the enormous international presence in the UAE (roughly 85% of the total population is made up of expats from some 200 countries). We drove in tandem by 4WD, leaving the glitzy bright lights of Dubai and crossing the desert border in Al Ain; similar surf trips are also available in Oman's capital, Muscat, with local operators. Our eight-hour journey seemed to traverse barren desert the entire way. The only other people that travel this route regularly are local residents or workers transporting goods between countries.

We passed rolling dunes and camels nonchalantly strolling in the distance. We occasionally drove through sleepy towns that smelled of sweet shisha, where the melodic call to prayer hummed in the background. There was excited nervousness in the car the closer we got to the coast. We were all hoping for waves, but it's not exactly a spot where one can rely on surf cams. The swell is predicted the old fashioned way, by reading a combination of swell and wind charts.

Then, as we came closer to the point itself, we finally saw the waves, perfect 6ft sets breaking off the headland. Even though we were not the first to see them, it felt like this was a frontier, like we were pioneers about to conquer a virgin break. And the truth is, there are still undiscovered spots along this stretch of coastline. One guy in our group had begun to open his door before the bus even came to a complete stop.

Unlike the opaque waters of the Persian Gulf in the UAE, the sea here is a dark blue. We immediately took off our shoes and walked into the ocean. It was lukewarm and yet completely refreshing. Aside from a row of blue-and-white fishing boats docked near the headland, there was nothing on the horizon except sand and sea. The nearest small town is 8 miles (13km) to the south.

A South African paddleboarder was the first into the water. He clambered over the rocks on the headland and paddled straight to the point; it wasn't long before he was ripping down the face of the beautifully peeling head-high wave. He made it look so fun and effortless that the rest of us sped up our pre-surf routines.

Once out in the water, many were struggling against a strong current on the paddle-out. I decided to walk up the headland and paddle out from the point. During a break in the sets, I launched into the ocean and paddled hard into the lineup.

The wind and current pulled me out of position easily, so I had to fight to maintain my position in the lineup. Thankfully, a wave was coming toward me pretty soon after I had arrived on the outside. I paddled hard – too hard – and ended up riding a big broken wave on my belly. But then a face reappeared on the wave, so I stood up and carved into it. It turned into a powerful, fast ride,

TURTLE NESTS

Between April and August, around five species of turtle nest on Oman's beaches. Beachside surf camps are prime spots to see green, loggerhead, leatherback, hawksbill or Olive Ridley turtles laying eggs in the sand. After roughly 55 days, the buried eggs hatch and the baby turtles emerge to make a break for the sea. Many of these species are endangered, and there are strict laws and penalties in place for those who disrupt the turtles or their habitats.

Clockwise from left: south swell at Joe's Point; a green turtle makes a break for the waves; scoping the Omani coast. Previous page, clockwise from top: empty waves are a sure thing at Joe's Point; the road less travelled in Oman; close encounters with the 'ships of the desert'

"Carl fired up a barbecue of locally caught fish and offered us a fatoush salad and lavash flatbread"

nearly all the way to shore. Instead of paddling back out, I walked back up the beach toward the point.

Out in the lineup again, I sensed movement under the water, then spotted a round shadow moving toward me. A turtle's head appeared; it took a gulp of air, then disappeared again back under the surface.

The conditions required constant effort and after just three or four waves I was ready for a break. We set up a line of folding chairs on a sandy knoll above the beach, the perfect vantage point for watching the surf. A couple of locals in their ankle-length white *dishdasha* gowns and *lihaf* headdresses walked past. I couldn't help imagine this as a future surf town, and to wonder if it was only a matter of time. But I quickly managed to pull myself back into the moment where, for now anyway, this was our undiscovered Middle Eastern surfing paradise.

ORIENTATION

Type of wave // Intermediate and advanced right-hand rocky point break, with a sandy beach section for beginners.

Best conditions // In summer and autumn waves typically reach 2ft–6ft, but it can also get very windy.

Nearest town // Al Ashkharah, which has ATMs, petrol, and coffee shops, is around 8 miles (13km) south.

Getting there // Most folks join a surf trip from the UAE (an eight-hour drive) or Muscat (a four-hour drive). Surf schools offering trips to Asylah Beach include the Ninja Surf School (www.ninjasurfschool.com) and Fahrenheit Beach Sports (www.alohaarabia.com).

Where to stay // Local surf operators will offer a choice of sleeping options, from camping in the desert to basic accommodation like the simple Arabian Sea Hotel.

Things to know // Campers should be aware that there are zero facilities on the beach: no food, water or toilets.

Opposite from top: the iconic Burj Al Arab overlooks Dubai's Sunset Beach; heavyweight company in Jiyeh, Lebanon

MORE LIKE THIS
MIDDLE EAST SURF MAGNETS

MUSTAFA'S A-FRAME, LEBANON

Lebanese surf culture dates back to the longboard era of the 1960s. The scene was centered around Beirut, Lebanon's charismatic capital, dubbed the 'Paris of the Middle East' for its vibrant art, fashion and music scenes, and for its charming café society. Beirut also holds its own in the wave department. Working on very similar swell conditions to the Israeli coast, Jiyeh is located only 36 miles (58km) north of the (closed) border with Israel, and some 12 miles (19km) south of central Beirut. The best-known break in the area is Mustafa's A-Frame, a consistent spot that can produce anything from tiny, clean peaks to solid overhead barrels. Nearby are a variety of breaks that come alive under meatier swells, including Saadiyat, a fun left-hand reef point to the north of town.
Nearest town // Jiyeh

SUNSET BEACH, UAE

Surfing backdrops don't get much more iconic than this: Sunset Beach sits to the right of the famous sail-shaped Burj Al Arab, one of the most famous buildings in the world and an emblem of Dubai. Surfers can ride swells nearly every day during the winter months at this public beach, when small waves break in crystal clear warm water on the soft sandy beach. People have been surfing in Dubai for decades, and before development, folks could surf up and down this entire coastline. After the construction of the World Islands and the Palm Islands off shore – which have blocked most of the waves – this is one of a handful of surfable beaches left in the area. It can get crowded but is a top beginners' spot in the region.
Nearest town // Dubai

RAMIN BEACH, IRAN

When it comes to adventurous surf trips, they don't get much more thrilling than a trip to Iran. It's off the surfing circuit due to challenging visa restrictions and few facilities. However, those who do make it here – with all their gear – are rewarded with empty southern beaches facing the Arabian Sea. The breaks here were first surfed just a decade ago by female Irish pro-surfer Easkey Britton; today, there's a tiny surfing community situated around Ramin Beach, with both men and women in the lineups. Admittedly, this area doesn't have the best waves in the world, but surfers will experience a rich culture and get the chance to ride waves in relatively uncharted waters.
Nearest town // Chabahar

URECA

*Alan van Gysen's obsession with seeking out undiscovered waves
brought him to a remote island off Equatorial Guinea.*

The eerie sound wakes me from a deep sleep inside my tent. I can hear it distinctly, above the symphony of crashing waves and the ceaseless singing of cicadas a few feet away. I sit bolt upright, tuning into the jungle.

I hear it again. *Scratch, scratch, swoosh.* Climbing out of my tent into the moonless night, I switch on my headlamp and cautiously search out the noise along the edge of the rainforest. Something huge and dark is digging amongst the stones down on the beach, flinging sand onto the dry leaves that litter the shoreline. My heart beats faster as I take a few steps closer. Then I see it. A giant Atlantic Green turtle, almost as big as a double bed, is working

meticulously to dislodge sticks, stones and sand in order to make a nest and lay her eggs on the same stretch of Bioko Island beach on which she was probably born many years ago.

Bioko Island is part of Equatorial Guinea, the small country that lies wedged inside the armpit of West Africa. With towering volcanic cliffs and dense rainforest, Bioko's remote location has made it a biological treasure trove. It's also rich in other treasure – oil, to be precise – and is ruled by a staunch military dictatorship. I'd been jumping through bureaucratic hoops for two years trying to get to the island by any means possible. But tourism is virtually nonexistent and inquisitive photographers are hardly the kind of

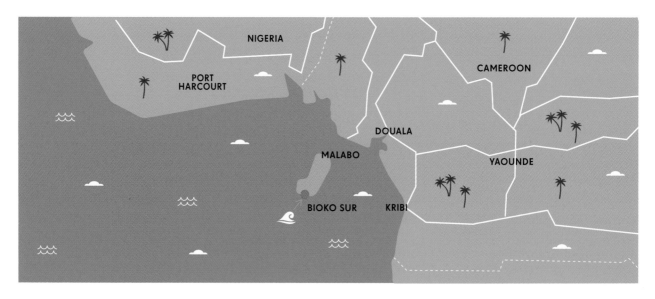

people they issue work visas to. Then, I found an in: the Bioko Biodiversity Protection Program (BBPP).

This collaboration of academics have been granted permission by the government to conduct conservation research on the island. They graciously agreed to host me, and a visa miraculously appeared in my passport. Fortuitously, their base camp at the mouth of the Moaba River is close to a couple of spots that looked promising, surf-wise, from the lofty heights of Google Earth.

Prior to the discovery of vast deposits of oil in 1995, the ex-Spanish colony of Equatorial Guinea was relatively unheard of, save for its colonial history and a bloody coup d'état, during which president Francisco Macías Nguema was deposed, tried and executed. In August of 1979, Teodoro Obiang Nguema Mbasogo (Nguema's nephew) took control of the government, and has ruled the country ever since. As Africa's longest serving president, he's been accused of brutal repression of opponents, electoral fraud and corruption. Today, Mbasogo's paranoia has resulted in a blanket ban on most forms of mass communication. This began in November of 2017, when the local internet was taken offline for a week during Equatorial Guinea's last election. Not wanting a West African 'Arab Spring', social platforms like Facebook and Twitter have been blocked ever since.

The capital of Malabo (on Bioko Island rather than the mainland) gives little of this turmoil away. Instead, it's surprisingly clean and well maintained. Few people actually take notice of me, but I'm flatly rebuffed when I ask permission to snap a portrait or two. I'm detained and very nearly arrested for taking photos of the beautiful neo-Gothic Santa Isabel Cathedral that lies in the centre of town, putting an end to my touristy curiosity.

From Malabo it's a three-hour drive to the south of the island. Our destination is Ureca, a small village that literally lies at the end of the road, from where we have to hike the rest of the way in to the camp. The drive passes through pristine equatorial jungle, complete with monstrous ceiba trees and a dizzying array of birds that flit beneath the forest canopy. Less appealing are the numerous bushmeat stalls that line the road, on which a variety of creatures hang by their tails: an African python, giant rats, small antelope, some sort of pig, a monkey, porcupines.

The tide is low, which makes the three-hour hike from Ureca to the camp easy going along compact, volcanic beach sand. The waves don't look great, though – mostly 1ft-high closeouts that dump straight onto shore. I swallow back the horrible, nagging doubt that I've come all this way only to get skunked.

At the end of a long stretch of beach, we cross another river before heading uphill and into the jungle for the final part of the hike to the campsite. We pass a massive spiderweb stretched across a gap in the canopy, its lethal-looking occupant hanging in the threads. Soon after, we drop back down toward the sea. The guide, Ivan, tells me we're close to our destination. I start to hear surf breaking, then catch a glimpse of a running wave through the thick bush. As we round the bend we see a hollow, peeling right wedging in front of a river mouth lined by cliffs. The steep canyon

THE MIGHTY JUNGLE

One of world's least visited regions, the area around Bioko's Moaba River is also among the wettest, receiving about 400 inches (1000cm) of rainfall annually. As a guest of BBPP you can observe and study alongside scientists and volunteers, getting up close with local turtle species such as giant leatherback, green, Olive Ridley and hawksbill, as well as the seven endemic primates including drills, black colobus and red-eared guenon.

Clockwise from top left: cliffs refract the Ureca swell just right; every session is an adventure; rustic living at the BBPP research camp. Previous page: a hollow, peeling right rewards those who make the journey to Bioko

All images © Alan van Gysen

behind us seems to be funneling the wind into a whispery offshore that blows straight out to sea.

Our contacts at the BBPP supply us with a tent, a tarp and a portable platform to keep our camp raised above the sand and the crawling insects. As the sun sets, it illuminates everything with an orange glow, like an old sepia lens filter.

The heavy flow of fresh water from the Moaba River is strange to surf in – the buoyancy isn't the same as fully salted seawater and it takes a few sessions to get used to. We take a long hike to Punta Santiago to hunt for more surf, but the trek yields no waves. Back at camp, it becomes routine to cool off under a nearby waterfall during the sweltering heat of the day.

The offshore bathymetry here fascinates me. A deep underwater canyon appears to focus the swell, while the cliffs refract it into peaks up and down the beach. Together with the shallow river mouth, the setup produces enough jungle wedges to keep us occupied as the days flow by.

Lying in my tent after the simple dinner we've become accustomed to, I hear the sound of rain, small drops at first that grow louder and more forceful until the tent is shuddering under their impact. I'm surprised it's taken this long for it to arrive. The southern coast of Bioko Sur is one of the wettest places on earth, but this is the first rain we've had in the week we've been here. We'd chosen to come in January because it's technically the driest month of the year, but 'dry' is a relative term in these parts, where rainfall averages over 400 inches (1000cm) a year.

I close my eyes and eventually the rain eases, until all I can hear again is the hiss of breaking waves and then the faint, unmistakable sound of one of the island's ancient residents returning home.

"I swallow back the horrible, nagging doubt that I've come all this way only to get skunked"

ORIENTATION

Type of wave // River-mouth sand-bottom A-frame wedge righthander.

Best conditions // Biko is only accessible during the dry summer season (November to February), and is best with light northerly offshores and a pushing or dropping mid tide.

Nearest town // San Antonio de Ureca.

Getting there // Fly in to Malabo International Airport (SSG) on Bioko Island via Addis Ababa, Ethiopia, from where it's a two-hour drive south of Malabo to San Antonio de Ureca, and a two-hour hike to the BBPP camp.

Where to stay // There are basic to luxury hotels in Malabo, and the BBPP camp closer to the wave.

Things to know // Visas are required for most nationalities. Due to numerous coup attempts, photographing official buildings or personnel is strictly prohibited. Bring a head-torch with a pure red light for turtle-watching excursions.

Opposite from top: Radiation Point off the island of São Tomé is one of the Gulf of Guinea's most consistent breaks; Nigeria's barrelling Lighthouse wave

MORE LIKE THIS
GULF OF GUINEA ADVENTURES

NACHO, EQUATORIAL GUINEA

The only other known, quality wave in Equatorial Guinea is also on Bioko Island. On the southern tip of Bioko Sur, between San Antonio de Ureca and the Bioko Biodiversity Protection Program's (BBPP) Camp Moraca, Nacho is about three hours hike west of Ureca along the shore. An exposed A-frame peak breaking over shallow reef and cobblestones, it's predominantly a bowly left and faces out unhindered to the Atlantic, harnessing any swell there is. Without a structure or person in sight, it can feel very isolated, and you need to take appropriate safety precautions. Probably one for the adventurous only, it nonetheless offers one of the most unique surfing experiences on earth: riding waves alone on the jungle-swathed edge of Africa.

Nearest town // San Antonio de Ureca

RADIATION POINT, SÃO TOMÉ

Some 250 miles (402km) south of Bioko are the islands São Tomé and Príncipe (also known as the 'Chocolate Islands', as they produce some of the world's finest dark chocolate). São Tomé is home to one of the Gulf of Guinea's most notable waves, Radiation Point (Praia de Algés). Just a short car ride from the city of São Tomé's airport, it is surprisingly consistent, as even local southeast windswell will wrap with enough size to ride, and the southwest wind is cross-offshore on the biggest outside section. It is a cobblestone right-hand point, and is best surfed on the lower to mid tides when it offers a long and running point.

Nearest town // São Tomé

LIGHTHOUSE, NIGERIA

About 420 miles (676km) northwest of Equatorial Guinea's Bioko Island, in neighbouring Nigeria, is Lighthouse. In the heart of the largest city in Africa, Lagos, it is one of the most unique waves in the world, as it didn't exist until industrious Lagosians accidentally created the left wedge by building a large shipping-lane wall to keep the giant waterway into Lagos safe. This exposed, consistent, powerful sand-bottomed left wedge is best surfed on the low to mid tides during the dry season (between November and February), which offers the best water quality as well as light offshore breezes. There are very few travelling surfers here, and only a handful of residents are willing to attempt to ride the powerful barrelling wave, so the water is never crowded.

Nearest town // Lagos

MALIBU

Former pro Jamie Brisick has traversed the globe in search of swell. But on one particularly well-known wave off the coast of Los Angeles, he found his blissfully dysfunctional surf family.

When I first came to Malibu in the late '70s, I took careful note of the surfers who gathered here. They checked the waves with a cool insouciance. They talked with their hands, as if painting an imaginary canvas. Some drank brown-bag beers and slept in their cars. Others were the sons of Hollywood royalty and lived in million-dollar beachfront homes. That socioeconomic diversity still exists. Los Angeles is a city built on status and hierarchy, but Malibu explodes such delineations. Jive-talking, parking-lot banter, the ability to connect with your fellow beachgoer – this is the stuff that carries currency.

I quickly learned that no matter what kind of surfer you are, or what part of LA you're from, the ride at Malibu starts long before you hit the water. On a big south swell in the summer, it starts miles away, as Pacific Coast Hwy teems with surfers from all over the city, their excitement palpable. Most days it starts in the parking lot, where it's customary to try to talk the attendant into letting you in for free, regardless of your age or the health of your bank balance. The lot is a true melting pot: a place where dusty old trucks with 1950s-era longboards poking out the back squeeze in beside shiny black Range Rovers with Firewires strapped to the roof.

MALIBU LAGOON

MALIBU POINT

BIG-SCREEN SURF

In the mid-1950s, surf girl Kathy Kohner relayed tales of her days on the sand and in the surf at Malibu to her screenwriter father, Frederick Kohner. Over a six-week period, Frederick wrote the seminal novel *Gidget.* And so it began...

From left: 16-year-old Kathy Kohner, the real-life inspiration for Gidget; longboarders love to 'dance' at First Point; Second Point is a hotspot for shortboarders. Previous page: LA's most iconic lifeguard tower

The parking lot scene is like a snow-globe miniature of LA life; there's an odd sense of comic despair that runs through the place. There's local ace Chad Marshall, one of First Point's premier nose-riders, prancing along with a rainbow-flag-bedecked 10'6". There's Malibu Carl – a fixture for 30-plus years, though he doesn't actually surf – bumming a cigarette from an unsuspecting Orange County kid who seems overly pleased to be part of the scene. There's two-times world longboarding champion Joel Tudor, up from San Diego to ride California's most storied point break.

My personal Malibu ritual is to hang and chat with the crew a bit. Being there liberates the spirit. I speak more frankly. Otherwise, dramatic things become funny. This does more to loosen me up than any kind of pre-surf stretch or warm-up.

Located 23 miles (37km) north of LAX, and also known as Surfrider Beach, Malibu is where *Gidget* happened. It's where the great design leap that was the Malibu Chip board – smaller, lighter, more manoeuvrable – happened. It's where Miki Dora famously dropped his shorts at the judges, media and spectators in the 1967 Malibu Invitational. And it's where *Big Wednesday,* set in a fictional Malibu, effectively happened. There might be better-quality waves in California, but nowhere holds more notches in the belt of surf history.

Even the iconic Malibu wall – which, these days, is usually hidden behind dozens of leaning longboards – harkens back to the Rindge Family, who fiercely guarded 'Malibu Rancho' from 1892 to the early 1920s. After unsuccessfully prospecting for oil in the region, they instead found red and buff clays and launched Malibu Potteries, a major supplier of ceramic tiles in the 1920s and '30s.

The wall is often splashed in graffiti ('Dora Lives', 'Vals Go Home'), but in fact it's a Malibu Potteries artefact. The history is felt every time I pass through the gap in the wall, the entrance to the beach – we call it the Pearly Gates.

But what matters most at Malibu is how you dance through the water. You're never alone out there. Even on the crummy days, the crowd is dense. The pecking order works on a sliding scale of skill level and years accrued in the lineup. Dogtown surfing legend Allen Sarlo still rips aged 62, and has put in nearly half a decade – he gets any wave he wants. Parking Lot Teddy does not rip, but he's there every day from dawn till dusk, and has been for 20 years, so you don't want to drop in on him. Nonetheless, drop-ins are frequent. At First Point, I often see three, four, even five surfers on one face. Over time, I learned when – and when not – to join in on these party waves.

This is where the chaos of Malibu functions fine, so long as you understand the nuance. At first glance it looked like a free-for-all. But looking closer, I learned that those multiple surfers on that one wave have shared history and knowledge. I've even come to love these well-choreographed ménages a trois, quatre, cinq.

Once, at the tip of First Point on the high tide, I took off on a sweet, bending, waist-high wave. I was riding a borrowed 11ft board, fire-engine red, a quasi-canoe. In a low crouch, I angled right. When a towheaded pre-teen kid paddled for it, I did not call him off; I welcomed his shared line, almost paternally. But when a third surfer dropped in, creating a rail-banging sort of kid sandwich, I became a bit concerned. The sun was low, the water was dimpled gold and Crayola-blue, the wave was zippering fast.

"There might be better-quality waves in California, but nowhere holds more notches in the belt of surf history"

I grabbed my outside rail for stability, and so did the kid. A fourth surfer dropped in, a tall, lean girl on a yellow soft-top. She wore a red bikini and a black baseball cap. On some primal, purely heterosexual level, she completely stole my attention. For a few seconds, we were a waveriding family (though I was still trying to place the guy between the woman and the kid). The wave peeled away. The kid's board nearly scalped me. The girl disappeared.

Malibu is a kind of anarchic experiment that somehow works. It teaches us about our surfing selves. I've seen terrible fights over waves. I myself have barked at dropper-inners, and fallen into pathetic bouts of wave rage. But over the decades I've come to learn that the only way to surf Malibu is with levity. You *will* get dropped-in on, that's a simple fact of surfing there. The key is to laugh, to practice humility, to be grateful for whatever little piece of peeling water the wave-gods send your way.

And what a wave it is! Los Angeles' entire coastline is blessed with surf, but Malibu's quality is unsurpassed. It has a pulse and momentum to it. You feel the swell bending down the point with resolve. And your job – you, the surfer – is to piece it all together, to make the right move at the right time, so that you ride to the very bottom and step off onto the shore with grace.

In those moments, it's not unlikely to hear a hoot and to look up toward the parking lot and see cheering, applause. We're a beautiful family in that parking lot. In fact, I recently shared those exact words with a fellow Malibu surfer. 'We are', he agreed. 'But be careful: you start hanging out in the Malibu parking lot too much, and you become the Malibu parking lot.'

ORIENTATION

Type of wave // Right-hand point break. First Point is the most machine-like, but Second and Third offer racy, less crowded peelers.
Best conditions // Summer, summer, summer! South and southwest swells wrap around the point best.
Nearest town // Malibu.
Getting there // Surfrider Beach is 45 minutes' drive north of Los Angeles International Airport (LAX), along Pacific Coast Hwy.
Where to stay // The Surfrider Malibu, across the street from First Point, looks straight out onto the break. There is good camping further up the coast at Leo Carrillo beach.
Things to know // Longboards tend to be the equipment of choice at First Point, shortboards and hybrids at Second and Third. The lineup here is friendly, but respect the crowd.

Opposite from top: beginners flock to San Onofre for its gentle, rolling beach break; Steamer Lane in Santa Cruz is experts-only

MORE LIKE THIS
SURF'S HISTORIC LANDMARKS

WAIKIKI, O'AHU, HAWAII

There is the wave. And there is the culture, and the history, and the lineage. Waikiki is in the same vein as Malibu: it's where the great Duke Kahanamoku got a mile-long ride in 1917; where Jimmy Stewart, Gary Cooper, Montgomery Clift and Babe Ruth caught their first waves in the '50s; and where the beach boy ethos – part surf instructor, part entertainer, part gigolo – originated. (One story has a strapping beach boy and a smitten *haole* (foreign) girl making love while riding a wave under the full moon.) Waikiki does not have a parking lot scene, but it has board-rental kiosks, and surf instructors who harken back to the beach-boy days. Catching a wave at a spot like Queens or Canoes is as fun as it is nostalgic.

Nearest town // Honolulu

SAN ONOFRE, CALIFORNIA

San Onofre, at the north end of San Diego County, is awash with surf history. It became one of California's premier surf hangouts in the mid-1930s, when dudes from San Diego to Santa Cruz would ride the soft, rolling swells by day, and gather around camp fires to talk and play ukuleles by night. From 1938 to 1941 it was home to the Pacific Coast Surf Riding Championships, which drew the Golden State's hottest surfers. Advances in board design (the Malibu Chip) saw postwar waveriders move on to more challenging breaks, but by the '60s, San O and, specifically, Old Man's (the main break) would become a hotbed of sweet nostalgia. And it has been that way ever since. Here is where multigenerational families hang, where a relaxed, barefoot tenor prevails. Here is the antithesis of the high-octane shortboarding scene.

Nearest town // San Clemente

STEAMER LANE, CALIFORNIA

Steamer Lane has been the epicentre of Santa Cruz surfing since the 1940s. A reef/point break with several spots to ride, it is crowded like Malibu, and steeped in history like Malibu (the Santa Cruz Surfing Club was formed in 1938). Steamer Lane is where Pat O'Neill and Roger Adams invented the surf leash in 1970. And it has a terrific parking-lot scene. West Cliff Road lines the cliffs that drop down to the break, so close you can hurl an apple core at your buddy as he rides past. Or you can heckle wittily from your elevated perch, which the Santa Cruz locals do most mornings. Hundreds of contests have taken place here, most notably the O'Neill Coldwater Classics in the late '80s. And there's the Santa Cruz Surfing Museum, at the base of the Mark Abbott Memorial Lighthouse, which traces over 100 years of surf history in Santa Cruz.

Nearest town // Santa Cruz

PAVONES

Many know that Costa Rica's most famous wave is one of the longest lefts in the world. Kitt Doucette says too few know about the town's past.

It was long past nightfall when I finally arrived in Pavones for the first time. We bumped slowly into town after a 12-hour white-knuckle ride through the pouring rain, full of wrong turns and washed-out roads, potholes and sketchy river crossings. It was 2003, and Costa Rica's most famous wave had yet to surrender to the masses. Anyone wishing to experience this legendary half-mile lefthander would first have to endure a long and unpredictable journey to what still feels like the edge of the world. Any wave that requires this much effort to get to sears itself into a different part of your brain.

The only light in town was coming from the cantina, where a couple of bare bulbs buzzed above a rusty refrigerator and a few tables. I jumped out of the truck and ran across the cantina's cement patio to get a look at the wave. It didn't matter that it was dark, I could still make out the ruler-edged racetrack spinning down the point. As it did, bioluminescence flashed in the darkness.

But all great waves eventually end up on the map. And in a country like Costa Rica – known for its wave-rich Pacific Coast – it was only a matter of time before Pavones was designated the country's most valuable surf resource. My own trips to Pavones increased in frequency as the journey got easier. Since that first trip, I've been back dozens of times, usually with my good friend Trevor, a longtime Costa Rica resident and stylish goofy-foot.

Like Pavones, Costa Rica as a whole has changed a lot in the last few decades, successfully capitalising on its off-the-grid tropical paradise feel, and on its cultured population. The standard of living and general happiness quotient of the locals – ticos – is famously high and, because of that, they're famously friendly and welcoming. Ticos are quick to share their *pura vida* ('pure life'); the phrase is

as much a lifestyle here as it is a greeting. The country abolished its military in 1948, and has remained an extremely safe and easy place to travel in a region that, for the most part, is currently headed in the opposite direction.

Costa Rica is also blessed with surf – perhaps more than almost any other country its size. One could actually surf both coasts in one trip, and there are plenty of waves to choose from. The Pacific coast is like a warm-water California, with lots of fun waves and beautiful, wide-open beaches. Pavones, however, is one of the best waves in all of Central America, with three main sections which, when they connect, create a leg-burning speed run.

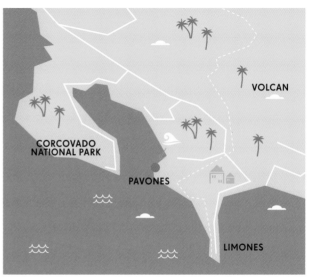

These days, the town itself is a sort of classic surf outpost. Pavones is now a straightforward two-hour drive from the airport in Golfito, with road signs – albeit covered with surf stickers – leading the way over fresh blacktop and across sturdy bridges. The change is good, but having witnessed the town's transformation, I can't help but think of its past every time I visit – a past I learned about during that very first visit.

After dropping our bags that night, we drank a few beers while watching wave after wave flash and roll along the point in front of us. We rented a couple of basic rooms right above the bar so we could be as close to the break as possible. At high tide, we would sometimes hear waves slapping into the retaining wall a few feet below our beds.

The next morning, we paddled out at first light. The swell had dropped a little, keeping whatever locals were around in bed. It's hard to believe today, but there was no one else out. We traded waves all morning, overhead-height and outrageously long. We were struck by how the wave never seemed to close out – it just eventually moved faster than we were able to surf. Multiple surf sessions each day became the routine. At night, we'd play dominos and smoke dirt-weed doobies. And thankfully, it was a time when some of the locals could still vividly recount Pavones' wild beginnings.

The Pavones surf breaks were first ridden by surfers exploring the Central American coastline by boat in the early 1960s. A few years later, a freewheeling waterman, surfer and rumoured smuggler

from California named Dan Fowlie, aka Danny Mac, flew over the area during a good swell. Stunned by the perfectly shaped lines he spotted below, Fowlie spent a week cruising the portside bars in Golfito, asking who owned the land. As the story goes, he plunked down US$30,000 in cash and walked away as the new owner of 250 acres (102 hectares) surrounding one of the best lefts in the world.

Fowlie kept on buying as much land as he could, eventually building an airstrip and lumber mill. Over the next 20-plus years, he carved an entire town out of the jungle, complete with a schoolhouse and a church. He was beloved by the local families and fisherfolk, who started calling him 'El Rey de Pavones' (The King of Pavones).

In the mid-1980s, Fowlie was charged with drug trafficking. While he maintained his innocence, he was sentenced to 20 years in jail; Pavones fell into disarray. Mired by labour disputes, the banana plantations around Golfito were being closed. Squatters took over the town, some of the land was sold, then some more, and farm equipment was stolen. Adventurous surfers continued to pass through Pavones – some even stayed – but lawlessness reigned. It all came to a violent head when a gringo named Max Dalton was shot and killed in 1997 during a land dispute with local squatters. The distrust, violent threats and land disputes continued, and Pavones actually dropped out of the surfing spotlight for a while.

Danny Mac's private airstrip is long gone today. So is the old cantina we stayed in – it burned to the ground a few years back. It was the transformation of Costa Rica itself over the years that

> *"The wave never seemed to close out – it just eventually moved faster than we were able to surf"*

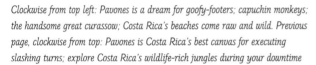

Clockwise from top left: Pavones is a dream for goofy-footers; capuchin monkeys; the handsome great curassow; Costa Rica's beaches come raw and wild. Previous page, clockwise from top: Pavones is Costa Rica's best canvas for executing slashing turns; explore Costa Rica's wildlife-rich jungles during your downtime

FEATHERED FRIENDS

Named after a Costa Rican jungle bird that looks (and tastes) remarkably similar to a turkey, Pavones is known for the numerous tropical birds that call the area home, including scarlet macaws and toucans. The area attracts as many visiting birders as it does surfers, the latter descending to take advantage of the smaller swell and clear skies of Costa Rica's 'summer' months (December to March).

sparked Pavones' resurgence. Tourism, not banana cultivation, is now the country's biggest industry, and Pavones has changed with Costa Rica. The town is yet another hotspot for yoga retreats, eco-lodges and bird sanctuaries. Tensions mellowed and the road got better.

And, of course, a truly great wave never changes. I still love it when I can connect all the sections of its racy face. I love seeing that beautiful wall, stretching out in front of me for hundreds of feet, begging for high-lines and speed runs.

Walking back up the beach after yet another 'longest wave of my life', I still always picture Danny Mac stopping in the shade of the cantina to grab a bottle of cold beer, before carrying on to the top of the point for another wave. Interestingly, change has erased a lot of Pavones' lore. These days, as surfers from all over the world feast on *gallo pinto* (rice and beans) and drink cold Cerveza Imperial in the town square, local groms sit in the lineup daydreaming about sponsorship. Many visiting surfers can spend an entire week here, or even two, without ever learning about Danny Mac and the area's controversial past. Even so, history is still being written.

Danny Mac actually outlasted his jail term. Now in his 80s, he has been allowed to return to Pavones, and is currently fighting to regain the land he says was stolen from him. Meanwhile, an American-owned, multi-million dollar condo development at the top of the point is also underway. It should be another interesting battle over the soul of Pavones.

ORIENTATION

Type of wave // Long, left-hand river-mouth point break.
Best conditions // Higher tide helps the wave connect, but once it gets to 8ft and above, low tide is hollower. Look for a strong south swell with some west in it.
Nearest town // Pavones.
Getting there // It's a trek, no matter how you slice it: the fastest way is to fly into Golfito then drive for two hours to the end of the road (a 4WD isn't always necessary, but often is). There's also a daily bus between Golfito and Pavones, but journey time is four to five hours.
Where to stay // Cabinas Carol is a cool hostel owned by an Italian surfer; it's also posible to find a private house to rent near the point.
Things to know // Costa Rica is as well known for its rainforests and wildlife as for its surfing. Be sure to explore the nearby waterfalls and jungle trails.

*Opposite from top: the heavy
A-frame at Playa Hermosa; Playa
Negra is on the surf-rich Nicoya
Peninsula*

MORE LIKE THIS
COSTA RICAN CLASSICS

PLAYA NEGRA

A great place to escape the gringo hordes of Tamarindo, nearby Playa Negra has an international flavour and a cool, cultured vibe. It's just a quick trip down the northwest coast from Nicoya, the main city of the Nicoya Peninsula. Playa Negra has a punchy and nicely shaped right-hand reef break that fires during a northwest swell. There's also a sandy beach break for beginners, just south of the reef break. The white-sand beach fronting the break is stunning, and there's a cool little surf hotel right on the wave. Playa Negra town is walking distance from the beach, and has a lot of great restaurants and accommodation options.
Nearest town // Playa Negra

SALSA BRAVA

Salsa Brava on the Caribbean coast is Costa Rica's answer to Hawaiian juice. This powerful top-to-bottom tube over sharp volcanic reef is capable of handling the biggest swells the Caribbean Sea can throw at it. Fickle and difficult to ride, with a twisting channel – and usually ending on dry reef – the right is the better, longer wave. But the left off the peak can offer quick, chunky tubes as well. Beware of the Caribbean beating that this wave is capable of administering. The powerful currents, shallow reef and shorter-period waves produced by storms on this side of the country keep you on your toes. Nearby Puerto Viejo is a small party town on the beach with a Caribbean flavour, and is worth some time even if Salsa Brava isn't breaking.
Nearest town // Puerto Viejo

PLAYA HERMOSA

Just south of Jacó, one of Costa Rica's original surf meccas, Playa Hermosa is one of the heaviest breaks in Central America, and is the location of several high-profile contests. There are several quality beach breaks along the coast here, but they're all fast, hollow, and can get very powerful indeed. It's also possible to be surfing Playa Hermosa the same day you arrive in Costa Rica, as it takes just over an hour to drive from San José to this gorgeous black-sand beach. Fly in on the red-eye and you could surf the famous sand-bottom A-frames for a couple of hours before getting a breakfast of delicious *gallo pinto* at one of the beachfront restaurants.
Nearest town // Jacó

MAVERICKS

In this excerpt from his book, The Fear Project, Jaimal Yogis recounts his insane journey to surfing – and surviving – his very first monster wave in California.

'm not sure why I opened the book. I already knew what it said.
'Best Size: Triple-overhead to 8oft faces.
Ability Level: Nothing short of Flea, Laird or Neptune (Flea and Laird being two of the best big-wave surfers in the world; Neptune being a god.)

Hazards: Death by drowning, sharks, run over by a whale, a trip through the rocks, hypothermia, broken boards, ego deflation.'

Surfline's *California Surf Guide* isn't helping my situation. Seeing the dangers in print changes things. I trip and fumble as I walk around the house, wiping counters that don't need wiping. I don't eat. I check and double-check that I have everything, but still feel vulnerable, exposed. Something must be missing. Music. Music will help, I'm thinking. Here we go, the Felice Brothers, a favourite. But the normally soothing sounds are grating. Darwin comes to mind: 'When fear reaches an extreme pitch...the mental powers fail.'

I get what's happening here. For the last couple of years I'd been talking to some of world's top scientists and psychologists about how fear works and how to, you know, keep kicking butt when you feel like curling up in the foetal position. I actually incorporated years of interviews and research with my own personal experience to create *The Fear Project*. The especially brilliant part of the plan? Making myself the guinea pig. Yes, after a decade of working my way up to feeling marginally comfortable at anything served up by Ocean Beach, San Francisco's occasional big-wave spot, I'd put my theorising to the test and make a quantum leap south to the death-wave, Mavericks. It has all seemed so brilliant. Until today.

In the parking lot, a silver Tacoma rumbles into the slot next to me. Inside is Ryan Augenstein, a pro-surfer who competes in the annual Mavericks contest. Augenstein looks casual, like he's going out to breakfast. I envy him. Then, an SUV full of men who look like they could be the Rolling Stones' bodyguards rolls up. Behind the wheel is Jeff Clark – the Jeff Clark who discovered these waves. These guys are the gatekeepers. What. In the hell. Am I doing here?

Unlike Ocean Beach, the paddle-out won't be hard. The simultaneous beauty and deception of Mavericks is that there is a deep-water channel, allowing surfers to literally paddle out on peaceful flat ocean, then approach the takeoff zone between set waves from the side, often still with dry hair. With a blue October sky above, I feel lighter with each stroke toward Mavericks. Dr Lardon's technique of a 'positive anchoring thought' comes to mind, too, and

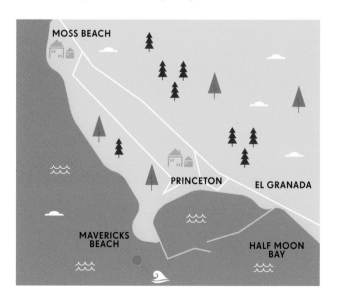

I start chanting in my head: 'I do this every day. I do this every day'. Nonetheless, when I finally see the pack, my stomach knots.

There are maybe 15 of them, floating near a patch of kelp, practically shoulder to shoulder. People had told me that the takeoff zone was small at Mavericks, but I had no idea I'd be practically holding hands with them. It's deceptively flat out here between sets, almost calm. But when a wave finally comes, the tone changes.

When the first green wall – tall as a four-storey building – marches off the horizon and pushes onto the reef, the base of the wave (the cauldron, as it's called) drops below sea level, sucking in its gut. There is the hook as the swell boosts to full height, and then that weightless, eerie quiet as the lip falls toward the sea. When the lip connects, forming a vapid core as big as the Holland Tunnel, the explosion of white blows higher than the wave itself, 40ft up; and the sound, Jesus – an explosion.

Behind this monster there's another monster, and a surfer is going. I recognize his paddle and his wetsuit. It's Alex Martins, one of the Mavericks competitors who occasionally fixes my boards at his San Francisco shop. He pops to his feet quickly, composed even as he rides down, down, down. Something shifts in my brain. I know Alex. Alex is human. I am human. I have dreamed of doing this from the age of 12. People do this. I can do this.

I paddle closer to the pack, nodding and trying to look manly and confident. Nobody acknowledges me. The other faces are familiar, but only through surf media: Flea, Grant Washburn, Tyler Smith, Skindog. The minutes pass, the minutes turning to strange, trancelike hours of watching; hours of gradually moving deeper into the path of the beast, hours of hedging, second-guessing. I try to cheat inside and paddle for the smaller sets – small, meaning, oh, just a few giraffes high – but at the top, I'm looking over the edge of a cliff as it crumbles. Everything in me wants out and back and away. All I can think is that this is where fear makes sense. Mark Foo died on a day just like this, his body floating in a lagoon after catching an edge on an 18ft wave. Mark Foo, who never came back – never. But I've trained for this. The statistics are on my side. You must push

ALIENS AND A-FRAMES

Locals have long reported seeing flying saucers streaking across the sky near the giant golf ball-like structure perched on Pillar Point, just east of Mavericks. This house-sized globe is actually a sensitive radar instrument that tracks missiles being shot from Vandenberg Air Force Base. Air Force insiders say the UFO sightings are missile tests, but those explanations don't satisfy UFO enthusiasts. Perhaps an intergalactic big-wave invitational is in our future.

Clockwise from top left: the opening ceremony of the WSL Mavericks Challenge; surviving the Mavericks drop; the surf shop owned by local pioneer Jeff Clark. Previous page: the Mavericks swell regularly reaches 50ft

past instinct. This is the greatest of human feats. This is philosophy, science. This is... Oh, mother f–

A rampart of green almost twice as big as anything that has yet come, far outside, has eclipsed the sky. And so the mayhem begins. Everyone scraping for the horizon. Most make it over, but it's too late for me. I'm in the dragon's shadow now. Automatically, I fling my board forward and dive down into the pocket. Diving deep, deep, into the murk, hoping, praying. I'm somehow suddenly through. I breathe air, but just when I think I'm safe, I feel the tug. My board is caught in the vortex and the leash is yanking me down. One last gulp of air, and... Darkness.

I'm under, pulled deep, deeper than I've ever been before. The green murk turns to black. I take a guess as to which way is up and swim. The light must be around here somewhere. Please, please, lighter, lighter, and – inhale. Yes. No! On the horizon, the next wave, equally ugly, impossibly high, is plunging down. An avalanche of foam mows me down and I'm back into blackness again.

But once I see that everyone survived (including myself), another shift occurs. I have genuine information now. The horrible unknown – 'what will it be like to get smashed by a four-storey wave?' – is now demystified. I'm tired and hungry. I've been out for four or five hours and I haven't caught a wave. While I have physical energy

left, my real fatigue goes deeper. What I'm really tired of is hedging, doubting, feeling like I don't belong. The whole time, I've been waiting for that perfect fearless state. But the fact is, the fear is not going to leave. I'm not in any peaceful, meditative state. In fact, after hours of botching opportunities, I'm incredibly agitated. I take a few deep breaths. *Just let the fear be there*, I tell myself.

I'm a little hesitant to call what happens next letting go. It's a more primal surrender to whatever outcome – yes, even death – and a simultaneous sharpening of the senses. Instead of feeling weaker by embracing fear, I'm flooded with a surge of power. And as soon as this mental shift comes, I'm almost magically in position. The wave is coming right to me, too fast it seems, but I don't care.

I turn my board toward land and paddle. Suddenly, I'm on my feet looking over the mountain's precipice, and when it boosts to full height, the whole ocean hiccups. I scream down the wall so high above me, it's perfectly surreal. I look over my left shoulder at the houses of whitewater and they are just there, just houses of whitewater. Everything is big and beautiful and fast. I ride a football field of water, thinking nothing at all, the avalanche on my heels. The wave flattens, then reforms into a second frothy bowl. I drop down this ledge, half the size of the original. It slingshots me forward. Then, seeing the wave is going to close, I pull off the back, skimming and skimming and skimming across the flat sea.

Lying down on my board, there's a moment before I snap out of my trance and realise what has just happened. The fear has dissolved. It will be back, of course, but for now, there is this moment when only faith remains. And I belong here. I belong here, too. And while I don't know it yet, for weeks, months, even years to come, the memory of this one wave, the raw joy, will permeate my life and alter it.

> *"The horrible unknown – 'what will it be like to get smashed by a four-storey wave?' – is now demystified"*

ORIENTATION

Type of wave // Deep-water A-frame monster with a long hollow right, and a short hollow left. Doesn't break until triple-overhead.

Best conditions // October–April. Long-period west swells create terrifying slabby bowls. Breaks on all tides, but best on mid to low incoming tides. Do not attempt with a south wind.

Nearest town // Half Moon Bay.

Getting there // Half Moon Bay is an hour's drive south of San Francisco.

Where to stay // From camping at Half Moon Bay State Beach (a decent beach break) to a room at Half Moon Bay Ritz, there's a big range of prices and options here.

Things to know // If you're wondering if Mavs is the right place for you to surf, it's probably not. If you're serious about attempting Mavericks, there is now a big-wave safety course run by some of the best (www.bwrag.com).

MORE LIKE THIS
PACIFIC OCEAN POWERHOUSES

NELSCOTT REEF, OREGON

Unlike many of the Pacific Northwest's waves – which are usually guarded by fierce locals, dense forest and rugged cliffs – Nelscott is a reef break that lies almost a mile (1.5km) offshore. Waves with faces of 30–40ft are regular in winter on the inside reef, and can jump up to 60ft or more when breaking on the outside ledge. A regular spot for Oregon's underground big-wave chargers, Nelscott was thrust into the wider surfing spotlight with the debut of the Nelscott Reef Big Wave Classic, an invitational competition, in 2005. Since then it has attracted some of the world's best, who come to take on massive swell in frigid waters teeming with apex predators of the deep.

Nearest town // Lincoln City

KILLERS, MEXICO

Baja California's famed sea monster off the Todos Santos islands was discovered by San Diego surfers decades before Jeff Clark began his solo kamikaze missions at Mavericks. As at Half Moon Bay, an underwater canyon off these islands funnels and focuses winter's giant west and northwest swells onto a deep-water reef, causing the waves at Killers to stand at least twice as tall as other spots nearby. The dark-blue righthanders then detonate over the deep-water reef. When it's triple-overhead-plus, a lip as thick as a car can throw top-to-bottom at Killers. The water here is a more inviting blue and 10–20°C (50–68°F) warmer than Mavericks, and the barrel pitches about 20% less aggressively.

Nearest town // Ensenada

OCEAN BEACH, CALIFORNIA

Grant Washburn, Danny Hess, Bianca Valenti, Mark Renneker, Alex Martins – these are just a few of the Mavericks regulars who live a few blocks from Ocean Beach in San Francisco. Big-wave riders love 'OB' for many reasons. The 3-mile (5km) stretch of beach break is open to swells from anywhere in the Pacific, and the sandbars can usually turn just about any size swell into a rideable wave. From 1ft summer log days to 20ft winter A-frames, if there's a bump in the water, Ocean Beach is open for business – and packing a heavier-than-expected smackdown (think Puerto Escondido beatings in water temps of 53°F/12°C). Ocean Beach can attract thousands of surfers when it's clean and small, but once it's double-overhead-plus, mother nature is the VIP bouncer. With complex wave fields and only luck-of-the-draw channels, you'd be hard-pressed to find a more challenging paddle on a big day.

Nearest town // San Francisco

SAQUAREMA

After a few sessions in and around Rio de Janeiro, Ben Mondy could see why Brazilians approach surfing with the same fervour they do football.

It took me 30 years from the first time I saw a Brazilian surfer to actually visit Brazil. It was 2017, and I'd been invited to cover the Championship Tour (CT) event in Saquarema, about 70 miles (113km) east of Rio. Between heats, I paddled out during a freesurf and was sitting in the channel as Lucas 'Chumbo' Chianca dropped into a wave I was sure would kill him. With the 17th-century Church of Our Lady of Nazareth perched above the wave, I watched as Chianca swiftly spun into position, performed three powerful paddles and stroked into a huge wave. But as he popped up, the nose of his board was lifted by the strong offshore breeze, leaving just the tip of his trailing backfin as the only part of his surfboard in any

contact with the Southern Atlantic ocean. He airdropped from the lip – a precursor to a horrific wipeout for almost any other surfer. But Chianca had grown up in Saquarema, was pushed into his first wave by his father on this very beach aged just three. Now 22, he's won the Best Performance award at the prestigious Big Wave Awards and clinched Big Wave Tour wins at Nazaré and Puerto Escondido. So perhaps I shouldn't have been so surprised then when Chianca landed at the bottom of the wave, compressed his knees, and remained glued to his board as he made his bottom turn to safety.

It was the late 1980s when my surf-obsessed friends and I had that first sight of a Brazilian surfer. We had wagged a day off

PRE-PORTUGUESE

Thousands of years before surfers descended on Saquarema, its indigenous Tamoios people were revered for their skills as fisherfolk and watermen. When the Portuguese arrived under King Dom João III in the 16th century, they too were impressed by the locals' advanced canoeing skills. That, of course, didn't stop them from claiming the area as their own and, despite legendary and fierce opposition from the Tamoios, quickly establishing a base.

school and travelled an hour by bus to watch Surfest, the annual professional comp held at Newcastle Beach in Australia. Here, we got our first glimpse of Fabio Gouviea who, along with Flavio Padaratz, would go on to become the first Brazilian surfer to make a global impact. Almost 40 years later, Brazil is the undisputed global surfing superpower. Gabriel Medina became the first Brazilian to win a World Title in 2014, and repeated the feat in 2018; Adriano de Souza chipped in with another in 2015.

Surf culture first exploded on the beaches of Rio in the early 1960s, with its epicentre at the city beach of Praia do Arpoador. This was the location of Brazil's first world circuit event in 1976, and since then Brazil has been a regular stop on the CT circuit (Kelly Slater claimed his seventh World Title here in 2005, and Mick Fanning his first in 2007). Brazil's CT location shifted over time, shuffling between Rio and Florianópolis in the south. However in 2017, the CT found a new home in nearby Saquarema.

With its low-key surf vibe and clean waters, Saquarema reminded me of Byron Bay minus the Scandinavian backpackers and overpriced healing crystals. Despite being so close to Rio, Saquarema also has real natural beauty, being framed by the Atlantic on one side and lagoons, plains and mountains on the other.

I checked in at the Aloha Pousada, your typical family run accommodation, just a few steps from the beach. I was greeted with some freshly baked bread and homemade jam by my host

Maria, and a detailed surf report from her partner, Nunes. As I scarfed down the bread, Nunes grabbed my board, strapped it to his quad bike and waved for me to jump on.

As we scoured the relatively undeveloped beach for the best breaks, it was strange to think we were less than 100 miles (160km) from Rio. Rio has world-class waves, for sure, but the lineups are like the city itself: the crowds are thick and ferocious. Passing through Rio, it was easy to become distracted by everything *but* surfing – the dancing, the drinking and the eating. But in Saquarema, it's easy to remain single-minded.

The locals in Saquarema are largely left alone to make their own rules. It is very much a surf town, especially in the winter months when the non-surfing tourist numbers dwindle. Surf shops and surfboard repair signs are dotted along the beach roads, and the restaurant menus celebrate the local breaks and local heroes.

Surfing is celebrated here for good reason. The 2640ft (800m) stretch of Itaúna Beach is what draws people here. It doesn't quite have Arpoador's surf history, nor the variety of Florianópolis' many beach breaks. However, Saquarema has power, consistency and quality. It's a true surfers' break, without any distractions. Which is why, by the 1980s, Saquarema had become known as the 'Surf Maracanã' after the iconic football stadium in Rio. At Itaúna Beach, a channel runs out of the natural lagoon on the western end, creating big swells that can hold shape – a rarity in Brazil.

From left: Malia Manuel of Hawaii shows off at Saquarema's Oi Rio Pro; the town comes alive during the annual competition; Saquarema's beaches offer a quiet escape from Rio. Previous page: Brazil's Adriano de Souza is one of many local phenoms

"Saquarema became known as the 'surf Maracanã' after the iconic football stadium"

Thankfully, Saquarema mostly dished out forgiving and fun sessions during my trip, rather than the blood, thunder and heroics I witnessed with Chianca. The area is full of multi-generational surf families, and this translates into the lineup, where it was almost always a friendly vibe. I'd often be joined by a blur of groms popping airs at will, whose natural exuberance was kept in line by dads, mums, uncles and cousins.

Of course, as with any surf spot, sometimes there were no waves at all. But when there are zero waves to be had, there's no better place to be than a Brazilian beach. I would simply join the bikini- and Speedo-clad locals sunbaking, eating pastries from the local bakery, drinking cold beers and playing soccer in the sand until the sun went down. No one does beach culture with more fun and zest than the Brazilians, and I'd argue that the people of Saquarema do it better than anyone else.

A few days after that memorable session with Chianca, I met up with him again to watch the contest – along with 10,000 others, who were passionately supporting the Brazilian surfers. It was especially fascinating to see, considering what an individual sport surfing is. But patriotism clearly runs deep in Brazilian surfing.

Afterward, Chianca and I went for an acai bowl. 'We are so proud of our surfers', he said to me, 'and I'm proud to have grown up in Saquarema – this sleepy town has helped Brazilians become the best surfers in the world.'

ORIENTATION

Type of wave // Powerful beach breaks.
Best conditions // The winter storm season from April to October delivers the biggest swells and lightest winds.
Nearest town // Saquarema; Rio is a two-hour drive south.
Getting there // Nearest airport is Rio de Janeiro (GIG); there are regular buses and airport transfers to Saquarema.
Where to stay // There are inexpensive *pousadas* (small hotels) a short walk from the beach. Aloha Pousada, Pousada do Suico and Pousada Catavento cater for surfers and backpackers.
Things to know // The Oi Rio Pro is the CT event that has put Saquarema on the global surf map. It runs in May each year and crowds swell during this week, creating a great party atmosphere. The chance to watch the world's best surfers compete on quality waves, while scoring a few yourself, make it a great time to visit.

Opposite: Brazil's Fernando de Noronha archipelago offers up tubes and tropical perfection

MORE LIKE THIS
THE BEST OF BRAZIL

MARESIAS

Located on São Paulo state's northern coastline, 100 miles (160km) north of the capital city itself, Maresias is a beautiful 3-mile (5km) stretch of beach that offers great waves, natural beauty and no small amount of sophisticated fun. Initially known as one of the country's most consistent and best barrelling beach breaks, it has gained recent recognition as the home wave of the two-times world champion, Gabriel Medina. The wave helped him hone his incredible technique, as it offers punchy days for airs and rotations in the summer, but also long walls and powerful, hollow barrels during the autumn and winter months. Maresias was once only accessible via a long dirt road, and attracted only the most intrepid of surfers; new roads, development and deforestation have now improved access, but not to the extent that it has lost its sleepy coastal feel. But Maresias does heave a bit on weekends when the São Paulo socialites pile in. Luckily they tend to hit the bars, posh restaurants and all-hours nightclubs rather than the barrelling waves.
Nearest town // São Paulo

FERNANDO DE NORONHA

The Fernando de Noronha archipelago lies 220 miles (354km) from Brazil's northeastern coast, and is best accessed via a flight from the coastal city of Recife. The view through the plane window reveals a chunk of volcanic rock measuring up at just 10 sq miles (26 sq km), as well as 20 smaller islands, and gives a great overview of what this aquatic wonderland has to offer: glinting turquoise sea, pristine sand and many, many waves. There's a smattering of quality reef breaks and point breaks on the 'big' island, and a ton of quality beach breaks – including a barrelling left at Cacimba do Padre, the location for the annual Hang Loose Pro. Thanks to its distance from the mainland, the surf arrives quite clean and is normally bigger than at other breaks around Brazil. The best Fernando swells come from winter storms in the frigid North Atlantic, so prime surf season is December to March (summertime in Brazil). That means the water is bath-warm, and the predominant winds are offshore.
Nearest town // Vila dos Remedios

IMBITUBA

Located in the bottom-third of the southern state of Santa Catarina, the small city of Imbituba may not offer the aesthetic natural beauty of Saquarema or Fernando de Noronha, but the beaches and waves are among Brazil's most consistent. The best beach breaks are at Praia Rosa, but the money break is Praia Vila, a clean and consistent wave that, in large south to east swells, can hold the biggest waves in Brazil. Being so far south, the water is a little chilly: rubber is required all year round, especially in the winter when the swells are most consistent. Out of the water, the Santa Catarina province and its capital make much of the area's German heritage, with Alpine-style architecture and lots of beer drinking around the huge annual Oktoberfest; you'll also find a quiet, rural vibe in the small, friendly fishing villages.
Nearest town // Imbituba

CORTES BANK

Pro big-wave surfer Greg Long is one of the most powerful watermen on the planet and a pioneer in his sport. The wave he loves most is the one that almost killed him.

The way I fell off my board was nothing out of the ordinary – not much different to numerous other wipeouts I'd had over the course of my career. But there's a different sort of energy at Cortes Bank. There's so much water moving and it's incredibly violent. And what really took it from being a bad wipeout to the wipeout that nearly cost me my life was the hold-down.

I figured it would probably be a two-wave hold-down, so I decided to swim for the surface and get a quick breath. Just as I was about to get my head above water, the second wave landed on top of me, and actually knocked the wind out of me. That was the pivotal moment. That pushed me back down into what became another two-wave hold-down. And I was out of air. But I knew not to take a breath, no matter what. If you voluntarily take a breath underwater, that water goes straight into your lungs. Whereas, if you hold your breath until you black out, your body's natural safety mechanism – where your larynx closes off your airway – kicks in. Eventually, I just couldn't hang on any longer and I blacked out. It was a long time before my safety team got to me and pulled me out of the water.

But, the greater the challenge, the greater the reward, right? To this day, that's what motivates me to ride big waves.

Cortes Bank is 100 miles (160km) off the California coast. There's no landmass in sight. The waves get pulled up from 2000ft

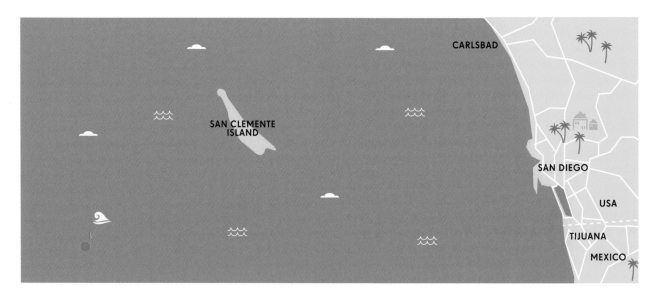

CARLSBAD

SAN CLEMENTE ISLAND

SAN DIEGO

USA

TIJUANA

MEXICO

below, and then they hit this huge seamount really abruptly. The currents out there are really extreme. Cortes has tons of weird boils and deep spots. I was drawn to it because it was just such an unknown frontier, a bit mysterious, and no one really knew all of its faces. And coming into my 20s, I was looking for the greatest challenge I could find in big-wave surfing. I felt it was possible that I had the greatest big wave in the world right at my back door. Based on its symmetry, I felt it had the potential to hold surfable 100ft waves.

I was born and raised in San Clemente, California, and my first experience on a surfboard was just like a lot of kids from the area. I was five or six and my dad, a lifeguard supervisor for all the state beaches, took me to San Onofre, a really popular place to learn. But with my dad, we were never just going surfing. We would sit and study the break, identifying the safe zones and any potential hazards. He taught us to spearfish and body-surf – I guess I had a sense of comfort in the ocean that probably exceeded a lot of kids my age. I'd surf Trestles every single day in the summer. We'd ride our bikes down there at 7am and not leave the water until sunset.

I made my first trip to a big wave when I went to Baja California, Mexico to surf Todos Santos. I was 15. I was lucky to have been invited by a few older guys like John Walla, who is a rock-solid waterman. My first day I was surfing 15–20ft faces. I remember one 25ft face where a bunch of us got caught inside; I got the wave right on the head. As odd as it sounds, it was almost more fun than the waves I actually rode that day – a different sense of accomplishment, I guess. After that, I knew that big-wave surfing was all I wanted to do.

A few years later, 2001 or so, I was surfing Todos on a particularly big day; that same day, John Walla was actually captaining a boat out to Cortes for Peter Mel and a few others. That was when I first became aware of Cortes Bank. I researched everything I could about the place – the bottom contours, footage of other guys surfing it – and I wanted to surf it the next opportunity that came up. Cortes breaks all the time, but you need the right weather to accompany it – calm enough to get a boat out there, for one. And Cortes will sometimes just go to sleep for an entire season; sometimes two. I became obsessed with it. In 2004, I finally went out.

Its unknown is what's so appealing about it. Your horizon line extends 360 degrees, so you've got no reference point as to where you are in the lineup. We actually drop three buoys – one on the inner part of the lineup, one outside and a little bit wide of the channel, and one out back – and use those as points of reference. Often things go bizarrely quiet – just this stillness that literally makes you feel like you're on the edge of the earth.

Strangely, my interest in Cortes sort of waned after that first trip, but I always kept a close eye on it, and surfed it any time conditions aligned.

In 2012 we decided to launch a big paddle-in mission – we wanted to paddle into the waves instead of using Jet Skis. This was

UNDERWATER ISLAND NATION

In 1966, a group of American businessmen tried to start their own independent nation on the submerged island of Cortes Bank, free from the constraints of US law and taxation. They planned to harvest and process seafood, especially abalone, which led the media to coin the project Abalonia. But the plans died when the freighter *Jalisco*, which was to form the core of the island's base, was smashed up by big waves in a storm. The shallow shipwreck remains there today.

"Often things go bizarrely quiet – just this stillness that literally makes you feel like you're on the edge of the earth"

the session where I ended up having my big wipeout. When the support Jet Skis pulled me out of the water, I was still unconscious. But they got to me in time. I still had oxygen in my lungs. Once on the big boat, they got my airway clear and then I just started trying to take a few breaths on my own.

The wipeout haunted me. I even felt some resentment towards Cortes – I sort of dismissed it, like 'oh, I don't need to go surf there again'. When I finally got back in the water at Mavericks, I was almost in a catatonic state. I just sat out there and froze my ass off. I didn't even catch a wave. Then, I slowly did begin catching some big waves, but of lesser consequence. Still, being *under* a wave would sometimes trigger those feelings of panic. And the idea of going back out to Cortes was unthinkable.

I ended up taking a few months off. I didn't even talk about big-wave surfing. I actually began accepting that if I never wanted to surf big waves again, it was totally okay. And that was actually one of the greatest gifts. In retrospect, the experience put into perspective what was important in my life. Awards, accolades, achievement – none of that registered. I just thought 'I'm still alive – I can still walk down to the beach, jump on a longboard and, you know, go surf with my pops.' That's when it all kind of shifted for me. And then I was able to go back to trying to ride big waves again, but without attachment or expectation. The confidence started to trickle back in.

Two years later, literally the day after the Mavericks contest, there was this beautiful window of fun swell for Cortes. We flew down on the night of the contest, literally walked right onto a boat at Dana Point at 10pm, and started motoring out. We surfed it the next day.

Clockwise from top left: Jet Ski safety crews are as skilled as the surfers; Cortes Bank on a 'smaller' day; Greg Long hopes to ride the world's biggest wave here one day. Previous page: Long pushes the limits of big-wave surfing

ORIENTATION

Type of wave // The Cortes Bank A-frame breaks off an underwater island. Locals believe that in the right swell conditions, it could hold a rideable 100ft wave.

Best conditions // The wave is only rideable when storms are big enough to create swell, but not so big that they make it impossible to reach Cortes by boat.

Nearest town // The wave breaks roughly 100 miles (160km) west of San Diego.

Getting there // Private boat charter.

Where to stay // Surf House in Encinitas.

Things to know // This is a wave for the world's best big-wave surfers only. It starts and ends in water deeper than 1000ft (300m), and waves here are reported to move 50% faster than those on the North Shore of Hawaii, making paddling into them almost impossible. Instead, most surfers get towed into them on a Jet Ski.

Opposite: the original big wave at Waimea Bay hosts the most revered event in surfing, the Eddie Aikau Invitational – aka 'The Eddie'

MORE LIKE THIS
BUCKET-LIST BIG WAVES

WAIMEA BAY, HAWAII

A jaw-droppingly beautiful spot on the North Shore of O'ahu, Waimea Bay has been the ultimate proving ground for big-wave surfers for the last 50 years. Deep-water swells hit a lava shelf to produce a wave that rises up savagely to heights of 25–30ft. Even if you can handle the wave, jostling amongst the crowds in the lineup is another matter. In 2009, Greg Long earned his place in surfing folklore here at the Eddie Aikau Big Wave Invitational, a contest which only takes place in waves over 20ft. Long, who was just 25 at the time, won the comp with a rare 100 points, beating Kelly Slater in the process.
Nearest town // Pupukea

GHOST TREES, CALIFORNIA

Originally known locally as Pescadero Point, Ghost Trees is a storied big-wave spot off the Monterey peninsula that, for a brief moment in the late 2000s, looked like it was going to rival its hard-hitting Californian neighbour, Mavericks. Then, in 2009, the NOAA (National Oceanic and Atmospheric Administration) banned Jet Skis from the area to protect local marine life – this meant surfers could no longer tow in to the waves here. Paddling into these waves is not necessarily impossible, but with faces as high as 60ft and a brutal scattering of rocks just below the surface, even Long has decided to let Ghost Trees lie for now.
Nearest town // Pescadero

ALEJANDRO SELKIRK ISLAND, CHILE

Some 500 miles (805km) off mainland Chile, this rugged, remote island is named after Alexander Selkirk, a Scottish sailor who was shipwrecked nearby – an experience that inspired Daniel Defoe to write *Robinson Crusoe*. In stormy weather, local fisherfolk on this beautiful volcanic island have long steered clear of the spots which give rise to giant waves, but in recent years surfers studying the maps and charts have arrived to ride them. In 2019, a group of Patagonia-sponsored waveriders made it out here; the wind ruined their plans that time, but they and other big-wave hunters are sure to return, as it remains one of the only known big-wave spots in the world that has yet to draw the big names.
Nearest town // Santiago

SUNSET BEACH

O'ahu's North Shore is surfing's ultimate testing ground. Beau Flemister says
his lifetime of sessions at Sunset are what define him as a surfer.

'd waited underwater, counting the seconds evenly to let the notorious Sunset Beach West Bowl sneaker-set roll over me. Eyes open, I watched the explosive columns boil above my head. Then I felt the tension in my leash suddenly vanish with an undeniable *POP*. Not good. Not good at all, I remember thinking. I kicked toward the light, broke the surface, and gasped for air.

In the soupy white foam, I looked around at the handful of others that had also bailed their boards – but all had boards still attached to leashes. A couple surfers glanced at me – at the poor, unlucky, boardless creature treading water in the worst place on the island – and I will never forget their expression. It's one you hardly ever see during a North Shore winter's cache of ego and hyper-masculinity: pity. Indeed, Sunset rarely shows pity to locals *or* visiting takers. Which category I fit into, I wasn't quite sure.

I was 18 years old when I moved back to O'ahu after a five-year sabbatical on the East Coast of the US. I was staying in the dorms in 'Town' (Honolulu), enrolled at the University of Hawaii. And while my major was still very undecided, I was decidedly resolute on packing all my credits into Tuesday–Thursday courses so as to maximize a higher surfing education on the North Shore. By the start of the semester, the winter season had already begun.

I'd load boards and any takers into the car and make that 50-minute drive from campus to the North Shore a handful of times every single week, over that last batch of pineapple fields outside of Wahiawa, always trying to gauge the size of the surf by the whitewater lines flickering on the horizon: 6–8ft? Bigger? We'd quickly learn that on the North Shore, if you had to ask, then, yes, it was surely bigger.

But returning home to O'ahu I had a unique perspective. Part tourist (*haole*), part resident (*kama'aina*), I had a sort of dual citizenship in both worlds, often questioning my own local-ness (*kama-kinda*). Just as they call Honolulu 'Town', locals call the North Shore 'Country'. Indeed, the place can seem like its own separate nation-state, complete with its own language: '*chout, u faka!* is blunt shorthand for telling someone to watch out. Country seems to have its own systems of law and justice. The lifeguards are known to look away when a fight from the water bleeds onto the beach.

So a trip back to Country was always a new adventure, as navigating these nuances on land can be equally as treacherous

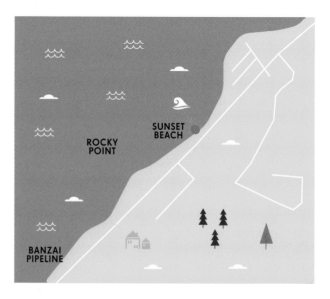

as on the ocean. One learns to drive slow down Ke Nui Rd, the parallel lane stretching from Log Cabins to Kammie Land that smells of plumeria flowers and sun-screened flesh; and even slower, still, through the neighbourhood behind Sunset Point, as per the many hand-painted 'Watch Out For Keiki' (children) signs diligently enforced by vigilante residents surveilling transgressors.

As a returning local, I re-learned the dance steps to the so-called Seven Mile Miracle, while simultaneously rediscovering Country's customs and culture. On the North Shore, for instance, there's just as much nuance in the tautness of your shaka (not too tight, nor too loose) as there is at a punchy surf break like Rocky Point. I remembered I could score a meal at the Foodland supermarket from the dubious hotplate section for under eight bucks; and which line to avoid at Ted's Bakery in the morning. I smiled at strangers on the beach paths – not letting my gaze linger long – and walked the tightrope, both in the lineup and out. It doesn't take much to spark a confrontation here, whether by paddling too close to a local, or being far too cheerful at a backyard party. Indeed, I was once snapped at by a Pipeline icon for not picking up a piece of trash on the beach that I hadn't even seen while taking a look at the surf. So, you learn to look harder.

Guys who might be superstars back home in California or Brazil amount to nothing until they've proven themselves in the water here. In the Country, mettle is the most valuable currency there is. It can be hard to tell if the North Shore is nothing like the cult-classic movie of the same name, or exactly like it.

But I'd also rediscovered that surfing the North Shore isn't all just groundshaking Banzai Pipeline. Sure, Pipe is undeniably the most sought-after, picture-perfect wave on the coast, but it's only that for a very certain level of advanced surfer. Within those Seven Miles, there's also the leg-burning brilliance of a north swell at Laniakea; or the playful righthanders for longboarders and learners at Chun's Reef. Halfway through the winter, a sandbar forms just north of Pipeline at Ehukai Beach Park, with playful turquoise peaks spitting both ways over soft golden grains.

I wanted to ride a big board and challenge myself – and for that, there's always good ol' Sunset Beach, the OG of big-wave surf spots, a spot that can hold a wave bigger than 12ft (Hawaiian size) without closing out. The thing about surfing Sunset Beach on a bigger day is that whether you actually catch a set wave or get your ass handed to you, you always feel like you've accomplished something. You were out there that day, a feat in itself.

Predictably unpredictable, straying from the relative safety of a giant channel, the playing field out at Sunset is just as they say – way larger than it looks. Be it the currents, the shifting peaks or the utter space in the lineup, it's easy to get lost out there. Whereas, at 10ft Pipe, you can avoid the peak and dip in and out of the pack from the channel, 10ft Sunset has a way of sneaking up on you – like a truck rounding a corner when you thought it was safe to cross. Many say that a 12ft day at Sunset is more hectic than an 18ft day at Waimea Bay.

NATIVE LEGENDS

Sunset was a part of Hawaiian lore long before Westerners first surfed here. It was originally known as Paumalū ('taken secretly'), a name prompted by the story of a local woman who caught more octopus than was permitted, and was punished by having her legs bitten off by a shark. It's also said that, in order to prove himself, Prince Kahikilani paddled 100 miles (160km) from his home on Kaua'i just to surf the notorious Paumalū waves.

*Clockwise from top left: surf aside, O'ahu's
beaches are some of the world's best;
Australian pro Stephanie Gilmore surfs
Rocky Point; Hale'iwa has an authentic
small-island feel. Previous page: US pro
Brett Simpson takes on Sunset Beach*

"It can be hard to tell if the North Shore is nothing like the cult-classic movie of the same name – or exactly like it"

Oddly, the lineup at Sunset is a mishmash of egos and ages, from living legends sitting deep on the North Peak to World Tour warriors on the Inside Bowl. And then there's always the odd local kid, who looks barely nine years old, that makes you think 'well, if she's out here, then I've got nothing to worry about...'

Well, nothing other than that notoriously shifty West Peak bowl, that pops up out of nowhere. Which is precisely what got me treading water that day sans surfboard, near the end of my first winter back. I remember the long swim in that had me kissing the sand on the shoreline. I remember deciding to get a thicker leash before I surfed here again. I remember wanting to add another day of courses on to the next semester and clarify that 'Undecided' label for self-preservation.

And 18 years later, having surfed Sunset every winter since – including *big* Sunset, dozens of times – I still feel like a visitor. Or a tourist. Or a hopeless devotee making my weekly pilgrimage. Whatever it is, every trip to the Country still has me wondering, needlessly, if I remembered my passport.

ORIENTATION

Type of wave // A powerful, consistent right-hand reef break.
Best conditions // Tides don't matter much here, and Sunset breaks on any glimmer of a swell, from 2–15ft (Hawaiian size). It works on west, northwest, north and northeast swells, but is perfect on a 10–12ft westerly.
Nearest town // Hale'iwa.
Getting there // The North Shore is a 40-minute drive from Honolulu (HNL) airport on O'ahu.
Where to stay // Turtle Bay Resort is a 15-minute drive north of Sunset. There are homestays and B&Bs in the area, and a backpacker hostel near Waimea Bay.
Things to know // A bigger board – over 8ft – is recommended. Not only is it fun, but you'll catch more waves. It's very easy to get caught inside at Sunset, because the waves move fast. If you paddle for a wave here, commit.

Opposite: Hawaiian pro Kalani Chapman sneaks in a Pipeline session before the Billabong Pipe Masters

MORE LIKE THIS
TITANS OF THE NORTH SHORE

BANZAI PIPELINE

Unanimously recognized as the most desirable (and most photographed) wave on earth, the Banzai Pipeline – and its right-hand cohort, Backdoor Pipe – draw in the cream of the surf world and thousands of fans each December for the year's final (and often world-title-deciding) CT event, the Pipeline Masters. Many pro surfers (mostly Hawaiians) have crafted entire careers from surfing this one wave well. As gorgeous as it is dangerous, Pipeline's reefs serve up impossibly steep, intense and hollow left-hand tubes, at any size from 2ft to 12ft, from October to April. Made up of three consecutive breaks (First Reef, Second Reef and the rarely surfed Third Reef), Pipeline often hosts a tight pack of 50-plus surfers. As a spectator, if you happen to miss the Pipeline Masters in December, there's at least three more contests to witness there (Pipe Pro, Da Hui Backdoor Shootout and Bodysurfing World Championships) staged later on in the winter season.
Nearest town // Pupukea

ROCKY POINT

The punchy, hollow and often shallow reef break of Rocky Point (aka Rockies) lies some 1200ft (366m) north of Pipeline. Comprised of two waves (Rocky Rights and Rocky Lefts), splitting both ways in front of an exposed reef point, Rockies is known as the North Shore's premiere high-performance wave – this is the spot where a Dane Reynolds or Mason Ho practice their 360-degree aerials in front of an ever-present line of photographers manning tripods. Not reserved only for pros, Rockies is often considered an intermediate bridge between a softer wave at, say, Pupukea, and an advanced wave like Off the Wall or Pipeline. With the lefts preferring a more northwesterly, angled 3–4ft swell, and rights reeling down the line with a more north angle, Rocky Rights can serve up pretty tasty tube rides on waves of up to 6ft before the stretch of coastline between Ehukai and Kammies closes out.
Nearest town // Pupukea

LANIAKEA

One of the longest waves on the North Shore, the inviting right-hand reef break at Laniakea (aka Lanis) can feel more like a world-class point break when the conditions are optimal. For instance, on a north-angled swell, Lanis can break from the top of the point outside for over 300ft, with multiple tube sections along the way, and hold up to 10ft solid. With a large channel to paddle out on the Hale'iwa-side of the break, less experienced surfers often hang on that last peak that breaks into the channel, while more advanced surfers sit on sections of the wave up the point. Lanis isn't as shallow and intense as its neighbours, but if you wanted to work up to it, try Chun's Reef just to the north; it's a great spot for learners.
Nearest town // Hale'iwa

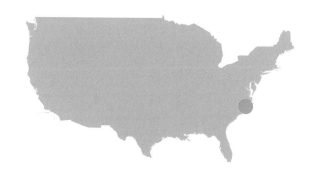

OUTER BANKS

The East Coast of the US has plenty of great waves. But none, says Matt Pruett, have the raw power and wild setting of those that break off North Carolina's barrier islands.

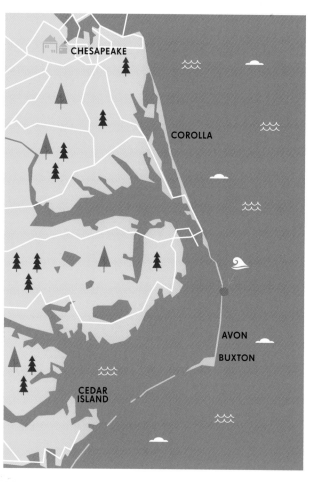

CHESAPEAKE

COROLLA

AVON

BUXTON

CEDAR
ISLAND

You know you truly love a place when you love it at its worst. That's what I keep telling myself as a galaxy of mosquitoes and horseflies swirl in the sweltering air outside my truck windows, ready to pounce. A miasma of car exhaust, tanning lotion and restaurant grease seeps through the cracks. A cacophony of horns, sirens and country music blasts my ears. It's July on the Outer Banks of North Carolina, my home for the last three decades. And I ain't too stoked.

Hwy 158, the main thoroughfare connecting the habitable parts of our sandbar, is a bumper-to-bumper boa constrictor of vehicles towing watercraft of all sorts. Drivers with licence plates from Quebec to Florida, Pennsylvania to Utah are all clustered together like human papilloma, and I try to imagine why they come. Every summer. What fantastic concoction of sea-glass sculptures, swaying sea oats and surreal sunsets, shipwreck dives and lighthouse strolls, playful porpoises and feral horses could seduce so many to this otherwise boring, frail strip of peninsulas and barrier islands?

Admittedly, it's not a bad problem to have. After all, visitors are the vessel that keeps our economy afloat. And I can only assume many come looking for the same liberty, detachment, or some other derivative of the same dream that's kept me here all these years. Perhaps we're even kindred spirits. As a teenage transplant in the early 1990s, I too was seduced. The Outer Banks to me back then was romantic. It was punk. It was haunting. But perhaps more important than anything else, it was where I first got barrelled.

Tubed. Pitted. Slotted. Piped. Shacked... Whatever you want to call it, getting barrelled is the absolute zenith of the surfing experience, and a milestone for any grommet. Before experiencing my first legit tube at Rodanthe Pier that day – getting behind the curtain, over the foam ball, out with the spit – I was just another kook from Virginia. Immediately afterward, however, I remember thinking to myself: 'I'm gonna move here.' I even remember whispering to myself 'then live here until I die.'

I can't remember the exact high school melodrama that had me so edgy that day, but whatever it was got swiftly silenced in sea foam, drowned in heaving saltwater and smashed to detritus atop a shallow sandbar. The thrills were nonstop. Every time I surfed, my wave count was through the roof. And I wasn't even very good yet. Nevertheless, these heaving emerald bombs detonated all around me, equally grotesque and gorgeous, with no-one mining them but me. I never saw another surfer all day long.

Blessed with a 230-degree swell window, the Outer Banks coastline is a veritable catcher's mitt for anything the Atlantic throws out. On rare world-class days, wintertime nor'easters have been known to produce a poor man's Skeleton Bay at the Lighthouse; while a tropical south swell can reveal an everyman's Burleigh Heads; and a sneaky, wind/groundswell mix could very well spawn a miniature Supertubos.

"It's our third day of a fun 6ft swell. My skin is burned, my eyes are bloodshot, and I have indigestion from Carolina BBQ"

That was the clincher for me, and probably every local surfer who decides to post up in the Outer Banks for life. Whether you're at Hatteras Lighthouse or Kitty Hawk Pier or any anonymous shore break in between, a good session on the Outer Banks is a microcosm of the most coveted part of the American dream: freedom. No toll booths or parking meters. No blackball or beach badges. None of the draconian hassles or antiquated ordinances that have become emblematic of so many other East Coast beach towns. Just mile after mile of free, easy access to weatherbeaten, dune-framed beachfront from which to pick your peak. Add a 4WD vehicle and a reasonably priced beach-driving permit, and you'll

think you've landed on Tatooine (or whichever *Star Wars* planet has the best surfing).

That's the ideal that nurtured me as a young surfer and, today, keeps the mid-life crises at bay. It's exactly what I'm chasing today, as I sit trapped in a traffic jam, stalked by flying insects. Because just up the road, right over the next bridge, beyond a certain dune somewhere along the Pea Island National Wildlife Refuge, is Isolation Incarnate.

That's not to say the Outer Banks isn't on the surf map. Indeed, it is in fact ground zero for any respectable East Coast surf trip – as it has been ever since the early 1970s. Despite its popularity, though, the surfing experience here is still a uniquely raw one. Shipwreck- and rubble-strewn beaches shake their sugary fists at the horizon, smack dab in the crosshairs of hurricanes. And that's not to mention all that comes with cold fronts. Perpetually flooded, it's a miracle these stilted homes haven't been blown off the map (knock on driftwood). Until then, surfers will keep coming. Top amateur competitors and their associated entourages descend here every September for the ESA Eastern Surfing Championships.

Granted, New England can hold more size, New Jersey gets more razor-perfect, and Florida is certainly more user-friendly. But none of those places can translate long-interval energy

Clockwise from top: feral horses graze along the Outer Banks shores; find the right spot and you might have the wave to yourself. Previous page: hollow, shreddable bliss in the Outer Banks

ORIENTATION

Type of wave // Beach breaks.
Best conditions // Head-high to 2ft-overhead surf; offshore (westerly) winds; incoming tide. Best in autumn.
Nearest town // Nags Head.
Getting there // The Outer Banks are around 1½ hours by road from Norfolk International Airport. A 4WD vehicle is recommended during your stay.
Where to stay // Nags Head has a lot of good motels, accommodates the most surf shops, has the most piers, and hosts the most surfing competitions.
Things to know // Bring all your wetsuit gear, regardless of season. The upwelling that often accompanies summertime offshores can cause water temperatures in the Outer Banks to plummet. Also, a gunnier surfboard with a bit more volume up front might help for taking steep, late drops.

and short-period windswell – and everything in between – into hollow, shreddable bliss at the drop of a hat. Swell energy is rarely a problem. Finding the right sandbar, on the other hand: therein lies the challenge. And that's what keeps us on our toes. Checking it hard. Driving and scouring, jogging and searching for that constantly shifting shallowness – swell after swell, season after season – until we stumble upon that distinctly OBX, sand-bottomed slab, dredging 50ft off the beach and blowing its guts out. Often without another soul in sight.

Today, we're on our third straight day of blazing sunshine, offshore winds and a very fun 6ft south-southeast swell from a cheeky low pressure system (a rarity this time of year). I'm starting to look like Papillon. My skin is burned and my eyes are bloodshot. My armpits and thighs are rashed and my muscles feel like overcooked ramen. I have indigestion from the Carolina barbecue I inhaled for lunch, my voice is scratchy from saltwater, and I've got another sand-spur stuck between my toes. Oh, and I'm still idling in traffic with the sea-glass hordes.

There are thousands of them, and only one of me. But I can't help smiling and, if we make eye contact, throwing 'em a shaka. Because there's really only one small difference between us. A tourist says: 'I'd like to live here.' A local says 'I'm gonna die here.'

Opposite: offshore of West Palm Beach, Reef Road is a big-wave break in a region better known for its pretty palm-lined streets and tropical vibe

MORE LIKE THIS
EASTERN USA'S BEST BARRELS

LIDO BEACH, NEW YORK

It's no longer a secret that a legitimate, thriving surf culture exists a mere 45 minutes by train from one of the world's greatest cities. Long Island boasts some of the heaviest, hollowest beach breaks on the entire US Eastern Seaboard – and Lido Beach has long been dubbed 'Escon-Lido' for its Puerto Escondido-like girth and power. During optimal conditions (south-southeast swells, north wind) ushered in by any properly directed nor'easter, low-pressure system or tropical swell, Lido's scattered sandbars are responsible for more broken boards, limbs and egos than you're likely to find at most East Coast beach breaks (most of which can't handle more than 8ft faces). Lido can easily hold double-overhead-plus energy, and it's nothing but barrels.
Nearest town // Long Beach

REEF ROAD, FLORIDA

Believe it or not, surf-challenged Florida has a legit big wave, even requiring Jet Ski tow-in on occasion. The Reef Road sandbar, some way offshore near West Palm Beach, is capable of handling the largest north-northeast swells (and not much else, given the shadowing from the Bahamas), and its predominantly left-hand lineup offers an adrenalized, polychromatic spectacle unlike anything else on the East Coast. Tropical flora and azure seawater aside, when it's really pumping here, Reef Road is a full Black Diamond, with viper-quick closeouts, below-sea-level double-ups, torrential currents, various species of shark and maddening crowds. It's probably one of the most dangerous surf spots in the southeast US.
Nearest town // West Palm Beach

BAY HEAD, NEW JERSEY

With hundreds of jetties and groins dotting the coastline of New Jersey, and many Army Corps of Engineers dredge-and-fill projects, every township in this state has its day. In terms of slam-dunk consistency, however, it's hard to beat the mile-long (1.6km) Bay Head zone, which features longer jetties than those further south. Preferring powerful southerly swells, Bay Head can handle anything from waist-high to double-overhead energy, often producing razor-perfect tubes funnelling the whole length of a shallow sandbar. It might be crowded with surfers, and it will be restricted by local ordinances, but if you can't get barrelled at Bay Head, then maybe getting barrelled isn't for you.
Nearest town // Avon-by-the-Sea

PUERTO ESCONDIDO

*Chas Smith finds that no amount of tequila can drown out
the fear of facing Mexico's heaviest wave.*

There is no better feeling than sitting on a sweltering beachfront patio in Mexico, languid fan spinning overhead, sipping a still-cold margarita – salt, rocks – nibbling shrimp tacos garnished with fresh pico de gallo. Which is why I couldn't quite understand why my knees were pulled to my chest like a frightened little kitty cat, why my heart pounded so hard that I thought it might leap right out of my throat. The chair underneath me quaked and my senses returned. Because this sweltering patio fronts Puerto Escondido, home to Mexico's biggest, most notorious, dangerous, famous and superlative wave. I could hear it thundering on the sand, snapping boards in half, eating grown surfers whole.

I'd come to the Mexican Pipeline, as it's called, to test myself – to push beyond what had become my comfort zone: namely soft southern California reef breaks, groomed Australian point breaks and shoulder-high tropical barrels. Being a surf journalist opens up a world of ease and, as I looked at myself square in the mirror one day, I was disappointed with the tanned, softened visage looking back.

I wasn't always such a baby. I'd grown up on Oregon's rugged coast, paddling out in my two wetsuits toward walls of mess – giant, freezing slabs that wanted to maim, chew, destroy; into rip currents that sucked my Xanadu and Rusty all the way to Japan. The entire coastline of Oaxaca has fun, reliable surf. But the wave, or rather waves, that put Puerto Escondido on the map are the heaviest, largest sand-bottomed monsters that break at the southern end of a broad 1½-mile (2.5km) beach named Playa Zicatela. Ostensibly, there is a right, ominously called Wheelchair Bar, and a left that hammers 600ft further down called Far Bar. Athough, traditional ideas of 'right' and 'left' are loose here. Being

sand bottomed, they each depend on proper bars to form, so both waves often appear just as one terrifying closeout.

The reason for its ferocity, geographers say, is the large trench that amplifies unfiltered Pacific rage into a condensed area. The sandbars may not always be consistent, but the swells are entirely dependable. From late spring until mid-autumn, Puerto Escondido rarely drops below head-high and regularly exceeds 15ft. Southern mainland Mexico is hot, humid and sticky, and the air temperature often matches the water temperature.

The town of Puerto Escondido perches right above the main beach in a colourful tangle of jungle. Cute, brightly painted

ice-cream shops sit beside porticoed knick-knack stores selling Day of the Dead statuettes. Music hangs in the air, children laugh, dogs bark. It is Mexico done right – just the right amount of hotels, bars and restaurants; just the right amount of convenience, with a strong local vibe. Buzzing, but never overly crowded.

Before paddling out, I stood shoulder to shoulder with tourists on the beach watching the monsters rise up and roar. I was clutching a 5'11 thruster – a board that was far too small for the break – with wax that had melted off entirely. But not paddling out was no longer an option – personal shame is one of the greatest motivators in surfing, and I would not have been able to live with retreat. After many deep breaths, I trotted to the water's edge and pushed off.

Paddling felt surreal, wild, like I imagine sumo wrestling might feel. The energy was overwhelming. The brine swirled around me, pulling my arms this way and that, taking me where it wanted. I had never felt that sort of raw intensity in any ocean, even Oregonian ocean, and I wondered how in the world those brave men and women out at Bars were able to keep their bodies from being drawn and quartered, much less catch waves and sometimes succeed.

A non-set nugget popped up in front of me. Not a proper Puerto Escondido nugget, as I had drifted too far south but, still, a wave – a wave at Puerto Escondido. I spun, paddled twice, popped to my feet, sped toward the shoulder and arrived safely in an imaginary channel, feeling like a legendary conqueror. 'I've got this!' I said to myself as I paddled south toward bigger and bigger waves, until I

HIDDEN MEANING

Escondido translates as 'hidden', and local lore has it that the town got its name thanks to the shenanigans of a ne'er-do-well pirate. He and his crew had just raided nearby Huatulco, snagging a young maiden in the process. As they sat anchored off an empty stretch of coast, the woman sensed her opportunity, swimming to shore and disappearing into the jungle. When the pirates couldn't find her, they told their captain she was 'escondido.'

"I could hear it thundering on the sand, snapping boards in half, eating grown surfers whole"

Clockwise from top: checking the swell off Puerto Escondido; surf travellers descend during the summer months. Previous page: Puerto Escondido's big wave

was sitting only a few hundred feet away from Wheelchair Bar. It was breaking much further outside than where I was, but it would be my inevitable next stop.

Then, the horizon darkened, ugly and mean. The sun blotted from the sky. Uh oh. I had gotten lucky, apparently, and been in some bizarrely eternal long-period swell, but now was the moment of truth. Now was the time to etch my name in the big-wave annals and be celebrated for all time. I span, paddled twice – and slipped off my board. I was subjected to the worst pounding of my entire surfing life.

I was pummelled in the torso, legs and head, my face driven toward the sand bottom and rubbed along it, exfoliating every single pore. I barely made it to the surface before getting drop-kicked three more times and miraculously washing up on the beach next to the tail half of my broken board, right in front of those same tourists. I looked up at them with swollen red eyes. One of them smirked while the rest pointed out to sea and gasped.

Afterward, I stumbled through town in a daze. I found an open patio, languid fan spinning overhead. I ordered a margarita – salt, rocks – and shrimp tacos garnished with fresh pico de gallo. I was still scared. But I had done it. And after two more margaritas – oh, and after snagging a new board – I'd do it again. Being physically terrified is a rare pleasure, as an adult.

ORIENTATION

Type of wave // Extremely heavy beach break.
Best conditions // Breaks year-round, but biggest from April to September.
Nearest town // Puerto Escondido.
Getting there // Fly to either Mexico City or Oaxaca City, then hop on a commuter flight to Puerto Escondido; you can also drive from Oaxaca City in 7½ hours.
Where to stay // Puerto Escondido is a very established surf destination, overflowing with cool, moderately priced pensions and hotels.
Things to know // There is a serious local crew that surfs around Puerto Escondido, and they should be respected. Go out of your way to be polite and deferential.

*Opposite: Barra de la Cruz, one of
Mexico's powerful sandbar breaks*

MORE LIKE THIS
THE BEST OF MEXICO

PASCUALES, COLIMA

Pascuales is said to be the perfect training ground for anyone keen to tackle the better-known waves of Puerto Escondido. Located near the township of Tecomán in the state of Colima, Pascuales roars to life with any hint of south swell. Coming out of deep water, deceptively powerful peaks wedge up on the black sand, offering both incredible tubes and big wipeouts. However, on smaller swells, perfect A-Frames dot the beach, though they're often busy with a regular crowd of surfers who prefer less adrenalin in their life. Mind you, with no other quality waves close by and the small town providing barely the basics, this is no honeymoon spot. Pascuales is all about paddling out when it's big, getting barrelled, and enduring bad beat-downs.

Nearest town // Tecomán

BARRA DE LA CRUZ, OAXACA

One of the most perfect (and contentious) point breaks in the world, Barra de la Cruz is the first Oaxacan wave that captured the attention of the global surfing population. Some 2½ hours east of Puerto Escondido, Barra was burned into the broader surf consciousness as a result of the 2006 Rip Curl Pro Search; although the promo material didn't name the wave (referring to it as 'La Jolla' instead of Barra de la Cruz), or even the town where it was being held, the event changed this sleepy Mexican hamlet forever. Since 2006, Barra de la Cruz has undergone significant development, including the relocation of the river mouth as a precaution to protect a newly built beach restaurant. The wave hasn't broken quite like it used to since the river mouth was shifted, but it still belongs on anyone's Mexico bucket list.

Nearest town // Barra de la Cruz

LA PUNTA, OAXACA

There's more to Mexico than right points, as impressively demonstrated by La Punta, just south of Puerto Escondido's pounding beach break. Peeling off a series of rocks at the top of the point of Zicatela Beach, and then running along the sand for several hundred feet, La Punta is still the archetypal Mexican point, only it's a left. Whilst it might not be as hollow as some of its right-hand counterparts, La Punta offers a mellow respite to goofy-footed surfers whose bodies have been twisted into awkward positions at nearby Puerto Escondido. As a result, La Punta has the tendency to be crowded, and the locals don't suffer fools if a gringo should drop in out of turn.

Nearest town // Puerto Escondido

SOUP BOWL

In a region not known for swell, Alex Wade learned that this famous wave in Barbados is as technical – and fun – as any break in the world.

Zed Layson, one of the best surfers on Barbados, is not a man to hurry. He's so chilled that sometimes it's difficult to imagine he was tearing up the island's premier wave, Soup Bowl, when he was 19 and coming joint first in a contest with a certain 11-time world champion from Florida. But tear it up he did, and has done many times since. But Zed's unstudied Bajan languor has a very definite upside: if he happens to impart any sense of urgency when he speaks, you listen. 'Today's the day', he tells me, leaving no room for manoeuvre. 'We're going in an hour. Let's do it.'

But I wasn't so sure. If conditions were anything like they were a few days ago, I'd be signing up for carnage. 'Just right for you', he reassures me. 'Come on, get your board, and get Harry, too.'

Harry is my son. He was 13 at the time. We'd both been surfing Bajan waves for four to six hours a day, for the previous 10 days. We'd scored perfect head-high swell at Freights, a beach-reef setup, as well as fun lefts at Surfers' Point, where Zed runs a surf school and rents out apartments. Harry was a talented grom, who'd take on just about anything; I had been surfing long enough to hold my own. As amped as we were feeling after this surf trip from heaven, I still wasn't so sure about Soup Bowl.

I didn't want a perfect trip to end with bad memories. And as counterintuitive as it might sound, the conjunction of 'perfect' and 'surf trip' in the Caribbean is not a chimera. Sure, most surfers with time and money to spare opt for Indo, Sri Lanka or Hawaii. But the Caribbean shouldn't be written off, especially for those looking for something a little less obvious. There are well-established surf scenes nearby, in places like Puerto Rico, the British Virgin Islands and the Dominican Republic – even Jamaica has an interesting waveriding subculture.

However, the Soup Bowl is arguably the Caribbean's headline wave. There's surf here 355 days a year, the sea and air temperature are always around 27°C (80°F), and even in the near-constant onshore breezes, there are barrels galore, as well as long, walling sections. And between surfs, Barbados is as good as the Caribbean gets.

Two years previously, I'd been on Barbados for work. In my downtime, I hit the lively outdoor market, Oistin's Bay Gardens, in the southeast (which is near two other great waves, Freights and South Point). I explored lush rainforest amid the hills of St Joseph, lounged on the west coast's beaches, and discovered

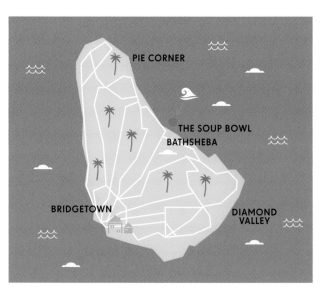

PIE CORNER

THE SOUP BOWL
BATHSHEBA

BRIDGETOWN

DIAMOND
VALLEY

remote empty bays. Sustenance is as simple as pulling off the road at one of the local 'fish frys' and feasting on barbecued swordfish and marlin steaks.

But I'd also managed to surf for a few days and, in that time, I'd decided to scope out Soup Bowl. The day I'd turned up it was 6–8ft and pumping: crystalline grey-blue walls were lashing across the reef, being shredded by the local crew. It was captivating, for sure, but it was way out of my league. But the truth is, like all surf spots, it doesn't fire quite like that every day. And according to Zed, there's a backdoor for surfers like me and my son.

The problem was that just a few days earlier I'd stood on the low cliffs at the fishing village of Bathsheba, watching messy onshore set waves pulverise the reef. That day it was actually double-overhead and no one was out. Russell Winter and Ben Skinner, two of the best British surfers ever – let alone of their generation – were also on the island and thought about it. 'It's doable', said Skinner, a British longboard champion who's also excellent on a shortboard. Winter concurred, but they both still decided against Soup Bowl that day.

Yet, here we were, sitting in the back of Zed's car as he drove the sugarcane-lined island roads on the way to the wave. Before we knew it, Soup Bowl was in front of us. Zed and another local powerhouse, Christian, started waxing their boards. Harry was just as quick, perhaps blissfully ignorant. Was I being a bad surf dad?

In front of us, the vast Atlantic Ocean looked a bit lumpy, thanks to a light onshore breeze. But the wave looked... doable. And then I saw a set. It appeared out of nowhere and was

"A few days earlier, it was double-overhead and no one was out. My son Harry waxed his board, perhaps blissfully ignorant – was I being a bad surf dad?"

SLATER-ENDORSED

Eleven-times world champ Kelly Slater is a Soup Bowl fan. No surprise, given what he told the *New York Times* in 2009: 'I've been going for over 20 years, and I'd put Soup Bowl as one of the top three waves in the world. It's got a really good curve and allows all sorts of manoeuvre and airs. The only problem is the sea urchins all over the bottom – just don't fall and you're fine.'

easily twice the height of the waves I'd been watching. Zed had warned me about this: Soup Bowl is a wave where you've got to be on your toes. 'Come on, let's go', he said.

Zed's voice never seemed to leave any room for indecision. Christian was already in the water, paddling swiftly to the lineup, thanks to a channel. Zed led the way, then it was Harry, then me. Even if my mind was full of doubt, even though I was half-praying for a cast-iron excuse not to paddle out, I knew I had to. There was no turning back now.

Then, seemingly without any real effort, Harry and I were sitting in the lineup. Yes, this is definitely doable, I thought, watching as Harry whipped his 5'10" board around, paddled, and caught his first wave of the day. He flew down the face, hit the top for a couple of turns, and kicked out with the biggest grin on his face I'd ever seen.

Next, Zed made a drop and rode with such style and self-possession that, just for a moment, I wondered what all the fuss was about. Christian had paddled further along the reef, eyeing up the lefts that work on smaller days.

Then, a wave with my name on it loomed in the near-distance – and I mean loomed, in classic Soup Bowl style. At first, it looked to be no more than a few feet high. But waves at Soup Bowl have this odd way off revealing their true size only once they are on top of you. By the time I'd paddled and caught it, I realized I was flying down the face of a 6ft wave.

But I didn't make the drop. And the wipeout was heavy. Same for my next wave, too. Suddenly, to my intense, excessive, uncontainable and endless joy, I was powering down the line of a wall that seemed to go on forever. It was third-time lucky for me at Soup Bowl.

Clockwise from top left: weatherbeaten coastline near Bathsheba; Zed's Surfing Adventures has beds and boards; American pro Courtney Conlogue shows off at Soup Bowl; break-side provisions. Previous page: as well as its world-class wave, Barbados has some of the globe's most beautiful beaches

ORIENTATION

Type of wave // Right-hand reef break over coral.
Best conditions // Barbados is a year-round surf destination. The Soup Bowl is best between October and April, and works on all tides.
Nearest town // Bathsheba.
Getting there // Flights arrive at Sir Grantley Adams International Airport in Seawell. Hire a car and drive 15 miles (24km) north to reach Bathsheba.
Where to stay // Head to Surfers' Point, 30 minutes' drive south of Bathsheba, and stay in the one- or two-bedroom apartments at Zed's Surfing Adventures. You can hire boards from Zed, too.
Things to know // There are urchins on the reef at Soup Bowl; and when it's big, the rips are big, too.

Opposite: the island of Martinique has killer waves, a tropical vibe and a unique blend of French and Creole culture

MORE LIKE THIS
CARIBBEAN CLASSICS

MT IRVINE, TOBAGO

This superb right-hand reef break off the island of Tobago (part of the island nation, Trinidad and Tobago, off Venezuela), is not as powerful as the Soup Bowl, but it is arguably a longer, better-shaped ride. The locals are known to be enthusiastic on the better days and Tobago itself is a gem: two-thirds mountains, the flatter and drier west of the island hosts great beaches. Some spots still retain the sense of untouched isolation that persuaded Disney to set a 1960 adaption of the Johann Wyss novel *Swiss Family Robinson* here. Tobago's surf spots are pretty much all in the southwest, and there's great snorkelling and diving in many places, especially at Buccoo Reef Marine Park and in the northeast around Speyside and Charlotteville.

Nearest town // Scarborough

CANE GARDEN BAY, TORTOLA

The British Virgin Islands are home to what is likely the Caribbean's most famous surf spot, Cane Garden Bay: a freight-train, west-facing, right hand point that serves up 1000ft rides. Well known to US surfers thanks to its appearance on the front cover of a surfing magazine a few years ago, it fires in winter swells and has one or two sketchy sections breaking in just 1–2ft of water. But this is a wave that can be truly epic: it's one for fit, expert surfers only. Tortola itself is the largest, most populous of the British Virgin Islands, which are still recovering from the decimation wrought by Hurricane Irma in 2017.

Nearest town // Road Town

TOMATE, MARTINIQUE

Want to practise your French and try a slightly easier right-hand reef break? Head to Martinique, one of the islands making up the Lesser Antilles chain, about halfway between Venezuela and the British Virgin Islands. Tomate is a cracking, long righthander over sand and reef. It's mainly a winter wave, but there's always surf on the eastern side of the island. And there's always French, too – in the architecture, culture, cuisine and language (French is the island's official language). Add Creole and an array of West Indian and African influences, and of course surfing, and you've got a very unique paradise.

Nearest town // Fort-de-France

MONTAÑITA

Ecuador's surf capital has become quite a scene. Jade Bremner found
a fun wave, and discovered why dawn patrol is so unpopular here.

By mid tide, there are no less than three surf schools set up in the whitewater at the beach break off Montañita, Ecuador. So I decide it's time to walk north to La Punta, the wave that put this place on the map. It's slightly less crowded – but that doesn't necessarily mean there's room for me.

The other surfers greet each other with a nod or an 'hola'. There's only a dozen or so people in the lineup, mostly locals, and all of them can surf. I mean, really surf. The machismo is thick in the air; there is only one other female surfer in the water. And it feels competitive. This is, after all, where Ecuador hosts its national surf competitions. I'll be lucky if I get a wave, I think to myself. I wait my turn, showing a little extra patience and etiquette. Perhaps I'll score at least one ride.

One tattoo-covered surfer, built like a tank, paddles for a wave. He pops up smoothly, cuts back twice, and attempts an aerial on the closeout. It's 30 minutes before I hear any English spoken. I paddle nearer to two Australian surfers, and then realise I'm getting very close to some protruding rocks. But they slowly disappear with the rising tide. And the waves are also getting fatter and a little more forgiving, rolling in at about head-high. One comes straight for me. I paddle hard. There are two other surfers going for the same wave, but I'm closer to the point. I make the drop. It's one of just a couple waves I caught that day, but it remains one of the best waves of my life. I vow to return at dawn tomorrow to beat the crowds.

I had arrived in Montañita the night before. Reggae and chill-out music wafted through the air as I wandered the dusty streets. It was nice to stretch my legs after the three-hour car journey from Guayaquil. Flip-flop-clad patrons drank around tables outside colourful palm-thatched bars. Well-worn backpacker joints were

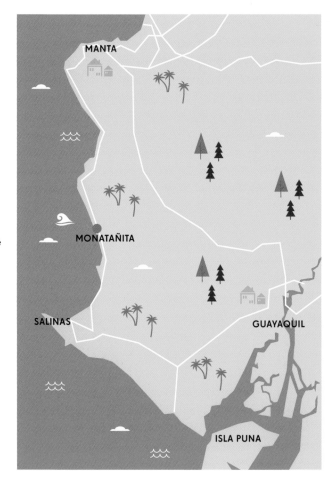

MANTA

MONATAÑITA

SALINAS

GUAYAQUIL

ISLA PUNA

© Israel Barona

"I'll always remember that wave because it was grace under pressure. No wonder people like to party here – I was in a celebratory mood myself"

decorated with surf paraphernalia. One entire road was lined with street carts stacked with bottles of liquor, selling cocktails to revellers from all over the world. I hear European, US, Australian and South American accents. Stalls are selling hippy bags and Rasta jewellery to tipsy tourists, while food vendors line stomachs with fried delights. It was already 10pm and the place was buzzing with people just gearing up for a big night out.

Montañita is actually a far cry from the sleepy little surf town I'd imagined on my way there. It quickly became obvious that most people come here to party rather than ride waves. But the festival vibe was infectious. I stopped to take it all in, ordering a zingy cocktail from a street vendor before searching for my guesthouse. It was only once I made my way to Playa Montañita, a five-minute walk northwest of town, that I was reminded of why I came. It was dark and much quieter; and to my left, I heard waves crashing in the big, black void of the Pacific Ocean.

My home for the night was Hostal Kundalini Montañita, right opposite the surf. I flicked off my flip-flops. There was the distant sound of someone strumming a guitar, laughter. I could see cherries from lit cigarettes burning in the distance. I couldn't wait to just wake up and surf, so I drifted off to the soundtrack of crashing waves and the distant, ever-present hum of dance music.

I was up just after dawn, well before the clubbers would emerge from their hangovers. I headed straight for the surf I could see from my bedroom window, a break known locally as Pueblo. The winds were gentle (around five knots) and there was 3–4ft of swell.

The modest town of Montañita only has about 10 streets and a fixed local population of 1000. But on weekends, the place swells in size when Guayaquil's heartiest partiers descend. It's hard to imagine Montañita as the tiny fishing village of the days before surfers discovered it in the mid-1960s, setting up camp under the phallic-looking rocky headland to the north. It's here that the famous rock-lined La Punta point break is located.

The dozens of guesthouse and hostels I passed had signs offering board rental and lessons. I grabbed a longboard from one of the guesthouses facing the beach, and within 15 minutes I was paddling out. It was October and, although the sky was cloudy, the temperature was notching 25°C (77°F) and the water was tropical-blue and a comfortable but refreshing 20°C (68°F).

It was still early, and there were only three other people in the water, likely locals catching a surf before heading to work. It was low tide as I paddled through the walls of whitewater. They had more power to them than it seemed, and an eight-second swell period wasn't allowing me much time to get past the sets. After a tiring 10

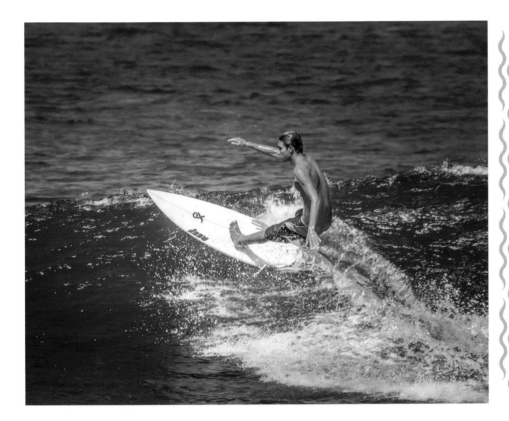

SIDE TRIP

Montañita gets all the surfing glory, but 2 miles (3km) to the north is the very sleepy (meaning less party-hard) surfing town of Olón, with a gorgeous, expansive beach and plenty of sand-bottomed waves for beginners. Post-surf, it's easy to explore the lush cloud forest of Cordillera Chongón-Colonche, home to jaguars, howler monkeys and macaws.

Clockwise from top left: Montañita turns on after dark; local snacks await on the beach; La Punta is a shortboard playground; the village offers one of South America's best surf scenes. Previous page: marvellous Montañita

ORIENTATION

Type of wave // La Punta is a right-hand point break over rocky reef; Pueblo is a sand-bottomed beach break.
Best conditions // Works all year but more consistent in the Northern Hemisphere's winter (December to May), with a north swell at mid tide.
Nearest town // Montañita.
Getting there // It's a two to three-hour taxi ride from Guayaquil to Montañita; taking a bus adds about 30 minutes to the journey.
Where to stay // Hostal Kundalini Montañita is an awesome little spot on the beach, with yoga and surf lessons (plus it's away from the nightlife noise).
Things to know // Longboards and shortboards can be rented by the hour. Lessons can also be booked at most guesthouses and hostels.

minutes, I was finally outside. I took a breath while looking back toward shore. A man was unfolding chairs on the empty beach and a vendor was pulling a boat-shaped cart selling ceviche.

In the water, I nodded to a young surfer about 100ft away. He smiled back. The break felt very chilled. When a set rolled in, I paddled for a wave, and easily rode it in cleanly until it closed out. I had several more great, easy rides – though I kept looking over my shoulder at La Punta, where the perfectly shaped waves were breaking off the headland. A woman at the surf hostel had told me that swells at the point produce 10ft-high barrels. Just as it seemed the rest of town was waking up, I decided to make my move.

The La Punta lineup had already established itself. An empty break in Montañita is a rarity, but my morning session had satiated me. At La Punta, waves were far from guaranteed – but all it took was one.

I'll always remember the wave that I caught at La Punta, not just because of the great ride, but because it was grace under pressure. No wonder people like to party here – I was in a celebratory mood myself. And no wonder dawn patrol doesn't exist here.

Afterwards, I decided to join the revellers and grab a cocktail. As chilled Ibiza-style beats thumped in the background, I sat back and stared at a gloriously red sunset poking through low clouds. It was already clear that tomorrow's session would be starting much later.

Opposite from top: close to Lima's
Miraflores suburb, Playa Makaha
makes an unlikely surf city of Peru's
capital; Chile's Pichilemu has waves,
wine country and wild beaches

MORE LIKE THIS
SOUTH AMERICAN SURF

MÁNCORA, PERU

In the same way Montañita has grown from fishing village to party-hard surfing epicentre, so has this larger Pacific Ocean beach town in northern Peru, around 2½ hours from the border with Ecuador. The water is warm, and there's a beach break and rocky point break, with a solid lefthander. There are also tons of rental places and surf schools that will hook you up with gear and a guide. Waves break all year round in Máncora, but the best arrive in spring and summer, when the tide is mid to high, with a west-northwest swell. It's very shallow at low tide, with exposed rocks.

Nearest town // Máncora

PICHILEMU, CHILE

Located around 120 miles (193km) south of Santiago, this surf town on the Pacific Ocean is flanked by spectacular cliffs and surrounded by the Colchagua Valley wine region. Remarkably, surfers only discovered this beach in the early 1980s. Today, waveriders stop in from around the world to tackle its gnarly point breaks. There's the Playa Principal de Pichilemu beach break for beginners, plus a fun point break named La Puntilla, a righthander which runs right for up to half a mile; when smaller, it's the ultimate longboard wave. Meanwhile, the rocky point, El Infiernillo, is a more intense, hollow ride, with a hard left-hand takeoff; it's favoured by shortboarders.

Nearest town // Pichilemu

PLAYA MAKAHA, PERU

If Playa Makaha sounds familiar, it's because this spot near Peru's capital is actually named after a heavy break in Hawaii. It's certainly no Hawaii, but as city breaks go, Peru's Makaha is one of the most fun waves out there, in one of the most unlikely spots on earth. South of downtown Lima, and a great escape from the city smoke, Playa Makaha is a pebble beach with a traditional pier, in the trendy area known as Miraflores. Makaha's lineups offer views of the city in the distance, and its long, clean lines favour longboarders and even learners – there are a handful of surf schools that rent boards right on the beach. Swell here is super consistent – there's something to surf every day for beginners – but it does get busy at the weekends. Do not surf here after rainfall, due to run-off pollution.

Nearest town // Lima

STONER'S

Surfer's Journal creative director Scott Hulet journeyed south to find out how Mexico's original secret spot was overshadowed by time and inclination.

In the spring of 1964, Long Beach surfer and photographer Leo Hetzel scrambled up a rock balustrade in the state of Nayarit on the Mexican mainland. Peering over the top, he copped the first surfer's view of a setup now known popularly as Stoner's. The lineup, as it remains today, was a warm green cove infused with fresh water from the adjacent river mouth. The atmosphere was silent, hot and thick. A set of waves lurched upward like cereal boxes on a conveyor line and chased themselves toward a beach of yellow sand.

Later that day, he told his pals what he'd found and the following morning, the crew logged the first tracks at what would be known for the next couple of years as 'the secret spot.'

Plotted on a graph, however, the life cycle of a surf spot usually describes a familiar 'up and to the right' motif, spurred by increased awareness and visitation until carrying capacity is met, exceeded, and then merely endured. The prime example is, of course, Malibu. Postwar population dynamics transformed that cobbled heaven into a Malthusian dystopia by the 1950s. For the first time, surfers seeking even a hint of freedom had to look elsewhere. Many of these refugees were seeking precisely what they'd lost: a wave like First Point.

Los Angeles big-wave carnivore Greg Noll went wave-hunting in Mexico. 'In 1954 I was living and surfing in Mazatlán by myself', he says. 'It had everything I was looking for. Just exploring around the coast, I found San Blas. The wave at Matanchén Bay wasn't big, but it was perfect – long, crisp rides.'

Like Malibu.

The following year, Noll returned to Mazatlán with a movie camera. The resulting footage appeared in Noll's first *Search for*

Surf film in 1957. Mexico, with all of its dark and colourful allure as portrayed in popular culture, found purchase in the minds of US coastal youth. The 1300-mile (2000km) run from southern California quickly became a rite of passage. Every surfer with decent wheels and a carnie roll crossed the line, plunging south across the Sonoran Desert. But this was the early '60s – and that entire diaspora numbered just in the dozens.

There certainly wasn't any sort of surf invasion taking place. The distance and expense in time and treasure were the first filters. The language barrier and parochialism were the others. And then there were the *jejenes* (no-see-ums). And the mosquitoes. Matanchén

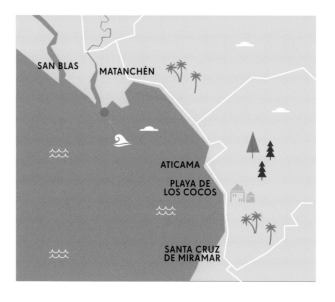

Bay is surrounded by an exquisite wetland, where cumulus swarms of bugs descend at first light. They back off to tolerable levels in the midday heat, but then find their tallest gear in the evening. The place is defined by them.

As a surf resource, Matanchen is also defined by a narrow swell window. One could sit, steaming and scratching, for months on end waiting for something – anything – to wrap in. For those lucky or stalwart enough to score swell, however, the main wave at Matanchen – Las Islitas – was the sort of experience one didn't soon forget. On a well-foiled period point tanker, one could stall and dance around the pocket for upwards of a mile. Factor in a local per diem of five bucks a day, including all of the rotgut Orendain tequila and liberally seeded Sierra sativa one could handle, and San Blas took on a certain Graham Greene-on-food-stamps appeal.

By the mid to late '60s, San Blas found itself a waypoint on the hippie trail, discussed in the same ecstatic manner as Goa, Kandahar and Cuzco. In California, surfing was revved up, feeling its oats as a bona fide countercultural indicator. *Surfer* magazine, hungry to feed its audience's voracious appetite for new discoveries, dispatched ace photographer Ron Stoner to head south. His photos become visual shorthand for surf exploration – his '63 Mercury Comet wagon, stacked with signature models and a crew of attractive vagabonds, became an archetype for the wayfaring waverider. For a brief moment, it almost got crowded. Almost.

Then, due mostly to the advent of the shortboard and partly to a natural urge to push south, seekers found themselves plunging deeper to hollower, more challenging waters. Stoner's – the spot that became a sort of avatar for tropical perfection in the '60s – found itself a forgotten backwater. Hetzel's baby was effectively left on the hospital steps by 1970.

But surfing never really buries its legends – it keeps them in a cool room, hits them with some makeup, and stands them up for another generation to appreciate. And there was no way the current crop of longboard hustlers would overlook a mile-long point wave, was there?

I myself hadn't visited San Blas in over 30 years, and that trip had been a memory-lane rumble back when I was corrupting the girl who would become my wife. I used to spend time at Stoner's, and had wanted to return. Somewhat sadistically, I saw it as a sort of test. Could she hang? (And how, as it turned out.)

This past summer found me in need of some plasma-warm point crumblers. Being cognisant of reports that Stoner's was essentially a ghost wave only galvanised my interest. A Mexican colleague, Mark Kronemeyer, picked me up in Mazatlán and off we went. Driving south through miles of mango trees and blue agave fields, we crossed the river bridge into San Blas three hours later. There were crocodiles lolling in the mangrove breaks. The old town centre had weathered well. It was vaguely quaint, lending a colonial charm to the pueblo I remembered as bedraggled.

BUGGING OUT

The 1951 opening of the Playa Hermosa hotel was supposed to turn San Blas into one of the premier resort towns in Mexico. It enjoyed a brief period of vogue after being discovered by the Hollywood glitterati of the time – Lee Marvin came to fish, Liz Taylor and Richard Burton stayed, Jim Morrison drank here. However, a severe mosquito problem proved too much and the guests just stopped coming. The ruins of the once glamorous hotel remain on the beach at San Blas to this day.

Clockwise from top left: street tacos in San Blas; Stoner's is Mexico's original secret spot; palapas and point breaks. Previous page: big moves on small waves

The next morning, we met a clutch of Kronemeyer's friends from Sayulita on the beach at the tip of Matanchen – gathered there at dawn, swatting against the onslaught. The waves where we had parked were utter dishwater, and did nothing to instill confidence, but we had come properly equipped. Well-versed in all conditions, our ad hoc group of surfers were far from hidebound, surfboard-wise. The previous day I had watched Dylan Southworth launch credible airs with no evident wave energy. Logjammer Israel Preciado chose artful, section-connecting lines. 'Taquito', Southworth's chica, styled the joint up with some effortless runs.

The jungle track was only driveable for a portion of the way to Stoner's proper, and even that required a 4WD. We parked on the sand at Little Stoner's, where teet-high rights whipped along a natural jetty before mushing off into a *quebrada* (ravine). The crew was amped, and out there in an instant. I had other bones to pick.

Rock-stepping my way north, out of site of the surfers, I found my way blocked by a small rock tower: Hetzel's perch. Clambering up the toeholds, I reached the top and peered over. It was 3ft and cracking perfectly into the cove. Flawless, really. Dozens of surfers were simply not there. They had been swept along with the current, down to Instagram dreams with better access, fewer bugs and a more open swell window.

Walking back down the beach to Littles, I saw another vehicle come to a stop at a respectful distance from our post. Two surfers emerged to survey the scene. The visitors took in the view, enjoyed a smoke, and started up their car. I was surprised to see them pull a U-turn in the sand, away from the empty perfection just out of sight. For an instant, Stoner's was gone, and Hetzel's jungle cove reeled off by its lonesome.

"Being cognisant of reports that Stoner's was essentially a ghost wave only galvanised my interest"

ORIENTATION

Type of wave // Right-hand boulder-bottomed point break.
Best conditions // April to September.
Nearest town // San Blas.
Getting there // Fly to Puerto Vallarta, from where San Blas is a 3½ hour drive north.
Where to stay // San Blas has been on the tourist map for decades and, as a result, has a wide range of accomodation to cater for all budgets.
Things to know // Stoner's needs a solid south or southwest swell to start working, but on its day, it is the best wave in the area. However, there are few regions better for surf exploration. A couple hours south of San Blas is Sayulita, another one of Mexico's great surf towns, and there are hundreds of quality breaks in between.

Opposite: Scorpion Bay is one of many desolate desert surf breaks along Mexico's Baja California peninsula

MORE LIKE THIS
THE BEST OF MEXICO'S BAJA

SCORPION BAY

In a country rife with quality right-hand point breaks, the thing that makes Scorpion Bay stand out is the sheer length of the ride. It needs a fair sized south or west swell to light up, but when it does it's truly a marvel. Depending on who you talk to, there are up to seven points within the bay that can actually link up to gift lucky surfers with rides over a mile long. These long rides don't come without a cost, however, as getting to Scorpion Bay entails a gruelling 14-hour drive south from southern California, or an 8-hour drive north from Cabo San Lucas. Scorpion Bay suffers from extended flat spells and unfavourable winds – oh, and there's the scorpions, just waiting to take refuge in the foot of your sleeping bag – but it's worth the wait.

Nearest town // Loreto

SAN MIGUEL

San Miguel is, without a doubt, northern Baja's best wave, a cobblestoned right point that rivals Malibu, Rincon or even sometimes J-Bay. It's consistent, groomed, long and reeling. Catching any and all west and northwest swells (which usually wash up in the winter), it can easily hold double-overhead size, getting better and better as it grows. It's also fairly easy to access: from the US/Mexico border, simply drive south toward Ensenada, pull into the marked dirt parking lot, pay a few dollars, paddle out, and surf some of the better, user-friendly waves on the peninsula. Too good to be true? Only sometimes. San Miguel's reputation has far preceded the visiting surfer, so the crowds can be very heavy. It also tends to blow out by mid-morning, so an early arrival is the call. Bring a high-performance shortboard, and a step-up for those big days.

Nearest town // Ensenada

SHIPWRECK

There are many breaks named Shipwreck or Shipwrecks, in various spots around the world, and every one of them seems to be really good. Maybe it's because trouble for ships – such as reefs, rocks and swell – are the ingredients for wonderful surf. And this right-hand point break on Baja's east cape follows suit. It can be found east of San José del Cabo, and a newish road makes the trip much easier than it once was. The wave itself is fast and long, racing over rock and reef, connecting all the way through on good days – which happen on south swells that hit from spring until autumn. Like most reef points, its best size is head-high up to double-overhead. While it can get crowded, the multiple takeoff spots thin the aggressive competition.

Nearest town // San José del Cabo

TRESTLES

Southern California's premiere high-performance wave is so good that the entire American surf industry wanted to be near it. Chris Dixon came chasing the same dream.

The first time I visited San Clemente back in 1992, at the ripe old age of 26, the only real knowledge I had of San Onofre and Trestles was that this 3½-mile sweep of coarse sand, date palms and fragrant chaparral was one hell of a place to surf. Up until then, most of my surfing had taken place along South Carolina's swell-starved sandbars. As a teenager, I remember drooling cereal milk on the dog-eared pages of neon-inked surf magazines, at photos of Trestles' teal-hued, kelp-flecked point break waves. It felt both dreamy and impossible – *'people actually live right next to waves like that? Waves called out by name in the Beach Boys' Surfin' USA. Waves filled with ripping punk rock surf heroes?'* Geographically and culturally, this Southern California Shangri-la was as far away from Myrtle Beach as the moon.

As I sat in the lineup during that first visit, a tattooed aerial specialist named Christian Fletcher launched himself 6ft into the sky. On that same visit, I vowed to one day call San Clemente home. I was just getting started as a writer. I wondered if I might even be able to wow the editors of *Surfer* magazine, which had been based here since the 1960s.

Two years later, I followed through on the promise I hade made to myself. I moved to San Clemente, and I did it after somehow convincing the venerable team at *Surfer* to enlist me as the magazine's first online editor. Still obsessed with Trestles itself, I went in search of an apartment as close to its hallowed peaks as I could afford. So, for the next few years, I shared a shabby $400-per-month south San Clemente triplex with a sardonic, wave-addled North Carolina transplant named Steve, who'd landed a night job filling vitamin supplement capsules with freeze-dried bull testicles.

It was impossible for me not to feel starstruck when surfing with my new co-workers. I was paddling out with guys like photo deity Jeff Divine, *History of Surfing* author Matt Warshaw, and Steve Hawk, brother of Tony and a former star reporter for the *Orange County Register*. And, out in the water, I was getting snaked by top pros like Chris Ward, Mike Parsons and Shane Beschen nearly every day. In the early 1990s, San Clemente itself was in its waning days as a sleepy California surf town, as the influx of pros and some questionable antics from surf industry staples such as the Lost surf team ushered in a new era – and a new reputation.

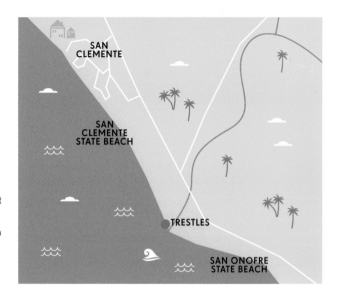

Lying halfway between Los Angeles and San Diego, San Clemente felt like a sort of So-Cal surf suburb. It's the southernmost town of Orange County, a coastal stretch of low-slung hillside homes with to-die-for views of the Pacific. The towns here are jarringly bisected by eight-plus lanes of the perennially busy Interstate 5, but the desert air is cooled by onshores and the area rarely sees more than 14 inches (35cm) of rain a year. To the Acjachemen Native Americans who lived here some 8000 years ago, the fertile river valley that defines Trestles and nearby San Onofre was a village called Panhe. Eons before construction of the train trestle that gave this place its name, they navigated waves on canoes of lashed river reeds. Panhe's creeks teemed with steelhead and salmon and the ocean with gamefish, abalone and mussels.

It's San Onofre's creeks – dry during summer and raging during winter storms – that make these waves so great. Through the millennia, their payload of sand and cobblestones has created a broad sedimentary reef called San Mateo Point, which rises from the depths at a perfect angle. It's this jutting chin along an otherwise fairly straight coastline that pulls in swells.

My roommate Steve and I would rise before dawn, load our wetsuits into backpacks, and strap our surfboards to bicycle racks (no cars are allowed to the wave itself, so you have to walk, bike or skateboard). I soon learned that each spot – from north to south Cottons, Barbed Wires, Uppers, Lowers, Middles, Church and The Point – offered a markedly different experience in terms

of setup and humanity. I came to revere Cottons Point, which sits directly in front of the cliffside manor that was once Richard Nixon's Western White House. I once sketched into one of the biggest waves of my life here.

Typically, though, Trestles doesn't really get that big. It's just amazingly, consistently fun. If the crowds weren't too insane, Steve and I would head just south to the surfing 'skatepark' of Lowers. It can get crowded, but it has achingly perfect rights and lefts. Unfortunately, the takeoff zone is so compressed that the scrum of pros and wannabes can be tricky to navigate. Over time, I learned to paddle out to the southerly corner of the lineup where, every once in a while, a wave would swing just wide enough to escape the clutches of the teeming hordes and allow me to score a flawless peak.

Eventually, Middles became my go-to. It's less consistent, but it's also less crowded, and the vibe is mellow. One clear winter morning in 1999, I paddled out at Middles before dawn. Save for a small pod of dolphins, I was all alone. The biggest set waves were about 3ft overhead, but thanks to the warm Santa Ana winds howling offshore, they were throwing out perfect almond-eyed barrels.

Out on the horizon, a big North Pacific set reared up. Sprinting hard, I narrowly scratched over the first wave; 12 strokes behind it loomed the wave I'd been waiting for all my life. As I dug for it atop an undersized 6'2" thruster, I remember catching a glimpse of the snowcapped Santiago Peak to the east. I was blinded by the spray,

> *"San Clemente was in its waning days as a sleepy California surf town. The influx of pros and questionable antics from surf industry staples ushered in a new era"*

taking off by feel alone. Then my vision cleared as I went into freefall with the lip. I was terrified my fins would fail to hold as I reached the wave's trough. But they did. The curl of the wave arced over my head. Then 3ft (1m) ahead, a pair of dolphins launched out of the wave's translucent face. I hollered and laid turn after parabolic turn as the wave unspooled for 500ft. It was – and remains – the best wave I had ever surfed.

I moved away from San Clemente in 2005, as my wife and I opted to raise our daughter, and now our son, along the genteel but surf-challenged shores of Charleston, South Carolina. Much has changed in San Clemente since I moved away. It's gentrified, of course, and has expanded some way inland. It's home to thousands more surfers, cars and homes. Perhaps, most tellingly, *Surfing* magazine has shut its doors, and is now a less relevant quarterly (its founder John Severson would surely be horrified to know that his pride and joy is today owned by the same publisher as the *National Enquirer*).

But Trestles will always attract the true at heart. The Surfing Heritage Foundation is here now, and so is *Surfer's Journal* magazine. Lost is still thriving here, and so are a slew of some of the best shapers and surf artists the world will ever know. This past Christmas, my now 10-year-old son and I paddled out for the first time together at San Onofre, just south of Trestles. To Fritz, a waist-high runner at Old Man's was a sheer revelation. He'd never ridden such a long, perfect wave in his life.

From left: San Diego County is home to many pros; Trestles is named for the railroad running past it. Previous page: South African pro Bianca Buitendag tears it up at Lowers

ORIENTATION

Type of wave // Left- and right-hand point breaks.
Best conditions // Low to mid tides; there's swell year-round.
Nearest town // San Clemente.
Getting there // John Wayne Airport in Costa Mesa is about 40 minutes' drive from San Clemente. From town, you'll have to walk, bike or skateboard to the beach.
Where to stay // San Mateo Campground is within cycling distance of Trestles; avoid San Onofre Campground due to crowds and train noise. There are lots of hotels and Airbnb options in San Clemente.
Things to know // Since the waves at Middles and Church typically move more slowly than the others, they're better for bigger boards. If you surf a longboard at Lowers, you'll get barked at if you use it to hog the waves. If Trestles is packed, head south on Pacific Coast Hwy to the Trails beaches.

Opposite: Blacks Beach in San Diego County has a scenic setting amid the Torrey Pines State Reserve

MORE LIKE THIS
SO-CAL'S CREAM OF THE CROP

BLACKS BEACH

Challenging, steep, fast and perfect, Blacks is one of California's most iconic waves. It's located in tiny La Jolla, at the base of a towering scenic bluff. And from this high vantage point, its waves are fascinating to watch. Just offshore from the beach, the 300ft-plus Scripps Canyon funnels deep, long-period swell energy into shore, creating wedging, barrelling peaks far bigger than those breaking just to the south or north. The canyon also funnels in Caribbean-blue water from those depths, making Blacks particularly dreamy. Unsurprisingly, Blacks can be plenty crowded, but the hordes are somewhat mitigated by the long walk in. Most either hike down Salk Institute Rd, which switchbacks down to the beach's southern reach; or take the Torrey Pines Gliderport trail, a scenic gem that drops out at Blacks' northern end.

Nearest town // La Jolla

HUNTINGTON BEACH PIER

During hot summer days, the sands and boardwalk of Huntington Beach are packed with every sort of human who calls So-Cal home, making this a fascinating – and sometimes disturbing – melting pot. However, Huntington is also home to one of Southern California's best stretches of beach break, which pulls in swell from every direction; the north side of the pier, in particular, can be heavy with pros feasting on wedging peaks, created as waves refract off the forest of concrete pilings. Typically, the pier's south side is a little less crowded, and the further you move away from it, the less crowded it gets. Be careful during strong south swells as the current can pull you right into the concrete pilings. Huntington is usually best during mid to low tides, when waves trip over the outside bars and then steepen into racy lines on the inside.

Nearest town // Huntington Beach

RINCON

Known as the 'Queen of the Coast', Rincon is arguably the premiere point break of the entire US West Coast. Situated right on the Ventura-Santa Barbara county line, and easily accessible from the highway, it gets incredibly crowded. However, if you do manage to snag a single, three-block-long wave from the top of the point at the indicator past the river mouth, and ride it all the way down through The Cove, your surfing life is, arguably, complete. Like Trestles, Rincon is the product of millennia of deposits from the mountains just inland (in this case from Rincon Creek). The Channel Islands block Rincon from summertime south swells, but this crescent of cobblestones is a magnet for winter swells from the west and northwest. And because it's spread out over three takeoff spots, it is actually possible to get a wave or two even when Rincon is packed.

Nearest town // Santa Barbara

TOFINO

On British Columbia's primevally wild islands in western Canada,
Sam Haddad discovered surprisingly tame surf – albeit, a tad chilly.

The wooden boardwalk snaked through a break in the trees, a gnarled and knotted mix of western hemlock, red cedar and Pacific silver fir. At the last plank, this thick vegetation gave way to a seemingly endless beach, empty of people, with a small but perfectly shaped wave breaking left and right. The sun was shining, the sky was a blinding blue. It was paradise.

Except, not paradise in the screensaver sense. It's not tropical; it's not even all that warm. In fact, each step here came with a crunch that brought me back to reality, for there was a thick layer of frost underfoot. The air was fresh enough to see my breath and make my eyes sting. And it was pretty hard to ignore the neoprene hood, gloves, boots and 5/4mm thick wetsuit I was wearing. Yet, here I was at Long Beach, near the small town of Tofino on Vancouver Island's west coast, running into the frigid ocean in December with my longboard under my arm.

It's not that I'll only surf in places where I can wear boardshorts and a bikini – I'm from England, after all – but I've always felt that proper cold-water surfing was the preserve of those far more hardcore and hardy than me. And until relatively recently, it sort of was. Especially here on the edge of British Columbia, where there is nothing between us and Japan, and the coastline is stacked with challenging swell.

Long Beach, however, is one of the gentler spots on the coastline. It even tends to close out when the swell gets too big. The beach is popular with beginners, as the waves are consistent and hold their shape nicely. On this December day, the waves were calm and clean, 2ft where I was, 4ft at most at other sections of the beach. But there was nothing tame about this place. This is the Pacific Northwest, a coast and climate that oozes roar and fury.

You don't get the odd piece of driftwood on the beach – there are whole trees washed up; I wasn't seeing single strands of seaweed, I was stepping over knotted kelp forests carpeting the sand.

Tofino sits at the top edge of what would be an incredible surfing road trip through the Pacific Northwest. The rugged landscape, fir-topped cliffs and biting cold are drawing more and more surfers attracted to a quieter, raw, nature-driven surf experience.

On the short drive south from Tofino to Long Beach, we pass Tsunami Evacuation Route signs. Meanwhile, we spot a bumper sticker that reads 'Tsunami Evacuation Plan: 1. Grab beer 2. Run like hell.' Storm-watching is, in fact, a big tourist market here in

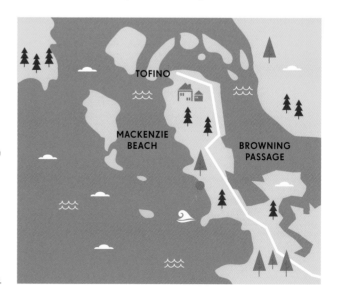

winter and local hotels even provide the wet weather gear. Heavy rain and fog are frequent. And the swell can get pretty wild, too. Yet, outside of these storm cycles, there are mellow beach breaks, such as Long Beach and Chesterman Beach to the north.

Surf culture is not new to Tofino. The original waveriders on Vancouver Island were the First Nations, the indigenous people who've lived here for the last 10,000 years. They used to shape the local red cedar trees into giant canoes, always asking the tree's permission first. The next people to surf here were hippies passing through town in the 1960s. Tofino's awesome nature and wildlife, combined with its edge-of-civilisation vibe (the first road wasn't built until 1959) attracted camper van-driving flower children from all across Canada, as well as a few draft-dodging Yanks.

Here at Long Beach, I'm imagining these pioneering surfers camping out in the lush old-growth forest behind me. Through cold, wet winters, and fine-but-fresh summers, they slept in their vans, tents and in shacks built from driftwood. Some even drove right onto the beach. An unlucky few lost their vehicles to an incoming tide.

In 1970, the Pacific Rim National Park Reserve was created amid concerns that Long Beach and the surrounding area were proving too popular for their own good. The park was also established to protect the forests from logging, which up until then had been the main industry around Tofino. In the early 1990s, the lumberjacks clashed with the increasingly environmentally aware surfers and First Nations people, leading to the largest act of civil disobedience in Canada's history, known as the Clayoquot protests, during which 900 people were arrested for trying to stop trees being felled.

It's a good thing they did. As I look around before paddling out, I see nature really is front and centre, just as it would have been for the First Nations people. Once out in the lineup, I stare

WAVES AND WILDLIFE

Vancouver Island's west coast is often called the 'Galapagos of the North' for its rich marine wildlife – from humpback and grey whales to dolphins, sea lions and salmon – which thrive here thanks to the vast offshore kelp forests. On land, it's not uncommon to spot black bear, bald eagles and even sea wolves, a unique species that has evolved to swim, and subsists on a diet of everything from seal and whale carcasses to barnacles.

Clockwise from top left: Vancouver Island's undeveloped coastline has changed little in thousands of years; the beaches are wild and wonderful here; catching a Tofino wave. Previous page: longboarders aren't the only ones who have fun at Long Beach

back into the forest, thinking about those original surfer hippies frolicking among the storm-twisted trees and rocky outcrops, as an atmospheric mist starts to gather at each end of this 6-mile (10km) beach. A sense of euphoric calm and awe at this remarkable landscape washes over me. I feel immense admiration for the First Nations people who preserved it so well, and who lived so symbiotically with the environment.

Thankfully, tourism has replaced tree felling as the dominant industry in and around Tofino. Nicknamed 'Tough City' by early settlers for its brutal winters and remoteness, it's no longer the same sleepy outpost, and now boasts smart hotels and and a great locavore foodie scene. There are no more wooden shacks along the beach; instead, there are million-dollar properties, many owned by celebrities.

But the shift feels discreet, low-rise, and low-key. And as an alternative to the fancier hotels, there is plenty of hip, design-led accommodation at lower price points. Tofino feels destined to remain an accessible and laid-back place to come hike, kayak, and, of course, surf.

I surfed for two hours straight, despite the cold, in waves that were as good as any I'd surfed before, from France to Indonesia. When I did finally paddle in, it was actually because my arms were done, rather than my internal thermometer. In fact, I've been far colder surfing in Cornwall.

Paddling back in toward the ancient forest, the low winter sun and fading light painted the sky in colours that seemed entirely unique to this part of the world. The cold had heightened my senses and once again reminded me of the rawness of this landscape. All I kept thinking was that perhaps cold-water surfing is not just for the hardcore, after all.

"I can see nature really is front and centre here, just as it would have been for the First Nations people"

ORIENTATION

Type of wave // Beach break with lefts and rights.
Best conditions // The spot is fairly consistent, only closing out in bigger storms.
Nearest town // Tofino is a 15-minute drive north, and Ucluelet a similar distance south.
Getting there // From Vancouver International Airport, take an internal flight to Tofino Airport, which sits just behind Long Beach. Or drive via the car ferry from Horseshoe Bay to Nanaimo, which takes just over five hours in total.
Where to stay // There is plenty of great beachside accommodation, from the swanky Wickaninnish Inn to Green Point Campground, right behind Long Beach.
Things to know // In summer, average water temps are 50–60°F (10–15°C); in winter they can drop to 40°F (4.5°C). A thick wetsuit (4mm-plus) is recommended, with a hood, boots and gloves.

Opposite: surfers willing to make the hike to Oregon's Short Sand Beach are rewarded with crisp and empty waves

MORE LIKE THIS
PACIFIC NORTHWEST WAVES

OTTER ROCK, OREGON

Often referred to as the Waikiki of the central Oregon coast, this mostly protected surf spot in Lincoln County is popular with beginners and longboarders. There is swell year-round and it is widely considered to be one of the best beach breaks in the Pacific Northwest. The rock that gave the spot its name may no longer be a haven for otters, but it is home to a variety of marine birds, including brown pelicans and cormorants. Larger mammals are never far away – grey whales can be seen off the coast from June through October. The nearby town is small but has good surf shops and places to eat. There is also great hiking, including a direct trail to the Devil's Punchbowl, a cauldron-like geological formation carved by the sea.
Nearest town // Otter Rock

SHORT SAND BEACH, OREGON

Short Sand Beach is a sheltered cove enveloped by cliffs and dense, old-growth coastal temperate rainforest. The only access is via a short hike through the forest from Hwy 101. This relative inaccessibility helped deter loggers back in the day, which is why so many ancient trees remain. Located within the Oswald West State Park, Short Sands is one of the most scenic spots along Oregon's coastline and a popular beginner's beach break. Though its proximity to Portland means it can get crowded on warm summer days, the surf is reasonably consistent, and it's easy to enjoy the cove without the crowds in the off-season. The break offers clean left- and right-hand waves, with a break mostly protected from the wind. The nearest surfboard rental is 10 miles (16km) north at Cannon Beach.
Nearest town // Cannon Beach

LA PUSH, WASHINGTON STATE

This remote, rugged stretch of coastline features dramatic fir-topped rock formations, jutting straight out of the sea. One of these is James Island – or A-Ka-Lat ('Top of the Rock'), as it's known to the Quileute Nation, who've lived on the north coast of Washington State's Olympic Peninsula for thousands of years. Tourism is a big part of the Quileute's survival and they welcome visitors, especially surfers, at the Quileute Oceanside Resort at La Push. The spot itself is a small protected cove at the mouth of the Quillayute River. It has a beach break for beginners, and more technical right and left point breaks that generally work best on a mid tide. Summer is the best time to surf La Push, though it can get busy at weekends.
Nearest town // La Push

POPOYO

Scott Yorko headed to Nicaragua so he could eat, sleep, and breath surf for an entire week — not exactly the right move for a new relationship.

'This is purely a surf trip. Nothing else', I said to Stef, the girl I'd been dating for only a few weeks. 'Are you sure you're down with that?' I'd been daydreaming about Popoyo for a while. It's home to Nicaragua's legendary reef break, where offshore winds blow 300 days a year and swells from all directions boost fast, hollow barrels right in front of the long, sandy beaches. When a short window in my September work schedule lined up with a weeklong forecast for consistent swell, I booked a ticket immediately, unconcerned with whether anyone was coming with me. But my excitement infected Stef and we were in that phase of our relationship where she was keen to show me she was game. She accepted my disclaimer, even assuring me she'd surfed before.

The thing is, Popoyo isn't exactly a great destination for a new relationship. It's one of those spots where life is reduced to eating, sleeping and surfing. No yoga retreats, no zipline canopy tours, and certainly no nightlife of any kind.

Popoyo is a place where abandoned beachfront mansions sit crumbling on their cracked concrete foundations. The wave was first discovered in the 1970s by Nicaraguan surfer Ronald Urros, but civil wars kept visitation at bay until 1990, when the country had its first democratic elections and the tourism ministry recognised surfing as an underexploited natural resource. In 1996, American expats JJ and Kimberly Yemma set up the rustic Popoyo Surf Lodge and began welcoming more and more surfers. But the vibe remains authentically Central American and locals dominate the lineup.

After flying into San Jose, Costa Rica (to save money), and driving north through the rainforest, we spent one night at the border, waking up to howler monkeys roaring in the treetop canopies above us. We then walked into Nicaragua and hired a taxi to take us to Las Salinas, the main strip of beachside hotels

and restaurants. The taxi hung a left onto a bumpy dirt road and pulled into NicaWaves, a clean and friendly American-owned hostel with a pool, private air-con rooms, and a houseful of guests glued to their devices. A tech bro from San Francisco hobbled around with bandages on his foot and reef rash down his back. 'I got a little too stoked', he admitted.

My own stoke was boiling over as I frothed to catch the tail end of the morning session. I quickly waxed my short board, while Stef rented a clunky 11ft longboard. We trotted 10 minutes down a dirt path through the jungle to the beach. Local dogs escorted us the whole way.

'Ok, have fun!' I said to Stef, as I ran towards the water. I paddled straight to the lineup and began feeling out the takeoff

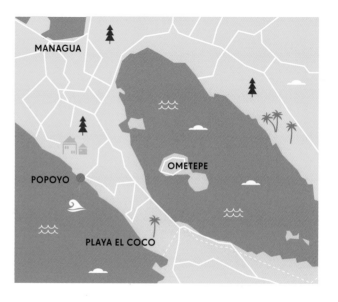

"The vibe remains authentically Central American and locals dominate the lineup"

zones, catching several lefts and pumping through the fast-moving sections. A year of living landlocked in Boulder, Colorado had me starved for that hydraulic flow state and I couldn't get enough of it. After an extra hour of milking the smaller waves well into midday low tide, I rode one in to the beach wearing a salty perma-grin. 'This is going to be an epic week', I said aloud to myself.

But then I saw Stef – standing right where I'd left her. She was trying to force a smile and there was blood trickling down her shins. After a thrashing in the shore break while struggling to control a massive fiberglass log, her surfing confidence tanked and, of course, I felt like a jerk for not taking a few minutes to help her get reacquainted. Apparently, her previous surf trip consisted mostly of pushing off the shallow sandy bottom on a soft top.

Nonetheless, the afternoon session, along with the next three days, continued to deliver the most consistent head-high waves I'd ever surfed, in bathtub-warm water. The locals took off deep and caught half the rides, but the vibe was 'tranquilo' with plenty of waves to go around. Stef wasn't quite ready to have another go.

After two nights at NicaWaves, Stef and I moved five minutes closer to the beach, to a rustic, thatch-roofed campsite called Camping Luna. After a lukewarm outdoor shower, we cooked pasta and beans in the outdoor kitchens. German backpackers with dreadlocks and soggy paperbacks, instead of devices, lounged in the hammocks, resigned to missing their upcoming return flights home. Without wi-fi or TV – or even much electricity – it was more communal and social.

Central America has seen surfers come from all over the world for decades, so there's no shortage of taxi drivers and English-speaking guides ready to help you find great waves. Especially for anyone from North America, the region is an easy, cheap destination for scoring surf year-round. Nicaragua is blessed with two major inland bodies of water – Lake Managua and Lake Nicaragua – which break up the American Cordillera mountain range and, therefore, funnel northeasterly trade winds onto the 150 miles (241km) of Pacific coastline. And there are far fewer crowds than in Costa Rica.

On our fourth day, we finally ventured north of Popoyo to Lance's Left, a nearby point break that is accessed by boat. Lance's is not a beginner's spot, so Stef sat on the boat, watching the waves break from behind and chatting with a British yoga teacher who'd tagged along for the ride. Back home, Stef is a serious mountain athlete who wins half marathons and tackles big backcountry skiing missions all year long. But she was still feeling gun-shy after her first session. However, in Popoyo, the surf bug is more persistent than the mosquitoes, and even she would soon be bitten again. That night, at Camping Luna, we feasted on lobster curry

MISTAKEN IDENTITY

Las Salinas' main break is misleadingly known as Popoyo, even though it's in front of a beach called Playa Guasacate; the actual Playa Popoyo is just on the north side of Mag Rock. Las Salinas itself gets its name from the beachfront saltflats where local artisans collect and boil down sea salt to sell at markets – the whole area is covered in a fine, powdery layer of the stuff.

Clockwise from top left: Nicaragua is a hit with visiting surfers; aerial moves on the Popoyo wave. Previous page: waveriding paradise

with a few Toña beers and the panoramic view of an stellar sunset.

On our last day, Stef rented a lighter 9ft longboard and together we waded out into Playa Sardina cove, just south of Popoyo's main break. She was a natural paddler, for sure, sometimes going too far outside. But the cove is sheltered from the open water by Mag Rock and has a shallower rocky bottom, with mellower waves trickling off the point. After a few failures to launch, a hip-high wave came along, with just the right amount of power. It propelled her forward and she popped up into a crouch. She then caught the thrust down the line, and rode it all the way into shore. I could hear her shouting with delight for the entire 15-second ride.

Stef paddled back out with a fire in her eyes, like she'd just seen the light and couldn't wait to do it again.

If nothing else, she was settling into the unique rhythm of a dedicated surf trip – deep downtime, often doing nothing for hours in preparation for the next intense session. And Popoyo is certainly the place to do this. Finding a place on the perfect wave opens Popoyo up to anyone willing to surrender to the flow – even newer couples still feeling out the convergence point of their respective agendas. Our Nicaraguan adventure was indeed a pure surf trip. But once Stef got her taste of the supernatural power of surfing, we both had all we needed.

ORIENTATION

Type of wave // Point break, split-peak rights and lefts.
Best conditions // Building high tide, year-round except during heavy October rains.
Nearest town // Las Salinas.
Getting there // Popoyo is a 2½-hour shuttle ride from Managua's Augusto C Sandino airport.
Where to stay // Stay at NicaWaves for comfortable amenities, Camping Luna for rustic and cheap, or Mag Rock for the best views around.
Things to know // Bring plenty of heavy duty bug spray and sunscreen, which are hard to find locally. There is only one small *tienda* (shop) in Las Salinas and they don't have much, although a well-stocked fruit and vegetable truck does drive around every day selling to people on the street.

Opposite from top: overwater living in Panama's Bocas del Toro islands; Santa Catalina was once Tom Curren's secret spot

MORE LIKE THIS
CENTRAL AMERICAN SWELL

BOCAS DEL TORO, PANAMA

Hailed as the best surf area on Central America's Caribbean coast, Bocas del Toro is an archipelago of nine main islands and a bunch of smaller cays and reefs providing a variety of wave types: from lefts to rights, for first-timers to pros. There are three main surf islands, so it helps a lot to have local knowledge here; hiring a guide will significantly up your chances of scoring good waves according to swell direction, tides and winds. Just 20 miles (32km) south of Costa Rica and 60 miles (97km) from the Pacific side, the Bocas del Toro islands have a decidedly Caribbean vibe and architectural aesthetic, with thatch-roof bungalows perched above warm, clear green-blue water. But the island vibes come with island prices, so this won't be your cheapest Central American option. January through March is the best window for waves.

Nearest town // Bocas del Toro Town

PUNTA ROCA, EL SALVADOR

Punta Roca is the most consistent wave in El Salvador, with something to surf here almost every day, in all conditions. It's a perfect, long right-hand point break that, on the best days, impersonates South Africa's Jeffreys Bay (minus the wetsuits and sharks). Also known as La Libertad after its port city namesake, the original El Salvador wave has power, kicks up frequent barrels, and is a fast, steep ride. Due to its proximity to town, the break can get very crowded with locals that rip, so dawn patrol is the best call to score. Another move to avoid the crowds is taking a drive north to check out other right-hand point breaks nearby: Cocal, La Bocana, Sunzal, K59, and K61 are just a few within a 30-minute drive. Some of these waves will be a little slower and less steep than Punta Roca, but that makes them a little more accessible for beginner and intermediate surfers.

Nearest town // La Libertad

SANTA CATALINA, PANAMA

The Pacific side of Panama is home to the biggest barrel in Central America, Santa Catalina. The main break is a right-hand point that is very consistent, and usually bigger than most spots due to the bathymetry (it holds waves of up to 20ft). Definitely for experienced surfers only due to its raw power, this was Tom Curren's secret spot during the '80s and early '90s until it got popular. There are smaller and friendlier waves in the area, too – like Estero, where sand-bottom surf kicks off consistent lefts and rights. All these breaks work best from April through October with south or southwest swells pulling rights off point breaks, but the size of the waves and remoteness of the location keeps the crowds minimal. Best to hit them at high and medium tide.

Nearest town // Santa Catalina

DITCH PLAINS

Just a few hours east of New York City, Montauk is a surf town like no other, with a surprisingly great point break. Chas Smith soaks in the over-the-top scene.

I was at Montauk's Surf Lodge one evening a handful of years ago, sipping a cocktail, surveying the decadence. What was once a simple dive bar, perched at the edge of town on the banks of Fort Pond, had been styled, fitted, reclaimed and transformed into the hottest summer spot east of Marfa, Texas. All manner of model, artist, actor, poet and lucky child with trust fund sipped passionfruit mojitos or watermelon, vodka and basil cocktails. Surf Lodge utilises a 'surf theme', though it's hard to tell if it's really for surfers. It's certainly for investment bankers who enjoy pairing mid-thigh designer surf trunks with a white linen button-up, and for interior designers with a knack for working thickly glassed longboards into casual beachy motifs. Then I spotted professional surfer Danny Fuller.

Now, Fuller was born and raised on the North Shore of O'ahu, and collects Pipeline's biggest and best waves each winter before travelling to Fiji, Indonesia and Tahiti to take on more tropical bombs. He's a charger in the truest sense of the word, a perpetual Eddie Aikau invitee. Yet, here he was in a place that rarely, if ever, gets bigger than shoulder-high in the glorious summer months.

'Danny, what are you doing here?', I asked him.

His answer was simple: 'I love it here in the summer.'

It makes a lot more sense than it seems. We all know, intuitively, that surfing is about much more than the simple act of riding a wave. It is a way of life, a way of being. As a professional hound, Danny travels the world looking for waves that demand full attention. They require singular levels of concentration, skill, ability and focus. In a place like Montauk, or surfing the mellow point at Ditch Plains, he can simply be a surfer. And, in many ways, being a surfer in Montauk during the warm summer months feels even better than being a surfer in places like Malibu, Hossegor or, say, Bondi. It feels pleasingly unique.

The town, perched at the very end of the Long Island peninsula, some three hours' drive from Manhattan in light traffic – double that on a typical weekend – has undergone a revival of sorts. The Hamptons, around 15 miles (24km) closer to New York City, has long had its reputation as a gilded playground for millionaires and billionaires. Montauk, on the other hand, was the blue-collar end of the road, where the mechanics, busboys, dishwashers and construction workers built homes and raised their families.

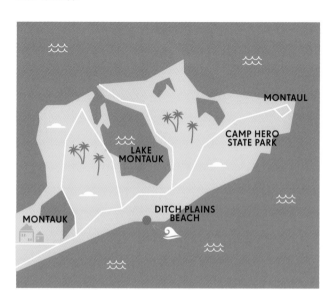

It is no wonder surfers found refuge here, especially in those early days, left alone and mixing in with the shark fishers and nobodies, drinking at bars that didn't know they were dives. A young army man named Richard Liewsinski is said to have been the first surfer. He drove up to Montauk in 1949 with a surfboard he had shaped using plans from *Popular Mechanics* magazine. But Long Island's last holdout was simply too enticing for the hipsters of New York City. Some 50 years after Liewsinski, empresarios like Jamie Mulholland and Jayma Cardoso – who introduced the very concept of 'bottle service' – and designers like Cynthia Rowley, known for gorgeously artistic wetsuit fashion, set up outposts that transformed the fishing outpost.

The pendulum has certainly swung here: weekend crowds have threatened to spoil the place for good, though acoustic sets by local musicians during the week quickly bring things back to earth. While the cultural co-option feels overdone at times, it's also why Montauk matters today. I've sipped cocktails at Surf Lodge, bathed in a setting sun, listening to Sune Rose Wagner sets, swayed around the fire at Ruschmeyer's, and watched the sun come up outside the Memory Motel, made famous by the Rolling Stones. I've eaten the best lobster of my life off a paper plate on Duryea's Lobster Deck.

I've also surfed surprisingly fun waves. A broad stretch of sandy beach that draws the most consistent swell on Long Island, Ditch Plains has been a surfing mecca, of sorts, since the early 1960s. In summer, the waves are silky, warm and predictably packed; in winter, they are mind-bendingly freezing, but can get ridiculously good. And the scene in the water is as entertaining as on land: I once found myself in the lineup with five male models who were in town celebrating a famous Hollywood producer friend's 40th birthday. The models wanted to go surfing, so I took them. I also took their waves, while they struggled with their 9ft soft-tops.

At Ditch, hardcore locals mix fluidly with Rolex-wearing stockbrokers, who drop in on runway models wearing Rip Curl trucker hats and pastel springsuits. It is the sort of crowd that

GHOST STORIES

According to some, the lighthouse overlooking Ditch Plains is haunted. Rumour has it that a young woman named Abigail, the daughter of a construction worker who helped build the lighthouse in the 1860s, still hangs around here. As the story goes, a young colleague fell in love with her; the father didn't approve of their shenanigans, so he killed the young suitor. Abigail then committed suicide herself – and is now said to terrorise surfers. Listen for hooting next time you drop in.

"It's the only place where big-wave hounds mingle with models and interior designers"

Clockwise from top: surfers flock
for larger waves around Montauk
in winter; Surf Lodge parties
are some of Montauk's hottest;
longboards await the Ditch
Plains wave. Previous page:
Ditch Plains is the East Coast's
coolest surf scene

would infuriate you elsewhere. But for some reason, here in
Montauk, it is an endlessly fun cross-section of surf culture: real
surfers, fake surfers, non-surfers, aspiring surfers.

After sessions, I follow a well-worn path to the usual spots to fuel
up, but also to mingle. The Ditch Witch food truck has all you need
for days when you don't plan on ever taking off your wetsuit. The
picnic tables at Joni's in town are always piled high with healthy
sandwiches and smoothies. I usually end up wandering through
town licking an ice-cream cone, shopping for some high-end gift
for my wife. I've even wandered through Montauk's Surf Museum,
where you'll find a medallion that surfers had to wear when the
town made them register as surfers so as not to mistake them for
local derelicts. In 1967 the city bosses wanted to outlaw surfing
entirely, as they felt it was drawing LSD-loving hippies.

And, of course, there are places like Surf Lodge. Indeed, it's
best to go in with an open mind as you try to fit in to this hipper-
than-thou universe, where the cocktails are wildly delicious and the
people-watching second to none – the only place where famous
big-wave hounds mingle with models and interior designers.

But there is nothing better than being a surfer, and few places
where it's so much fun as in Montauk.

ORIENTATION

Type of wave // Rock-reef A-frames.
Best conditions // Summer through autumn, with the odd
nor'easter that pushes proper surf up the beach.
Nearest town // Montauk.
Getting there // Montauk is 120 miles (193km) east of New
York City, at the far end of Long Island.
Where to stay // Montauk, East Hampton and the
surrounding towns cater to a wealthy crowd. Trendy hotels
like Ruschmeyer's and Sole East are fun, but you'll pay for it.
Things to know // Ditch Plains is the wave that is easiest
to access and breaks most consistently, making it wildly,
seriously crowded in warm summer months. Like, seriously
crowded. Enjoy the party, and party-waves.

Ditch Plains

Opposite from top: Maine is finally on the map for surfers; Nova Scotia's Bay of Fundy waves are still largely undiscovered

MORE LIKE THIS
NORTHEASTERN FRONTIERS

FORTUNES ROCKS, MAINE

Imagine even considering Maine as a surf destination two decades ago. Even one. Of course, the locals knew there were waves, but imagine anyone actually travelling for those waves? Imagine surfers hopping on a plane or packing up a car to access those waves? Such is the glorious moment we find ourselves in today. Maine is a now a true surf destination, and its Fortunes Rocks break is a very fine place to visit. The wave, just south of Portland, can be accessed by driving north on Maine's primary coastal road and turning right at the Episcopal Church. Once there, the enterprising surfer will find a beach break with both lefts and rights – head-high in winter, knee-high in summer – and a wonderful raw, newly discovered vibe.

Nearest town // Portland

NARRAGANSETT, RHODE ISLAND

Surfing in the shadow of a castle is rare, especially in the United States. Such uniqueness can be experienced in Rhode Island while surfing a peak that breaks off a sunken barge (now that's really exotic). Narragansett might not reach Indonesian consistency, and it certainly doesn't reach Indonesian warmth, but there are waves, lefts and rights, usually breaking in the cold winter. But fun, longboardable ankle-slappers can also be had in the summer, and after surfing, you'll find the most delicious lobster roll you've ever had (even better than in Montauk or Cape Cod). Also, visit Sid Abruzzi's surf shop, just a short drive away in Newport. The coldwater crowd has never been so cool.

Nearest town // Newport

THE BAY OF FUNDY, NOVA SCOTIA

While Montauk may be known as 'The End of the World', Canada's Nova Scotia is the *actual* end of the world. There it hovers, jutting out into the North Atlantic with its population of a few stalwart souls. But there are also slabs, points and unridden beach breaks lining its entire coast, just waiting to be discovered by adventurous surfers. The Bay of Fundy is a gorgeous oddity, with some of the craziest tides in the entire world – 160 billion gallons of water flow in and out on one tide cycle. More importantly, you'll find one of the longest rights in North America. Park in New Brunswick, ask around, and bring a board with volume.

Nearest town // New Brunswick

NIAS

After a devastating earthquake changed this iconic Indonesian wave forever, Ben Mondy paddled out to see if it still delivered the best seven seconds in surfing.

As I paddled out into Lagundri Bay, everything – and nothing – was the same. Nias has become an iconic backdrop in surfing, with dense, luminous-green jungle behind a perfect emerald peak. The sun-drenched horseshoe bay was still ringed by a mass of coconut palms; the sandy beach lined with stilted *losmen*, the two-storey guesthouses that had provided bed, board and local Bintang beers for three generations of travelling surfers. Nias had become the poster break for adventure. I took my place in the lineup, where a tightly knotted group of salt-blasted surfers from all over the world sat waiting their turn.

Having surfed this wave countless times before, I knew exactly what should happen as large, long-period swells march in uniform sets from deep in the Indian Ocean. The powerful wave would draw off the coral reef below and stand up in a feathering peak, coloured a distinctive emerald (or, as many say, Nias green) by the combination of tropical sun and jungle foliage. Muscle memory was preparing me for a relatively easy drop and a perfect, almond-shaped cylinder that spun mechanically down the reef for 1000ft into the safety of a deep channel. It isn't a long wave, but it's not for nothing that Lagundri is known to deliver the best seven seconds in surfing. Or was, anyway.

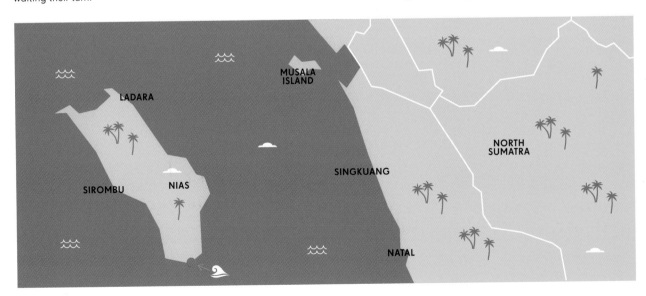

As I paddled into my first wave I noticed the usual emerald colour had been dialled down to dull jade. Instead of a perfect, almond-shaped barrel, the wave lurched forward, breaking faster and squarer than I remembered. Don't get me wrong, it was still an amazing wave. Possibly even still 'perfect'. But it was very different.

Located off the village Sorake on the western side of Lagundri Bay in Sumatra, Nias' wave was first discovered in 1975 by Australian surfers Kevin Lovett, John Geisel and Peter Troy. But the trio kept its location relatively quiet, determined to keep this true surfing paradise to themselves. However, as the saying goes, surf secrets are either too good to keep or not worth keeping. Word soon got out. The wave first appeared in surf magazines and movies in the early 1980s, and the break known simply as Nias quickly became a bucket-list surf destination.

Its isolation – on the southern side of the island of Nias, some 60 miles (100km) off the North Sumatran mainland – fed the mythology. After flying into Medan, surfers would endure a 10-hour bus trip, a six-hour ferry, then a six-hour drive to Sorake. Reaching Nias is still an arduous mission today. Flights from Medan to Gunungsitoli have shortened the journey, but the last leg often features treacherous roads and river crossings, which are especially tricky during the monsoon season. I once had to push a surfboard-laden van through waist-deep mud for six hours. My travel companions and I became firm friends before a single wave was ridden, and went on to become lifelong friends.

Needless to say, many of the surfers who made the journey tended to stay for the long haul. Many devotees would return each year and live with the same local families for months on end. It was a simple life based on a diet of home-cooked Indonesian food, fresh fruit, and incredible waves.

On March 28, 2005, an earthquake measuring 8.6 on the Richter scale struck Sumatra. The epicentre was just 50 miles (80km) from Nias. The force of the quake moved the Indo-Australian tectonic plate underneath the Eurasian Plate, and the whole island was levered up as if by a giant crowbar. Tens of thousands of homes were destroyed and nearly 1000 people in the area lost their lives. In some places, coral banks as high as 7ft (2m) poked out of what was once deep water. It was obvious that the quake would have had a dramatic effect on the sea floor and, thus, the waves.

I returned to the area a year later. Before I got to Nias, I took boat trips to world-class nearby waves like Bawa and Asu, places I had spent some of my most memorable days surfing. Both were unrecognisable, even unrideable. It turned out that hundreds of the area's waves were either lost or changed for the worse. But for some reason, it seemed impossible that Lagundri could have suffered.

I'll admit, I felt an odd sense of dread as I walked to the edge of the bay. And it seemed the water's edge had retreated out to sea, as if under the spell of a 60ft (18m) low tide.

This time, the surfers in the water could talk of nothing else but the quake. European backpackers, local grommets and Nias first timers sat wide, having recently graduated from Kiddies' Corner

POP CULTURE

In 1989, Coca-Cola made an ad featuring pro-surfers Luke Egan, Jodie Cooper, Stuart Bedford-Brown and Kye Fitzgerald travelling to surf an 'undiscovered' perfect wave (aka Lagundri Bay). When the technicolour waves of Nias were beamed into the living rooms of mainstream Australia and New Zealand, interest in the wave hit an all time high. Thanks to the ad's promotion, Nias saw its most crowded surf seasons ever throughout the early 1990s.

Clockwise from top left: surfers who journey to Lagundri Bay often stay for weeks; wet season woes; the wave is a favourite among the world's elite. Previous page: Nias' famous jungle backdrop is as iconic as the wave

"Devotees would return each year and stay for months with local familes – it was a simple life of home-cooked Indonesian food, fresh fruit and incredible waves"

and the Bubble (the more forgiving waves inside the bay that break when the swell is small). Further out sat the long-time Nias devotees: wiry American veterans, confident Aussie tube-pigs, Japanese chargers and Brazilian surf rats.

It took just one ride to confirm this wave was still very much alive. Some of the changes had even improved the break. The pre-earthquake version needed at least a 6ft swell to break, but now produced quality waves at half that size; and it had not become any less menacing on big days. It became clear that none of Nias' heaviness or hollowness had disappeared when the 2011 movie *Who Is JOB* was released, showing pro Jamie O'Brien surfing giant slabs at Lagundri. Hawaiian Mark Healey was credited with riding the biggest wave in the break's history during a 2018 swell.

During the first couple of years after the earthquake, many of us felt like those first surfers who discovered Nias all those years ago. We had to learn the moods of the wave all over again.

As in the lineup, there are more people in town every year. But so much feels the same, no matter how much it changes: the joy of scarfing down Kabu Nohi *losmen*'s signature nasi goreng and washing it down with a cold Bintang; the arduous journey to reach the wave. And while Nias is best known for its surfing past, it's interesting to reflect on the fact that, thanks to mother nature, its history is still being written.

ORIENTATION

Type of wave // Right-hand tubing reef break.
Best conditions // Most consistent in the dry season (May to September).
Nearest town // The small town of Teluk Dalam is the nearest place to gather supplies, but staying in front of the wave in the Sorake is the only real option.
Getting there // Nearest airport is Binaka (GNS), in the Nias capital of Gunungsitoli. There are daily flights between there and Medan, which has international air links with Jakarta, Denpasar, Singapore and Kuala Lumpur.
Where to stay // There's a range of *losmen* (guesthouses), plus newer resorts and surf camps.
Things to know // Malaria and dengue fever are still present on Nias. Gunungsitoli Airport doesn't accept boards over 6'8", and you can only bring three per passenger.

Opposite from top: South African
pro Michael February gets barrelled
at Keramas during a CT event;
Lakey Peak, Sumbawa

MORE LIKE THIS
INDO'S HEAVY HITTERS

HOLLOW TREES, MENTAWAI ISLANDS

Located on Sipura in the Mentawai Islands, the wave known as Hollow Trees, HTs or Lance's Right was discovered 15 years after Nias. While similar in terms of length and quality to the wave at Lagundri Bay, HTs is even more photogenic, and quickly became the new shiny object in the surf world (perhaps no other single wave has featured in more surfing magazines over the last two decades). In fact, some say HTs has taken over Nias' mantle as Indonesia's most dreamy righthander. Until recently, HTs was only accessible via chartered boat trips, but various camps now operate within walking distance of it. Unlike Lagundri, however, there are a dozen quality waves within a 10-minute boat trip from HTs, suitable for all levels of surfers.

Nearest town // Padang

KERAMAS, BALI

Rumours of a perfect righthander (in this land of lefts), hidden behind the rice fields of Bali's east coast, first surfaced in the 1990s. Yet Keramas somehow remained a relative secret until the millennium. But, of course, any wave of this quality with both a world-class tube and high performance potential (and a convenient location, just two hours from Kuta) could not be kept hidden for long. Fast-forward to today and Keramas now breaks 100ft in front of the pool of the luxurious Komune Resort. It hosts an annual CT event and is one of the most recognisable, accessible and epic waves on the planet.

Nearest town // Denpasar

LAKEY PEAK, SUMBAWA

While very different to Lagundri Bay (the wave breaks both left and right), Lakey Peak shares Lagundri's diehard following. Surfers tend to return every year, flying in from Bali to Bima Airport in East Sumbawa. As in Nias, accommodation was once mostly family-run *losmens*, but there are now several resort and hotel options, for every budget. Being heavily affected by the wet-season monsoon winds, Lakey Peak turns on from April through June. The perfect A-Frame peak breaks from three to 10 feet, and there are a half-dozen other waves, suiting all abilities, within walking distance of the accommodation.

Nearest town // Bima

ITANKI BEACH

Whether it's on snow or in the water, the island of Hokkaido is the epicentre of Japanese surf culture. Christopher Nelson immerses himself in the year-round life of glide.

Pulling up at the beach, we park along the road, joining a gleaming line of tiny, cubic cars and small, boxy mini-vans – tailgates open, wetsuits hanging, buckets beneath. Surfers sit in small clusters on the low wall, waiting and watching. From this vantage point it's only a short walk to the fine, dry sand. The tide is pushing off low and I watch a steep lefthander reeling from the end of the breakwater. I see a second follow the same track and am immediately digging in the trunk, pulling out my towel and wetsuit.

The first thing that strikes you about the remarkable Itanki Beach is that, on arrival, this 1.5-mile (7km) stretch of dull grey sand appears truly unremarkable. A short runway of coast road draws a line between the dusty warehouses and the steely shore, before the blunt cliffs force the tarmac to retreat inland. In common with many Japanese beaches, a tangle of concrete sea defences act to cushion this southeasterly facing bay, bookended between a small harbour to the north and a jagged point to the south.

When you take a breath, however, and look again, you see that those blunt cliffs are actually striated by bright white bands, topped with lush sasa bamboo. The sand, volcanic in nature, is *naki-suna* (singing sand), born of the seismic landscape. And those seemingly incongruous man-made obstacles actually serve to capture and groom shifting banks.

A wedging lefthander refracts off the harbour wall, launching skyward before tapering into the beach; a fun A-frame peak rears through the middle of the rocky barriers, spilling reeling walls. South past the breakwater, the beach opens up into a long, pristine curve, unrestrained by the engineer's pen.

Itanki is situated in Muroran, a small industrial town on the southeastern edge of Hokkaido. Famous as a port and a hub

for industry, it is a fascinating counterpoint to the vast, verdant landscapes of this large island. Tourism races past the town, usually hightailing it straight to the mountain resorts, with their glut of boutique hotels and, ironically, surf shops. In Muroran itself, infrastructure laid on for the more adventurous visitor is limited to a few hotels and basic hostels. In many ways, the beach at Itanki feels like ground zero for surfing in Japan's northernmost prefecture, but you'll find there are no actual surf facilities here.

Itanki aims out into the Pacific, hoovering up swells from any passing low pressure system and igniting during the August to October typhoon season. It is the best-known surf spot on the

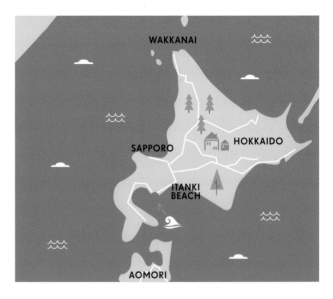

island and a regular contest venue. While Chiba, the Olympic star lying close to Tokyo, may have drawn the eyes of the world, most surfers know it often pays to push against the flow, to kick out towards northerly, less accessible reaches to reap hard-won rewards.

I launch from the beach and duck-dive the last two waves of a set. Opening my eyes underwater, it is surprisingly clear, the translucent green-blue of sand-weathered sea-glass. A small group of locals are sitting on the peak in the lull. I join the end of the line, nodding hello. My greeting is returned. Dark shadows furrow the horizon. A set approaches and the energy changes. The pack moves as one, paddling out and wide. Surfers pivot, one after the other, hooking into steep drops.

I wait my turn until I am on the peak. The next wave approaches, rearing, lifting. I angle my takeoff, pop, grab the rail and bottom-turn. Crouched on my backhand I look up at the feathering lip, release the rail and aim for the shoulder, holding the high-line for a fraction longer than instinct dictates before sweeping back down the face, revelling in that extra millisecond of flight. It is a wave that encourages smooth pace and flow. Some 200ft down the line I kick out, smile and begin the slow paddle back.

Japan has 6852 islands. Hokkaido is the second largest, the majority of it sitting at latitudes north of Vladivostok, Russia. This means that summer brings a fresh brightness, far from the sweltering humidity that descends on Tokyo and the main island. Typhoon season is dream-like: 3/2mm wetsuits, groomed offshores, and long golden days. However, when winter does arrive, it kicks down the door. Cold, dry winds sweep off the Siberian plains and, crossing the Sea of Japan, they greedily absorb moisture, arriving bloated with snow. For the year-round surfer it is time for the 6/5mm hooded wetsuits to come out of storage, time for thick booties to be prewarmed with flasks of hot water in preparation to wade through knee-deep snowdrifts blanketing the sand dunes.

Hence Hokkaido's legend as a winter sports destination, its fabled tree-runs drawing snowboarders and skiers from across the globe. The powder-shrouded terrain has shaped a specific approach to surfing here. With a love of both waves and mountains, pioneers such as Taro Tamai have pushed a style known as 'snow-surfing', in which long carves echo the surfer's line, harnessing the landscape in the way one utilises the whole face of a wave, using flow in perfect harmony with the environment. Like spring meltwater, this ethos has filtered back into the lineup, breeding an approach that is smooth and stylish – more soul-arch than air-show.

And this is key. More than the waves or the landscape, there is one thing that shapes the surfing experience here, that makes Itanki Beach such a singular spot. It is the people. There is a true heritage here, not a mere aping of California culture. Standing on the shore, I talk with Kazuhiro Miyatake, one of the first surfers on Hokkaido and a founder of the Itanki Beach crew. He learned *naminori* – wave riding – while at university in Tokyo in the late 1970s. He shares stories of the early days of surfing in the winter

HOT SOAK

Warm up post surf in a local onsen (hot-spring bath). Some onsen are outdoor, carved into the landscape; others more basic, municipal style. Leave your modesty behind: most are single-sex, no swimwear. You will be provided with a small towel for washing, but keep it out of the bathing waters (many people put them on their heads). Most onsen don't allow tattoos due to their association with Yakuza, the Japanese mafia – but times are changing, so be sure to check first.

Clockwise from top: grabbing a sunrise session at Itanki; onsen are the perfect antidote to cold-water sessions. Previous page: aspects of Itanki Beach

snow, those basic wetsuits no match for the frigid Pacific.

The first surfers here were regularly hauled out of the water by the local police, who had no reference point for what they saw. 'We had to obey the cops otherwise we would be arrested', he remembers, 'but when they went away, we went back in.' The burgeoning crew realised they needed to bolster their numbers to gain acceptance, and found unlikely recruits in the ranks of motorcycle gangs. Together, they formed the Hokkaido Surfing Association. The drive and determination required to overcome the social, political and meteorological climate has forged a hardy crew, with a distinct legacy.

It's lunchtime and Taro Tamai takes us to a tiny eatery close to a small harbour. The interior is compact and immaculately clean, a glass counter displaying little plates of glistening fish steaks and shellfish. The chef leans over and places a piece of *nigirizushi* on Taro's plate. The *neta* (topping) is prime-cut, marbled tuna. 'This fish tastes different to tuna caught later in the year; it was caught locally as it chased mackerel into shallow waters,' says Taro. 'It has a distinctive taste and a specific story. A good sushi chef can tell you the story of each fish here. I like that about surfing; every wave has a story, and they are different with every season, every time of the year.'

This is the way at Itanki. When you pause, take an extra moment, the full story is revealed. Like the mountains and sea, like the *neta* and the sushi rice, surfing and local culture are interwoven. On their own each is special, but when combined they produce something truly remarkable.

ORIENTATION

Type of wave // Wedgy left, shifting beach break peak.
Best conditions // Low tide on the push. It works all year on small to medium swell, but fires during the August to October typhoon season.
Nearest town // Muroran.
Getting there // Fly into Chitose Airport; Muroran is about an hour's drive south.
Where to stay // The no-frills Muroran Youth Hostel overlooking the beach is aimed at local workers and bikepackers. The mountain resort of Niseko (1½ hours' drive away) has excellent deals outside of the powder season.
Things to know // Summer sea temps are around 68°F (20°C), so a 3/2 mm wetsuit is plenty. Talk to locals on the beach here, and be respectful in the lineup, and it will be repaid in spades.

*Opposite: the Kaifu river mouth
creates intense and technical waves*

MORE LIKE THIS
JAPAN'S TOP SURF SPOTS

TSURIGASAKI (SHIDASHITA), CHIBA PREFECTURE

Chiba is the most popular and most famous surfing region in Japan – for good reason. The 37-mile (60km) stretch of Kujukuri Beach picks up almost any passing swell, making it super consistent. And its proximity to Tokyo has made it the go-to choice for a good proportion of the country's surfing population. The long stretch of curving shore, punctuated by large groynes, culminates with the easterly facing Shidashita break at the southern end. Sandbanks form around a series of breakwaters that protrude at a 90-degree angle from the beach, often producing long rights or fun peaks. If it's on, it's busy, but the beach to the north offers plenty of opportunity to spread out and find your place. Working at most tides, and offshore in westerly winds, this corner of the beach has good access and parking, and these factors have made it a regular contest venue and the host destination for the 2020 Tokyo Games, in which surfing will make its Olympic debut.
Nearest town // Chiba City

KAIFU RIVER MOUTH, TOKUSHIMA PREFECTURE

Japan is home to some world-class river-mouth surf that can serve up anything from fun, peeling walls in the small summer swells to heaving, grinding barrels during the August to October typhoon season. On the exposed southeastern edge of Shikoku – Japan's fourth largest island – is one such spot. Kaifu is a right-hand river mouth at the southern end of the long beach that fronts the town of Kaiyo. A small river runs into the sea adjacent to a working fishing harbour, where it deposits a tapering sandbank. When swell hits, it produces either long, tapering walls or short, heavy barrels, and can get very shallow on the inside section. Either way, you'll need to know your way around a lineup to surf here, as you'll be dealing with intense crowds or intense waves.
Nearest town // Kaiyo

NIYODO RIVER MOUTH, KOCHI PREFECTURE

Staying at the northern end of Shikoku island, there's another classic setup three hours west of Kaifu. Niyodo featured in many international surf magazines and is often the poster boy for Japanese river-mouth perfection. The waters of the Niyodo River are famed for their clarity and sacred power, but the real magic happens where they meet the Pacific. The sandbank here shifts around, depending on swell size, direction and recent outflow. Facing southeasterly and offshore in northwest winds, it delivers short lefts, but it's the rights that draw the crowds. *The Encyclopedia of Surfing* is glowing in its description: 'A right breaking sand bottom tube compared to Hawaii's Backdoor'. It's a popular spot with the hard-charging locals, but be respectful and you may just be afforded one of the best waves of your life. The break is visible from the coast road's bridge and there is parking to the west of the river.
Nearest town // Kochi

THE MALDIVES

In this tiny island chain in the Indian Ocean, waves are served up on a silver platter –
Janna Irons had no idea there was such a thing as too much surf.

From high above the Indian Ocean, 600 miles (956km) southwest of India and Sri Lanka, the Maldives appear out of nowhere, as hundreds of white and turquoise paint splatters glowing against dark blue water. It's breathtaking. But what struck me most as we began to make our descent toward the small island chain is that, although I had a good idea of the type of surf I'd experience over the next week, I knew absolutely nothing about the country's culture, history or life outside the water.

I blame surfing tunnel vision. And magnifying this was the fact that we'd opted to experience the Maldives via one of the ubiquitous liveaboard surf charters, a packaged experience where our days were planned for us, our meals served, and the experience sort of delivered to us on a customized platter.

As I stepped onto the blazing tarmac at Velana International Airport in the city-island of Male, the scene felt foreign, entirely different from the photos I'd seen of empty white-sand beaches and huts hovering over clear blue sea. Instead, the capital was packed with high-rises and bustling with people. In the distance, a group

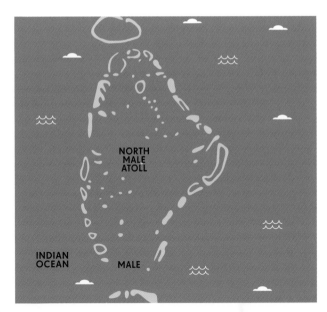

NORTH
MALE
ATOLL

INDIAN
OCEAN

MALE

of women took an afternoon swim in the sea, fully clothed, wearing hijabs. Wooden boats with exquisitely upholstered interiors ferried fancy honeymooners from the airport dock through cargo ships and fishing boats, to deposit them on bajillion-dollar yachts.

Turns out, a quarter of the Maldives' population live in this 2.2 sq mile (5.6 sq km) island. The rest of the nation's 400,000 inhabitants are scattered throughout the 1100-plus islands and sandbanks.

Known for its dozens of long, world-class reef point breaks, the Maldives is often thought of as a more mellow Indonesia. The breaks feature easier takeoffs and slightly less power, and fewer spots break over super-shallow reef. First discovered as a surf destination in the early 1970s by a pair of shipwrecked Australians, the surf in the Maldives remained a well-kept secret for over a decade until, in the '80s, the two launched the Maldives' first surf charter company, Atoll Adventures. These days, dozens of charter outfits and surf resorts accommodate an estimated 10,000 surfers each year.

With the promise of perfect 300ft rides, we decided to focus our trip on the Northern Atolls, one of three main surf regions. We heaved our longboard bags into the van. My four friends and I piled in, introducing ourselves to a couple of Australian women who'd recently became friends thanks to their mutual love of surfing.

Once on the boat, the captain, a cook and a surf guide welcomed us aboard our home for the next week – a 68ft cruiser – with a fruity drink. They showed us to our sleeping quarters below deck, a series of tiny bunk rooms with a narrow bed covered by a thin blanket, and cubbies tucked into the wall to stash our stuff. The cramped space smelled of must and exhaust.

Surf charters in the Maldives can be as luxurious or minimalist as you choose. Our budget demoted us to the latter. Nonetheless, for just a few hundred dollars a night, we received lodging, three meals a day and the promise of more waves than we could ride. As we slept, the boat slowly chugged toward tomorrow's surf break.

The next morning, we were all up before first light, unpacking our boards on the top deck, exchanging fin keys and surf wax. I could see the silhouettes of a few other boats anchored in the channel nearby; if I strained my eyes, I could just make out the legendary righthander known as Jails. As the sun peeked over the horizon, a perfect head-high wave peeled across the reef. Giddy, we piled our boards into the dinghy and motored out to the lineup.

We spent the next few hours exchanging waves and chatting with a dozen or so other surfers from around the world; some of them had chartered luxurious boats, with Jacuzzis and grand dining tables groaning with champagne and lobster. But even our budget experience provided a luxury I never knew I needed: a surf guide, whose only job was to get us to the best waves. Our guide knew precisely the type of surf we were after and would radio with other boats to check conditions and crowds, while continuously dissecting tide, swell and wind charts to put us in exactly the right spot at the right time. Often, the boats would trade off, with one group paddling out as another motored to a new spot. Despite thousands of other surfers, none of the crowds we experienced were anything close to those in Southern California or Hawaii.

Each morning, we'd be woken by the sound of the anchor dropping just before dawn. We'd sleepily emerge from our rooms and stir up an instant coffee. Then, they'd whisk us off to the lineup,

dropping us off right in position, and we'd each catch waves until we physically couldn't paddle out for another. Then, with a wave of the hand, the dinghy would reappear to whisk us back to the boat for pancakes and fresh fruit, or traditional Maldivian curries. Sometimes we'd stay anchored in the channel all day, surfing off and on. Other days, after a morning surf, we'd head off to another spot, passing a Club Med resort where pasty tourists played volleyball. It struck us that we had still not set foot on land, or seen a local village up close.

The days quickly blended together: surf, eat, sleep; surf, eat, sleep. By the fifth day, we were sunburned, rashed and exhausted. The swell had picked up and I just didn't have it in me to paddle out. I sat out the morning session, sipping coffee on the deck, watching my friends paddle into overhead lefts at a spot called Honkeys. Having surfed more waves in those past few days than we'd caught all year, we decided to spend the afternoon just floating in the clear blue water watching fish and turtles swim by.

On our final night, the air conditioner in our room began pumping out warm air. I pulled the pillow and sheet off my bed and carried them up to the top deck to sleep, only to find that a few of my friends – and the crew – had done the same. We laughed, lined up our lounge chairs and let the gentle breeze lull us to sleep.

Back at the airport, encrusted with salt and sunscreen, we slumped against our boardbags on the open-air terminal floor. A couple passed by looking relaxed, as if they'd stepped out of a spa. The man handed the boat driver a handful of bills and the woman looked down at us: a look of confusion mixed with pity. I smiled. The Maldives is certainly the place where two disparate versions of the Ultimate Dream Vacation come to life.

From left: Jails can be both fun and frightening; local life in the Maldives' capital, Male; hawksbill turtles roam the reefs. Previous page, from left: bioluminescent algae; duck-diving Honkeys, a North Atolls classic

ORIENTATION

Type of wave // The Northern, Central and Southern Atolls features every type of wave imaginable, most breaking over coral reefs.
Best conditions // The waves of the Maldives are best in spring and summer, with bigger sets arriving late summer. The ideal swell direction is southwest-southeasterly.
Nearest town // Male.
Getting there // There are regular international flights to Velana International Airport in Male.
Where to stay // There are several surf-charter outfits, as well as on-island surf resorts, all ranging from basic to luxurious. Most are all-inclusive.
Things to know // Bring at least two boards, one for smaller days and one for when the swell picks up. Also recommended are motion sickness pills, a first aid kit and antidiarrhoeal medicine.

Opposite: Cokes is a must-surf spot
while cruising the Maldives

MORE LIKE THIS
MALDIVES' TOP SURF SPOTS

COKES AND CHICKENS

For the seasick-prone, land-based surf camps are ideal. Located on the sandy shores of Thulusdhoo Island, a two-hour boat ride north of Male International Airport, is Cokes Surf Resort, where visitors have easy access to two of the best waves in the Northern Atolls: Cokes and Chickens. Named for the Coca-Cola factory on the island, Cokes is a hollow, fast righthander, offering reeling barrels, and is consistently bigger than other spots in the area. Nearby is its mirror image, Chickens (so-named for a poultry farm on a nearby island), which works on swells anywhere from 3ft to over 10ft, and provides rides as long as five football fields. Other nearby spots (reachable via the resort's surf-guide boats) include the well-known Jails, Honkeys and Sultans. Other perks of staying on the island include regular massages, beers on the beach and beds that don't sway with the swell.
Nearest island // Thulusdhoo

NINJAS

Sneak some surf into your all-inclusive family vacation. Located near all the best breaks, Club Med Kani Resort on Kanifinolhu Island is the four-star vacation experience that just so happens to have a perfect right peeling out front. Ninjas is a playful spot, perfect for surfers looking for a more mellow alternative to the reeling barrels at some of the other nearby waves. The imperfect reef bottom means it's slightly shiftier than the other waves in the area, but that unpredictability provides for fun turns. While you're having the time of your life, your non-surfing family can entertain themselves with activities like yoga, wakeboarding and games of Marco Polo in the infinity pool.
Nearest island // Kanifinolhu

PASTA POINT

If you're after a more exclusive Maldives experience, Pasta Point delivers. This is the wave that the founder of Maldives surfing, Tony Hussein Hinde, fell in love with upon being shipwrecked here in the '70s. Made famous by the World Qualifying Series surf contest in the early 2000s, Pasta Point provides long, peeling lefts that are protected from the wind, keeping the flawless faces perfectly intact. While the waves are generally in the 4ft–6ft range during the south swell season (May to August), they still break just as flawlessly at 1–2ft. But the best part about Pasta Point is that it's limited to just 30 surfers, all of whom must be staying at the luxurious Cinnamon Dhonveli Maldives resort on shore. From there, guests can paddle out directly to private surf sessions, as well as enjoy the resort's restaurants and bars, spend the day at the spa, take a submarine ride or just lounge in its over-water villas.
Nearest island // Kanuhura

HIRIKETIYA BAY

For Sam Haddad, this lesser-known break in southern Sri Lanka is one of the best family surf spots on the planet.

I didn't expect to fall in love with surfing again. Certainly not at 40, and deep into motherhood, which had limited not just my access to waves but also my strength, fitness and even my self-confidence. Yet, on a well-used rental longboard, in a dreamy horseshoe-shaped bay very far from home, where the jungle topples right into the sea, that's exactly what happened.

We were drawn to Sri Lanka after hearing the island described as a less-touristy alternative to Bali: a tropical wonderland, with incredibly friendly locals who loved kids. We'd heard it had much of the charm of neighbouring India, but without the daunting chaos. Sri Lanka is a country that still appeals to backpackers and adventure-

minded travellers but, as transport and accommodation options improve at a rapid pace, it's also beginning to attract older visitors and families with young kids. In fact, a friend suggested Hiriketiya Bay on the south of the island, specifically because the Colombo–Matara Expressway, which was finished in 2014, provided a relatively short transfer time (just three hours) from the capital's airport. Oh, and because of the waves.

The truth is, there are plenty of better surf spots in the world than Hiriketiya Bay. There are even better surf spots in Sri Lanka (especially on the east coast around Arugam Bay, where there are breaks that many would consider world class). But amazing waves

TANGALLE

WELIGAMA

HIRIKETIYA BEACH

MIRISSA

MATARA

attract amazing surfers, not to mention crowds. More importantly, we were after something very unique for our first family surf holiday. With our sons aged six and eight, we were looking for a more low-key experience. A place where the atmosphere in the lineup and on the beach was as mellow as the waves themselves.

A decade ago, the only people you'd find in the water around Hiriketiya were fisherfolk and local kids swimming. Then, in 2014, an Aussie surfer named Marty set up a guesthouse – surf tourism has been quietly growing ever since.

On our first morning, as we strolled down the dirt road from our guesthouse to the beach, enjoying the thick heat, we saw a troupe of at least 30 toque macaques. They were dancing along the overhead power lines as if performing a high-wire act, much to the kids' delight. We later found out that the monkeys enjoy the cables' electic fizz on their tongues so much that they often chew right through them, causing power cuts. Still, for us it was a perfect warm-up act before the main event.

Unlike a couple of other popular surf spots in the south, such as Hikkaduwa and Weligama, Hiriketiya is a small cove set back from the main coastal road, without obvious signposts. So it's not really somewhere you stumble upon – it's more a beach you hear or read about, which has added to the mythic status of the place.

Arriving at a beach you've only seen through filtered photos on the internet is always a risk. But Hiriketiya more than delivered on its promise of tropical perfection with local flourish. Bright green tuk-tuks with jazzed-up interiors rolled by; red-, white- and blue-painted wooden fishing boats lay idly on the sand, and there was an old yellow school bus repurposed to sell rotis and samosas.

There were also waves. Good ones. We saw a slow peeling lefthander that looked eminently rideable, even for the very out-of-practice. Then we saw a more advanced righthander over by the rocks. We even spotted a few gentle breakers, which I thought could be good for the kids if they decided to give surfing a try. The plan was to wait for the boys themselves to ask if they could give it a go.

The first day, they just swam and re-enacted scenes from *Harry Potter* in the shallows. Without a pounding shore break to worry about, the swimming is relatively safe close to shore. We could enjoy our good coffee, banana lassis and local King Coconut water without leaving our beach chairs.

Once the caffeine kicked in, I was ready to catch some waves – even if my children weren't. There were several friendly locals with decent rental boards set up right there on the sand. I grabbed an 8'2, but they had just about every shape and size you could want.

The water was bath-like, which is especially freeing coming from the crisp conditions in England. Paddling felt good and I quickly and easily reached the handful of surfers waiting their turn to ride the lefthander. The lineup was at least half women, a mix of Sri Lankans and Westerners, all ages and sizes.

As a nice knee-high roller headed toward me, I got into position. I felt it pull me so I went to stand, only to nose dive into oblivion. I guess it's not like riding a bike. Indeed, I wiped out on my next eight

BUDDHA'S WATCHING

At Wewurukannala Vihara, in the nearby town of Dikwella, you'll find Sri Lanka's largest seated Buddha. It was built in the 1960s, when ostentatious religious attractions were all the rage, but much of the temple itself dates back to the 18th century. To reach the Buddha, you first have to navigate the cartoonish Tunnel of Hell, which includes figures being disembowelled and hacked in half for their sins – perhaps a useful reminder not to take selfies.

Clockwise from top left: let the kids loose on a surfboard at Hiriketiya Bay; the local area is rich with non-surf excursions; a surf town on the rise. Previous page: Hiriketiya is tailor-made for lazy longboard sessions

waves, all slow peelers of between 2ft and 3ft. I actually began to consider the possibility that my days of surfing were over.

'You're trying to get up too quickly', said the kind voice of a local longboarder as she glided past, her wave-riding as stylish as her one-piece surf suit. 'Hold the rails for longer and relax...' The waves were small, but they had steep faces, which had made me panic into rushing my pop-up (instincts left over from trips to Bali and southwest France). But they weren't powerful, so taking my time was key. Plus, the conditions in Hiriketiya are so forgiving, it's exactly where you want to be when you're learning how to surf all over again.

The rest of the session was like a dream as it all came back to me. I ended up surfing twice a day – sometimes more – for the rest of the trip. I felt more stoked by riding waves than I'd felt in a long time.

However, there is no feeling for a surfer quite like the moment your children come to you asking if they, too, can give it a try. After making friends with some slightly older kids on the beach who were already decent surfers, our boys finally decided they were ready. And cheap private lessons with local instructors are easy to sort right on the beach if you just ask around.

For four days straight, they took a morning lesson from an instructor they both loved. He had them both standing up while pulling shakas within the first hour, and our eldest was paddling into and catching waves himself by the second day. He even began venturing into greener waves toward the end of the trip. While our six year old stuck to the whitewater – and still needed a push to get going – he was hooked. On one of his rides in, as I watched and cheered while standing in waist-high water beside him, he shouted to me, 'This is the best holiday of my life!' Regardless of the size or colour of the waves he was riding, he was a surfer. And perhaps he always will be.

"The lineup was at least half women, a mix of Sri Lankans and Westerners, all ages and sizes"

ORIENTATION

Type of wave // Beach break and left-hand point break.

Best conditions // Surfable all year. From March to July the swell can be bigger, producing more challenging waves.

Nearest town // Dikwella is a seven-minute tuk-tuk ride or 25-minute walk away.

Getting there // International visitors should fly to Bandaranaike International Airport in Colombo. Pre-book the three-hour transfer to Hiriketiya Beach.

Where to stay // Saffron House is a stunning villa, high on the headland above Hiriketiya, which has its own pool and walled garden (www.saffronhousevilla.com).

Things to know // The water temps are always above 75°F (24°C), but often closer to 85°F (30°C). Wear high-factor, waterproof sun protection. Beware of poor water quality after big storms. Women should dress modestly away from the beach.

Opposite, from top: Barra da Lagoa beach in Florianópolis has something for everyone; Bali's Legian Beach preps newcomers for Indo's more advanced waves

MORE LIKE THIS
FAMILY-FRIENDLY SURF SPOTS

SAYULITA, MEXICO

With its *palapa* (palm-leaf) roofs, brightly painted cafés and shops, and deep jungle backdrop, this tranquil surf village, just north of Puerto Vallarta on Mexico's Pacific Coast, is a top choice for a family trip. The water is warm, the waves are gentle, and kids can have lessons on the sandbar at the town's main beach. As they improve, there's also a long right-hand point break on the same beach, which is great for aspiring longboarders. Instructors are kind, laid-back and fluent in English as well as Spanish, and the town has loads of great foodie spots, including mouth-watering Mexican seafood places and streetside taco stalls that kids will love. Other popular activities around Sayulita include stand-up paddleboarding, mountain-biking and, in the winter months, whale-watching.
Nearest town // Sayulita

BARRA DA LAGOA, BRAZIL

Florianópolis – or Floripa as locals call it – may no longer be a secret rural idyll, but the laid-back capital of Santa Catarina state is still a place of rare natural beauty that's a far cry from the crowds and city-besmirched shoreline around Rio. An hour south of Rio by plane, the island has plenty of beaches for all levels of surfer, but the pretty fishing village of Barra da Lagoa, with its fleet of colourful boats, is one of the quietest and most family friendly. The waves are manageable, with both left- and right-hand breaks, and there are lots of surf schools accustomed to teaching kids in both English and Portuguese. There is also a reputable turtle conservation programme on the beach – children can learn about local species and how to protect them.
Nearest town // Florianópolis

LEGIAN, BALI

From Uluwatu to Padang Padang, Bali has long been renowned for its world-class surf breaks. But the Indonesian island can also be a great place for kids to stand up on their first waves, thanks to friendly local teachers, bath-like sea temperatures, and the consistent beach breaks that roll in at Legian near Kuta. These rollers have just the right amount of force to power foam boards forwards, but are also forgiving enough to paddle through. Legian is less chaotic than Kuta and more low-key than Seminyak, with a tropical holiday vibe and a solid choice of cafés and restaurants serving local and international dishes. Stand-up paddleboarding and wakeboarding sessions are also available.
Nearest town // Kuta

G-LAND

With almost too many idyllic surf camps to choose from these days,
Ben Mondy believes the first, on the island of Java, Indonesia, remains the best.

After another swig of medicine – a shot of local Drum whiskey – Dave Scard, the long-time guide at Joyo's Surf Camp at G-Land, gritted his teeth and placed a makeshift cast over his own back-bent leg. A few days before, the Australian had broken his tibia pulling into a large tube on the Javanese reef. He had two options: return to the closest hospital in Bali, or fly back to home to Queensland. Scard, however, chose a scarcely believable third option.

Using the fibreglass matting and resin he used to fix the many surfboards he snapped each year at G-Land, he made a cast and set the fracture himself. Because, here's the thing: Scard didn't want it straight, as most orthopaedic doctors would prescribe. Instead, he fixed his leg in the tube stance that would allow him to surf G-Land that bit better.

I had heard this tale before my first session at this legendary wave, located on the very eastern tip of Java. I was initially horrified. Scard's devotion was, clearly, insane. But by the end of that first day his actions seemed less insane. Perhaps even rational. Now, I have spent the last two decades trying to decode the many moods of this incredible reef. And I'm nowhere near done yet.

G-Land has inspired devotion ever since the first surfers set eyes on the wave. In 1972, when Americans Bob Laverty and Bill Boyum were flying over the very eastern tip of Java on their way to Bali, they looked out the window and saw a massive wave breaking on a reef beach known as Grajagan, at the edge of thick Javanese jungle. Once in Bali they set about finding it. Armed with 70cc Suzuki motorbikes, tattered naval maps and not quite enough food, they found the wave after three long days. It was as perfect as they dreamed it would be.

Knowing the wave was one of the best in the world, Boyum and his brother Mike established some basic accommodation. Their primitive setup was the prototype for the world's first surf camp. By the late 1970s, Balinese entrepreneur Bobby Radiassa had taken charge of operations. And the beauty of the Grajagan is that while many things have changed since those early days, most haven't.

Sure, the Suzuki ride to G-Land has been replaced by a two-hour speedboat crossing from Kuta Beach. And rather than mosquito nets hoisted on high wooden sleeping platforms (the local tigers were a concern), the accommodation is now feline-proof and air-conditioned.

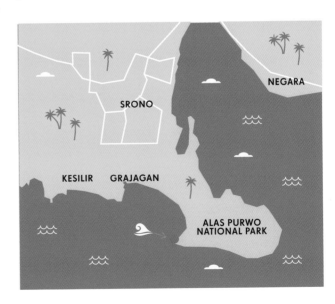

On that first day, I sat down at the camp's breakfast bar next to another guest. We both had books by Truman Capote; mine a battered copy of *In Cold Blood*, his *Breakfast at Tiffany's*. That started a conversation – and a friendship – that has endured to this day. After a breakfast of banana pancakes, mango smoothie and mud-thick Javanese coffee (a menu choice I've also stuck with for two decades), the empty lineup had me scrambling for my equipment.

But Matt, a G-Land veteran, advised me to slow down. He explained that the offshore breeze kicks in almost every day around 10am. Before then, the waves are lumpy and imperfect. Well, for G-Land standards anyway. That has the effect of making for lazy mornings, albeit ones laced with the adrenalin of anticipation.

After a few more chapters of Capote and a stretch, I felt the warm air start to blow off the jungle towards the ocean. The lumps were removed and the imperfections erased. The 10-minute walk through the jungle to the top of the reef was, and remains, a sensory overload. Every so often, a gap in the dense foliage revealed another section of the Grajagan reef, its perfect lefthanders roping down at breakneck speed.

At the tip of the reef you enter the water and make your way through a series of channels to the outside which, along with rips, tug you toward the outer wave known as Kongs. This receives the most swell and breaks even on the smallest days. It is also forgiving and provides G-Land's best section for intermediate surfers. On that first surf, a group of Irish first-timers and a pack of elderly South African longboarders were sharing the spoils. For me it was a great place to feel the power of the waves and take in the surrounds.

But looking down the reef, I could see the spray peeling off waves that I knew were faster, hollower and better. That was Money Trees,

SURFERS BEFORE SPECTATORS

For years, surf CT locations were chosen with the emphasis on filling seats rather than on quality waves. But from 1995 to 1997, the Quiksilver Pro was held at G-land, and this move to the jungle saw some of the best waves ever seen in a surf competition. As the 1996 winner Luke Egan said: 'It takes good waves to show people how rad this sport is.' This led to a shift for pro surfing and started the era known as the 'Dream Tour', with CT events in exotic locations like Tahiti, Fiji and Bali.

Clockwise from top left: surfers steel themselves for the paddle-out; Spanish pro Raúl García surfs G-Land; jockeying for the sweet spot. Previous page: South African pro Shaun Payne makes the most of the magic hour at G-Land

the most consistent and photogenic part of the reef. As a kid, I'd stared at a poster on my wall showing a lone surfer leaning against a palm tree watching this section's perfect green walls. The imprint on my malleable grommet's mind was so strong that I doubted whether the reality could ever match the mind-surfing. That was allayed as soon as I stroked into a low-tide wave that collapsed over the shallow coral slab at the tip of the reef. An adrenalin-fuelled highline barrel was followed by a 1000ft-long wall of green water that didn't have a single drop out of place.

After three hours, and with the tide pushing up, the final section of the reef, Speedies, sparked into life. It is a world-class wave and the jewel of all of G-land's many sections. My first wave started off with a relatively easy takeoff at the aptly named Launching Pads, before spinning down a 1000ft racetrack. It was here I saw Scard screaming through the 6ft green tube. His normal smooth style was a little tweaked, but the effectiveness couldn't be questioned. He may have been causing lasting damage – four months later he would have the leg broken and reset by a surgeon – but his stoke was undeniable.

Later that day, I sat with Scard, my new friend Matt, and the fellow camp guests, drinking cold beers and watching the sunset backlight the perfect waves. There were whales breaching out to sea, monkeys bathing in rock pools near the shore, and a mongoose sifting through the sand for crabs. Our evening was soundtracked by the roar of the ocean, the murmur of the jungle, and the laughter of surfers knowing they were in the right place at the right time.

Over the years I've had that same day repeated hundreds of times, with the subtle variation of every perfect wave. I have never once tired of the lazy-morning, two-surfs-a-day, beers-at-sunset, Indonesian-rice-dish-then-bed routine. Surf camps are everywhere now, but in my eyes, the world's first still has claim to be the best.

"I have spent the last two decades trying to decode the many moods of this incredible reef. And I'm nowhere near done yet"

ORIENTATION

Type of wave // Long lefthanders that break over a 1-mile (1.6km) stretch of coral reef.

Best conditions // The best waves occur in the dry season (from May to September), when the southeasterly trade winds blow offshore.

Nearest town // G-Land is 30 miles (48km), via very poor roads, from the small town of Banyuwangi. Realistically, the easiest way to get here is by speedboat from Kuta, Bali.

Getting there // All the G-land camps run speedboats from the beach at Kuta.

Where to stay // Bobby's Surf Camp and Joyos Surf Camp offer basic but comfortable accommodation, with views of the break.

Things to know // Most G-Land veterans time their stay when the tides are biggest, coinciding with the new and full moons each month.

*Opposite from top: Filipino-style
transport to Cloud 9; Siarago's surf
tower overlooks the Cloud 9 break*

MORE LIKE THIS
G-LAND DESCENDANTS

T-LAND, INDONESIA

Named after G-Land, T-Land does a
pretty good impersonation of its more
famous Indonesian cousin. Located off
Rote Island, near Timor, this left is as long
as the one found at Grajagan, making
it one of the longest waves in the world.
While it can also hold large surf, it is
nowhere near as powerful as G-Land and
can verge on playful. This attracts surfers
of much lower ability, and longboarders,
too, who travel to Nemberala beach to
get a taste of real Indonesian quality
without quite the same consequence.
Accommodation is available right in front
of the wave and the remote nature of the
island and its untouched natural beauty
add to the T-Land experience. After a
month here, you'll be ready for anything
G-Land can throw at you.
Nearest town // Kupang

KRUI, SUMATRA

It's perhaps a miracle that the Krui
coastline has remained such a well-kept
secret. This region of southern mainland
Sumatra rivals any part of Indonesia in
terms of consistency and quality of waves
and, by rights, should be better known. Its
location, a six-hour drive from the nearest
airport at Bandar Lampung (TKG), itself a
30-minute flight from Jakarta, has probably
been the biggest factor in keeping the
crowds down. But nonetheless, the
reputation of the area's most consistent
wave, Ujung Bocur (a long lefthander
with alternating barrel and turn sections)
has seeped through to the wider surfing
world; and when WSL world champion
Gabriel Medina turned up in early 2019 for
the Krui's first professional surfing event,
the word was really out. The best waves
are found from May to October when the
offshore northeast winds and southwest
groundswells are most common. There are
also a number of established surf camps
directly in front of the main breaks.
Nearest town // Krui

CLOUD 9, PHILIPPINES

On paper, the best wave in the Philippines
doesn't have much in common with
G-Land. Cloud 9 is as short as G-Land is
long, and as right as the Indonesian wave
is left. However, the two are linked by a
number of interesting factors and a shared
history. For one, they are both perfect
reef break waves located in equatorial
isolation. But aside from the world-class
quality of each wave, a more tragic shared
association comes through the infamous
surf character – and true surf explorer –
Mike Boyum. Boyum had helped discover
G-Land in the early 1970s and set up his
pioneering surf camp there later in the
decade. Some 10 years after that, Boyum
heard a rumour of a perfect barrel in the
jungles of the Philippines. He pitched
up at the remote village of Siargao and
stayed at Tuason Point, in front of the reef
that would become known as Cloud 9.
Unfortunately, his time there was short
and tragic; after a 44-day fast, Boyum
passed away in Siargao.
Nearest town // General Luna

PADANG PADANG

Jaimal Yogis made a painful offering to the reef gods in the hope that they'd allow safe passage through Bali's most celebrated barrel. Unfortunately, it wasn't that simple.

'The gods want you to get barrelled, mate – look at the Bukit!' It was a line I overheard from a drunken Australian on my very first trip to Bali. I didn't think much of it at the time. But a few days later, bobbing in the lineup of a break called Temples – teal lefts peeling beneath the Uluwatu shrine, with surfers disappearing like apparitions into glittery saltwater tunnels – I couldn't help thinking: *dude might be onto something.*

I was only just beginning to grasp the mystical perfection of Bali's Bukit Peninsula. Sure, it's overcrowded, overdeveloped, and often feels like an Aussie/Brazilian Spring Break music video, but no matter how fast it's changing, the magic isn't going away. World-class hollow reef breaks still dot Bali's southern peninsula like aquamarine gems in a necklace of sand and coral, a chain that culminates in an exquisite pendant known as Padang Padang.

This revered tube is a short ride compared to some of its epic, multi-turn neighbours, but Padang's purity of line (drop, bottom turn, run for cover, pray) and raw intensity rivals any of the best waves yet discovered in the Indonesian archipelago (that's more than 18,000 islands, by the way). I'd long felt that surfing Padang wasn't on the cards for me this lifetime. It was a wave where pros compete for barrels so deep they seem to vanish into a parallel surf-verse. But after spending several summers in Bali, I gradually came to see Bukit's breaks like videogame levels in which an average surfer like me could work up to a dream tube, or at least have fun trying. Some flesh would need to be offered to the reef. That's only fair.

Like many a pilgrim before me, I went straight from the airport to Kuta Beach on my first trip. I walked down lanes teeming with tipsy tourists and seemingly endless shops hawking penis-shaped bottle openers, then arrived at a rowdy beach where hundreds of surfers were struggling to ride murky brown shorebreak, and thought: *this is Bali?* Eager to get out, I bought a used board and hopped on a rented moped for the 1-hour ride to to the Bukit's southernmost point.

From the Uluwatu cliffs, I peered out at the Balinese Pipeline break. Like Bali's highways, Ulus had way too many people. But after Kuta, navigating the lava cave to the break felt like passing through the pearly gates. I paddled into the pack at Racetracks and pearled on my first three waves, a reminder I hadn't surfed a reef in years. After a few days, the barrel gods had seen enough. They tossed me onto the reef and blessed me with a bloody 'reef tattoo' over most of my back.

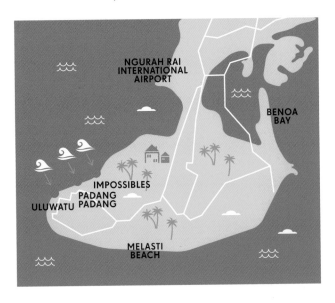

This wasn't my only mistake on this trip. I tried to be like the locals and walk without reef shoes across the football-size field of coral and urchins to Impossibles (gashes between the toes for weeks). I thought I'd outsmart the crowd and surf Middles at low tide with basically no swell (rolled over dry coral). I went too fast on the moped and slid out on a wet turn with my girlfriend on the back (we were ok, but I nearly got dumped on the spot). The basic lesson that the barrel gods seemed to want to instil in me was 'humble up'.

On subsequent trips, these lessons started to register. For starters, I skipped Kuta altogether. I also brought my own boards – a flat twin fin or quad for Impossibles and a more traditional thruster for Ulus and Bingin – the latter is basically a mini-Padang. I also started taking my first-off-the-plane sessions at the mellow, sandy bottom waves of Dreamland, a perfect level-one in the Bukit barrel videogame. I'd even soft-top a few at Padang Right, a beginner wave in the channel between Padang and Impossibles that stays waist high. Most of all, I was exercising patience. I had comfortable digs that looked right out on Padang. But when you're forced to gaze on the crown jewels every day, you start considering theft.

One dawn, I longboarded Padang waist-high with nobody out. Another time I surfed it head-high at high tide, when it was empty and just barely tubing. Neither of these counted as real Padang. But they got me acquainted with the reef and the soul of the place.

Then, towards the end of my third summer on the Bukit, when Ulus was maxed out and Padang looked like the Volcom Pro poster, I paddled through the channel with a friend to observe. Watching – and feeling – the thunderous, slabby lips throw, bash and devour barrel devotees, I found myself meditating on every excuse

THE NICKNAME GAME

Almost all Balinese go by the names Wayan, Made, Nyoman or Ketut, meaning first-, second-, third- or fourth-born. Sounds easy enough until you ask where Made's Warung is and get five different correct answers. With so many folks running around with the same name, a fun way to distinguish and learn more about someone is to ask if they go by a nickname. Many do, but may not introduce themselves this way.

Clockwise from top left: the front door to the Bukit's most perfect barrel; threading the needle; Pura Luhur temple, sitting pretty above Uluwatu. Previous page: perfection at Padang Padang

for why I didn't even want to be there. But there was a magnetism to this vortex. Even the surfers getting badly beaten were returning for more; the ones who made it out had a glow. They'd seen something in there.

Almost unconsciously, I drifted into the lineup. If you sat deep at Padang, the entry itself wasn't a Teahupoo-style maniac drop. Padang reared up, then gave a beat. It was about halfway into the drop that the wave hit the main slab and did its thing. Unless of course you tried to cheat inside slightly to outsmart the wolf pack, which I attempted at first and found myself promptly airborne. By grace alone I made the drop and whizzed down the face, grinning like I'd just escaped the cops. I hadn't.

Looking left, I was peering down the line of something that I didn't even recognise as a wave. It was a 50ft concave jade wall. It looked like every drop of water was going to fold and detonate at once. I wanted no part of this. But if I straightened, it would have picked me up and body-slammed me. My only choice was pointing towards the channel, trying to keep speed. I grabbed my rail and the world turned jade. There was a roar. I was in the dragon's throat and I was sure it would swallow. Yet, a second went by. Then another. I was still racing through this jade hall of mirrors. With each magnificent, eerie beat, I expected the worst, but the hall stayed open. During those three seconds of infinity, it looked momentarily like I was even going to be shot out in a burst of Bukit glory – yes!

No.

Instead, the lip clipped me at the end. I found myself cartwheeling and, once again, boom – another proper Bali tattoo on my back. It hurt like hell, but it was definitely the best place to go down. And even with the wind knocked out of me, I was happy paddling in to dab my wounds that morning. I had earned this one.

"I gradually came to see the waves like videogame levels – an average surfer like me could work up to a dream tube"

ORIENTATION

Type of wave // Heavy, hollow left-hand reef break. Usually packed.

Best conditions // May–September. Powerful, long-period southwest swell that can set up 8–20ft faces. Mid tide, light northeast offshore trade winds or glassy.

Nearest town // The fishing village and resort town of Jimbaran.

Getting there // Fly to Ngurah Rai International Airport in Denpasar, then drive, scoot, or take a taxi for the 30-minute journey to Impossibles Beach and Padang Padang.

Where to stay // Affordable and friendly Made Suardani has bamboo huts overlooking the wave. There are hundreds of inns, homestays and Airbnb options nearby.

Things to know // Unless you want to rely on cabs, you'll want to rent a car or scooter with surf rack. driving or riding with a surf rack is fun, but traffic rules are chaotic.

Opposite: heading out to surf Bingin,
one of the most popular breaks on
Bali's Bukit Peninsula

MORE LIKE THIS
THE BEST OF THE BUKIT

SANUR REEF, BALI

Sanur Reef is on the opposite coast of the Bukit Peninsula, 30–40 minutes by road from Padang. The wave peels the opposite direction to Padang (right), and generally only breaks during the opposite (wet) season, from November to March. No small wonder it's sometimes called an inverse Padang – but it would be better to call it Padang's fickle and tricky cousin. With a very shallow reef that closes out on the inside, Sanur needs a full to mid tide to keep it from completely shutting down. It also needs at least a head-high swell, which can be rare in the wet season. But if the right conditions come together, Sanur can turn into a 300ft bullet train with a gaping tube that rivals Padang's. Take extreme caution: the reef can quickly go dry, especially at low tide. And be extra respectful. The Balinese locals are some of the friendliest on earth, but they covet this spot when it's firing – for good reason.

Nearest town // Sanur

RACETRACKS, BALI

Uluwatu Bay is big enough to hold several football fields, and the ribbed reef can divide the territory into as many as six peaks. When it's head-and-a-half, and lining up perfectly, you'll occasionally see surfers connect a ride from the farthest corner, Secrets, all the way into the inside, Racetracks. But even on those rare days, it's usually Racetracks, the final section, that has the most consistent and impressive barrel. Racetracks is Bali's Grand Prix, and the usual starting line is a shallow, jutting mushroom of reef just in front of Uluwatu's cave entrance. The slurpy takeoff is followed by a pause. It then transforms from a rippable wall to a left-handed barrel that, on good days, is robotic in its dependability. On the wide swingers, there can be a second or even a third barrel. It's a long paddle back, a short way to the sharp coral if you fall, and as challenging as the Indie 500 to manoeuvre the crowd. But when you finally link it up, it's all worth it.

Nearest town // Uluwatu

BINGIN, BALI

If you're tube hunting and hungry to guarantee some coverage – replete with the option to buy a commemorative photo of yourself afterwards – then Bingin's your spot. On the positive side, Bingin is a barrel machine. When it's 4–5ft and the tide is right (low to mid), this reef will produce wave after wave with a nice, round, open tunnel that doesn't require an excessive amount of stalling or pumping to make it out of. Some call it a barrel school or mini-Padang. On the downside, the hundreds of cafés and inns in front of the wave have made it absurdly crowded. Locals who know the reef like they know their own palm tend to use the place like a barrel conveyor belt. Patience and respect are essential. Also, unless it's big and there's an opportunity for a turn at the start, Bingin is a quick drop, quick tube, then quick kickout kind of spot. Wait a beat too long and you'll be saying hello to jagged reef.

Nearest town // Uluwatu

THE MENTAWAI ISLANDS

Mentawai veteran Ben Mondy has learned that a great boat captain is the key to the perfect liveaboard surf experience in Indonesia.

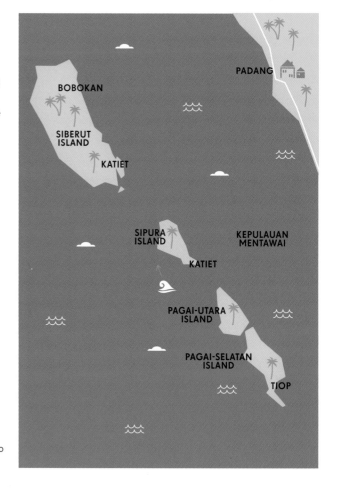

itting on the deck of the *Huey*, myself and its skipper Steve 'Sooly' Sewell watched the unmistakable figure of Angus McCracken stoke into a perfect 3ft wave at a spot called Macaronis. With his red hair and luminescent pale skin, he couldn't have been more Scottish if he was a wearing a kilt, drinking Scotch whisky and shouting 'Freedom' as he did his bottom turn.

That bottom turn was smooth, his line into the barrel perfect, the tube style compact and efficient. McCracken exited in a cloud of rainbow-spectrumed spray, before executing three vertical turns and wheeling off into the safety of the channel. Perched atop the aluminum wheelhouse of his converted Japanese government customs patrol vessel, Sooly smiled, raised his beer and hooted – the universal surfing signal for being stoked.

After 15 years operating boat charters in the Mentawai Islands off Sumatra, Sooly actually had little reason to seem so stoked. He'd watched a thousand surfers surf a thousand perfect waves in his time. He'd seen much better waves ridden by much better surfers. But seeing McCracken's smile, hearing his Scottish hoots, I realised just how much difference a dedicated and experienced captain like Sooly can make in a place like the Mentawais.

The Indonesian archipelago is fast becoming the gold standard for surfing boat-trips. Sure, you can hire surf charters in other parts of the world, but few other locations have the extensive mix of quality and quantity that this chain offers. They say there's never a guarantee of waves on any surf trip – the Mentawais beg to differ.

And a great captain, I was discovering, further stacks the odds in your favour. Sooly explained to me that McCracken had initially been in touch saying that he and his five surfing buddies wanted to experience their first ever boat trip, but had two primary concerns:

the cost and the crowds. So Sooly suggested an off-season charter in February, allowing him to both discount the trip and avoid the peak-season crowds. I'd been lucky to have done a few previous trips aboard the *Huey*, but only ever in the prime months between June and September. With room on board for one more, Sooly offered me the spot.

Funny enough, McCracken and his freckled cohorts struggled with the perfection of the Mentawais at first. Many waves were caught and wasted. Far more were missed altogether. But these missed opportunities weren't punished as they are when you have to go to the back of a long queue to get another chance. All our sessions featured just our boat crew alone, each of us with an all-you-can-ride pass to the Mentawais funpark. Sooly reckoned that of the 50 or so charter boats operating in the Mentawais during peak season, only a dozen were in the water that month.

Now, it's true that the swell here is nowhere near as consistent or as strong in the Northern Hemisphere winter months, so an off-season trip can be considered a relative gamble. But large waves were beyond the Scottish surfers' ability, and as the 70 islands of the Mentawais offer more than 100 world class waves along the chain's 115-mile (185km) length, we were rocking up to each and every perfect break, surfing head-high waves on our Pat Malone.

With its crystal-clear waters, palm-fringed lagoons, white-sand beaches and warm, gentle trade winds, this remote, inaccessible chain was once an untouched oasis. When the first surfers arrived in the late 1980s, its isolation was such that many of the local villagers had never seen Westerners before, let alone wave-riding. The first introductions were done in the channel when curious locals paddled their canoes out to trade wares and freshly caught fish – a tradition that still carries on today.

The off-season absence of crowds helped me to imagine what it must have been like for the first surfers who visited the Mentawais. Martin Daly, a surfer and boat captain who was operating a dive and salvage operation in the area, is credited with discovering many of the waves in the early '90s.

Word had spread by the mid-1990s, but that sense of remoteness still remains. Unlike the discovery of other world-class surfing destinations – Hawaii in the '60s, Bali in the '70s, France in the '80s – the Mentawais offered many barriers to entry. There was little or no infrastructure or public transport on the islands, making travelling in and staying there under your own steam virtually impossible. Additionally, the only way to access the sheer scope and variety of waves was by sea. This is what spawned the archipelago's surfing boat-charter industry.

And this kind of surf-travel was a revelation for many surfers. Like the Scotsmen, it was in the Mentawais where I myself first discovered the joy of jumping off a boat and paddling dry-haired to a perfect lineup. It was here I became accustomed to living a life at sea. And on what other surf trip can you jump off a boat and swim over the equator – naked?

BRUSHFIRE FAIRYTALES

In 2000, Kelly Slater gathered best mates Shane Dorian, Rob Machado and surf filmmaker Jack Johnson for a Mentawais boat trip. When Johnson wasn't surfing, he was filming from the tide pools and working on lyrics for a new song. His footage eventually became *The September Sessions*, which cemented the Mentawais' reputation among surfers more than any other film; his song, *F-Stop Blues*, appeared on his debut album *Brushfire Fairytales*.

Clockwise from top left: desert-island perfection in the Mentawai Islands; liveaboards offer a full surf immersion; barrel dreams come true for Peruvian pro Cristobal de Col in the Mentawais. Previous page: the world-class Macaronis wave

"They say there's never a guarantee of waves on any surf trip – the Mentawais beg to differ"

The early 2000s were a boom time. This was when Sooly brought his boat here, but he's one of only a dozen or so seasoned captains to have remained. 'I've seen a lot of operators come and go since then', he said. 'My first piece of advice is do your research and go with an experienced boat. There are cowboys out here. And safety is by far the single most crucial factor on any trip. Plus, experienced boat crews may cost a little more, but they guarantee more time in the water, whether you're a hardcore shredder or still figuring it out.'

And that was exactly why Sooly was hooting McCracken's wave. In a few short days we'd seen his crew transform from tentative wave-wreckers into pretty competent surfers. They surfed bucket-list waves like HTs, Rag's Left and Thunders, and here he was surfing a perfect Macaronis wave, one of the world's best, and surfing it well.

The Scots had been surfing an average of eight hours a day (a figure that would have been even higher if Sooly hadn't forced them to rest and rehydrate during the hottest parts of the day), but the acceleration of improvement was mindblowing.

'This is the most amazing, beautiful and consistent location for waves on the planet', Sooly told us. 'Sure, the crowds have increased, but a good captain will find you the pockets of magic that exist nowhere else in the world. No matter how long you've been here, or how many trips you've had, this place will blow every surfer away, every time.'

ORIENTATION

Type of wave // This isand chain boasts over 100 recognised surf spots. While 99% break over reefs, they vary from big waves to point breaks and fat, slow rollers.

Best conditions // Peak season is the Southern Hemisphere winter, from June to September. Shoulder- and off-seasons are becoming popular, with smaller swells but smaller crowds.

Nearest town // The waves are an overnight sail, or a five-hour speedboat ride, from Padang.

Getting there // Charters leave from Padang, which is accessible from many Southeast Asian airports.

Where to stay // There are more than 50 charter operations offering boat trips in varying degrees of luxury.

Things to know // Conditions during the first overnight leg of the charters can cause sea-sickness; but for the rest of the trip, you'll be sleeping in calm anchorages.

Opposite: Indonesia's remote Telo Islands offer a quieter alternative to the Mentawais

MORE LIKE THIS
LIVEABOARD ADVENTURES

TELO ISLANDS, INDONESIA

Just north of the Mentawais lies a more remote, and much smaller, cluster of islands that have yet to explode in popularity in the way of their neighbours. The Telo islands don't offer quite the same quantity and variety, but this is more than made up for by the lack of crowds, the beauty of the archipelago and the quality of the waves. The Telo also tend to require a little more swell than the breaks further down south, but as a result they also tend to be a little more forgivable and learner-friendly. Another massive plus is the presence of a world-class beach break, one of only a handful of quality waves breaking over sand in the whole of the Indonesian archipelago. Matt Cruden surfed breaks in the Mentawai Islands for 20 years, but loved the Telos so much that he moved there; he now operates the legendary charter boat *Mangalui,* and runs the Telos-based Latitude Zero camp.

Nearest town // Padang

CARIBBEAN COAST, PANAMA

Panama's Caribbean coast, between Bocas del Toro and the San Blas Islands, offers a huge variety of quality waves. Whilst many of the breaks can be reached by road, some can't, and island-hopping in comfort and style aboard a yacht is an adventurous and efficient way of scouring this beautiful coast. There is perhaps no more hands-on way to experience the biological wonders of the Bocas del Toro archipelago – or the white-sand, palm-lined beaches of the San Blas Islands – than by sea. Bocas del Toro is the better known surf destination, with its three main islands offering reef breaks, point breaks and of couple pumping beach breaks. A cruisy five-day sail east, the San Blas chain promises dozens of empty waves and hundreds of secluded coves. Sailing conditions are best from December to April.

Nearest town // Isla Colon, Bocas Town

BALI–LOMBOK–SUMBAWA, INDONESIA

Indonesia's original surfing boat charters, aboard traditional fishing vessels, followed this route eastwards to cater for travelling surfers who figured there must be more waves out there. With land travel sluggish, local operators offered cut-price deals to island-hop from Bali to Lombok, and on to Sumbawa. Over time, the boats have improved, but this wave-rich route is as perfect today as it was back then. A short crossing has you at Nusa Lembongan, with Shipwrecks and Playgrounds offering waves for experts and intermediates. Crossing the Lombok Straight, the next stop is the legendary Desert Point. It's as fickle as it is mythical, but after one good surf here, your investment will be paid back. The final hop is from Desert Point to Sumbawa, where stops at quality waves such as Scar Reef, Super Sucks and Yo Yo's bookend one of surfing's oldest, and still best, surf-charter routes.

Nearest town // Denpasar

HAINAN ISLAND

Jade Bremner headed to 'China's Hawaii' to check out the country's burgeoning surf scene. She discovered the perfect escape from its bustling cities.

It was hard to believe that one short flight had transported me from the chaotic roads, mega skylines and the din of development in Shanghai to a lush, seemingly deserted island paradise. But the teardrop-shaped island of Hainan, at the most southerly point of China, has a staggering 950 miles (1592km) of isolated coastland and a remarkably chilled vibe. Best of all, there are waves.

I was on a weekend vacation from my home city of Shanghai. With my longboard on my head, I walked barefoot under the bright morning sun toward the lapping water of the South China Sea. The beach was completely empty, but this wasn't a surprise. China is a country where basking in the sun has never been popular. A tan is a sign that you work outside (as well as a marker of poverty), and in the cities, people even carry umbrellas to shield themselves from the harsh rays. Beach holidays aren't exactly popular. Meanwhile, the averge Chinese urbanite knows very little about the sport beyond what they experience in the local Quiksilver shop, while buying lifestyle clothing – they certainly couldn't tell you who any of their most famous pros are (one being Hainan champ Monica Guo).

Hainan Island has the feel of Vietnam's tropical lowlands. The golden sand curled between my toes, palm trees lined the shore, and thick jungle-covered hills punctuated the landscape. I felt a rush of adrenaline when I clapped eyes on the rolling waves to the left of

"I'd stumbled onto one of the youngest surf communities in the world – and, possibly, a glimpse into China's future"

Riyue ('Sun Moon') Bay, as sets peeled perfectly off the main point. I could immediately see why many call this China's Hawaii.

Surfing first arrived on Hainan more than a decade ago. It was spearheaded by a Chinese-speaking Californian named Brendan Sheridan, who set up the first surf club (Riyue Bay Surf Club) and surf shop on the island. The embryonic community faced challenges, as the local authorities were at first confused by surfing, viewing it as dangerous. The police even had altercations with surfers, in which they destroyed or confiscated surfboards to try and prevent people from getting hurt. Nevertheless, Sheridan persevered, and the government has since done a U-turn on how they perceive surfers.

Now, with his surf school and organised surfing tournaments, Sheridan has managed to attract international stars like Robert 'Wingnut' Weaver (of cult surfing movie *The Endless Summer II*) to compete in the annual Hainan Open, an event that has helped to drum up publicity and raise awareness of the sport here. These days, there are around a dozen surf businesses on the island, and the official China Olympic Surf Team even trained at Riyue Bay in preparation for Tokyo 2020.

I arrived light on my feet, as I knew there would be plenty of rental shops near the beach. The main city of Sanya is clearly in transition: still rough around the edges, with signs of growth everywhere. It has the might of the Chinese government behind it (good highways, international hotel brands and a fancy new airport underway), but in between the mega-developments, locals live modestly.

My taxi passed through dusty, neon-lit streets lined with lively Russian vodka bars, and rows of stalls selling peculiar-looking street food. Eventuallly, we reached the much quieter southeastern beach town of Riyuewan, near Wanning. With a tropical feel, much like Southeast Asia, Riyuewan is considered the epicentre of Chinese surfing. There are other surf spots on Hainan Island, but the surf community congregates here, and it has the most options for accommodation and board rental. I checked into the Forest Inn Riyue Bay, just a short walk from the beach.

The next morning, I carried my rental board along the southern stretch of beach. Skateboarders practiced their tricks as reggae blared out of cafés. Inside one of the restaurants, I saw a group of Chinese surfers glued to a phone screen, studying videos of pros riding waves. I realise I've stumbled upon something special: one of the youngest surfing communities in the world – and, possibly, a glimpse into China's future.

At the water's edge, I hesitantly dipped my toes in the sea, unsure of the temperatures I'd encounter. It was warm and clear – the ideal boardie or bikini temperature. As I paddled out, I had that excitement that comes with not knowing a new setup. A woman smiled at me, immediately putting my mind at ease. There were about a dozen people waiting for waves at the bottom of the cliff at a spot known as Main Point. The sets were clean, 2–3ft high and breaking off a flat reef base. I began chatting with an American guy, who told me it actually gets pretty crowded at Riyue Bay on big winter days.

From left: surf travellers are discovering Hainan Island's quality swell; raw beauty along the Hainan coastline; delicious isolation at Sanya Beach. Previous page: Hainan's local surf culture is growing each year

HEAVEN OR HELL?

According to Tang Dynasty chancellor Li Deyu, who was exiled here as a punishment in AD 848, Hainan was the 'Gate of Hell', a 'damned place' where 'primitive' minority peoples lived under a scorching sun, plagued by humid weather and impenetrable virgin forest infested with mosquitoes, snakes and other critters. These days, however, its mosquito-free tropical climes are China's best-kept secret.

Apparently, from October to March, swells come in to Riyue Bay off of storms in the South China Sea, and it's possible to get barrelled at a point named Ghost Hotel, just a little further out from where I was sitting.

I began paddling for my first wave. There wasn't much power to it and so I stood up easily and rode down the face, turning at the bottom and slowly carving a super-mellow ride. I'd remembered one surfer telling me that good days can tee up 500ft rides in this very spot.

An easy paddle through the channel brought me right back into the lineup. Other surfers congratulated me. The relaxed atmosphere was pleasantly jarring – such a rarity at surf spots these days. This burgeoning scene, I imagine, is what it would have felt like in, say, California in the 1960s, before surfing became mainstream.

I sat on my board, scanning the picturesque bay and the surrounding dense green mountains. There was a construction site in the distance and the sound of drilling. It's the sound of progress, which I've become so used to while living in China. And it didn't puncture the calm in the lineup one bit.

By the time my session was over, there were a few people milling around the beach, including a couple of local ladies, faces covered, and another group sporting traditional *judao* bamboo woven hats, relaxing under a parasol and sipping coconut water. I just sat on the sand and watched a bit of surfing history unfold.

ORIENTATION

Type of wave // Left-hand point break over flat reef.
Best conditions // Works all-year-round, but more consistent and bigger in winter with a northeasterly swell.
Nearest town // Riyuewan, near Wanning.
Getting there // From Sanya Phoenix International Airport, taxis to Riyuewan take around 1½ hours. You can also get a train from Sanya to Wanning, then a taxi to Riyuewan.
Where to stay // Riyuewan has local inns, hostels and homestays catering to surfers, all of which are close to the beach. The Forest Inn Riyue Bay is a good mid-range choice, with simple rooms.
Things to know // Longboards and shortboards can be rented from Chong Hai Surf Club in Riyue Bay; lessons can also be booked here. When in China, search up 'Jalenboo Surf Club' on WeChat to access pages of useful info about the area.

Opposite: aprés-surf at
Kata Beach, Thailand

MORE LIKE THIS
SOUTHEAST ASIAN SURF

MY KHE BEACH, VIETNAM

Straight across the South China Sea from Hainan Island is Vietnam's famous 18-mile (29km) stretch of sandy coastline, known as My Khe Beach (or China Beach to some). It's more built up than Hainan, with high-rise apartment buildings and hotels along the bay, but the tropical look and feel of the landscape, complete with dramatic green hills, is very similar to Riyue Bay; the water temperatures are equally balmy. This fabled area is where soldiers surfed the windswell beach break during the Vietnam War, and since then, one of the biggest surf scenes in Southeast Asia has developed here. Waves break year-round, and there are several surf schools that also rent equipment.
Nearest town // Danang

KATA BEACH, THAILAND

Tropical Thailand is not really known for its surfing. But when the conditions are just right, you *can* surf in Phuket, on the Andaman Sea. Every once in a while, with gentle northeasterly winds, Kata Beach picks up a southwest swell, making it a great spot for beginners, or for those learning to surf from scratch. Located beneath a rocky headland, it's more reliable in winter – when there have been reports of head-high sets – but the warm blue-green waters are lovely at any time of year. Sadly, groundswell is blocked by the northern tip of Sumatra (which is around 186 miles/300km southwest of Phuket's southern tip). When there are waves, it gets crowded with foamies, but there's always a fun atmosphere in the water, with lots of kids on bodyboards.
Nearest town // Phuket

TAI LONG WAN, HONG KONG (CHINA)

The perfect antidote to Hong Kong's big-city hustle and bustle is this little beach, known as Big Wave Bay, just north of Shek O. This sheltered beach break, with rights, lefts and shifting peaks, has even been known to throw up a few barrels during typhoon season. The original Hong Kong Surf Club was established here more than 40 years ago. There's a tiny surf village, a small community of surfers and a few surf shops selling gear and renting boards (Ho Lok Shop is the place for gear rentals; they also have lockers, and serve cold beer and tasty bowls of fried rice). The beach itself is pretty small, with a little rocky headland and a lifeguard tower (plus a shark net to put your mind at ease). When on, it's a steep wave, which closes out fast and is better suited to a shortboard.
Nearest town // Shek O

THURSO

For British surf photographer Al Mackinnon, the barrels of Thurso, Scotland, were as elusive as Nessie. But since he first spotted them, he's known exactly where — and when — to look.

'd heard the rumours many times growing up. Supposedly, there was an Indonesian-style barrel at the end of the road in Caithness, right at the very top of Scotland. For a young grom who had grown up learning to surf on Jersey in the Channel Islands, way over at the opposite end of the UK, it may as well have been on the other side of the world. Eventually I got my driving licence and, in 2001, made my first pilgrimage to the mythical wave.

This was long before the advent of technicolour swell breakdowns or star ratings, especially for the UK. All you had to go on were the synoptic charts on TV or in the newspaper. Wind speed, fetch and position of the low-pressure system were all key, and you had to be able to read the squiggly isobars to predict a swell with any level of accuracy. When I saw one such promising storm brewing on the forecasts late in December, I decided to finally make the drive up.

I was living in Cornwall at the time, but my first tentative missions around Scotland and the greater UK had revealed waves as good, if not better, than in the country's surfing capital — except with nobody else around. As a result I started to dabble in photography, taking a camera along with me on my surf missions to record what I saw for posterity.

It was Christmas Eve when I arrived in Thurso under crystal-clear skies with a light offshore wind blowing. I drove east from the small town, down into a farmyard, past old stone buildings, and stopped alongside a couple of other parked cars that looked out across the bay, where an overhead north swell was running down the reef.

There were fun waves, to be sure, but there were no barrels. I looked further up the reef to a section that was much hollower and thought perhaps that was the wave. Just then a local who lived in

a cottage adjacent to the farm walked past. He introduced himself as Chris Noble, and told me that the section I was looking at was called Unsurfables. The wave in front of us was in fact the mighty Thurso East.

Chris paddled out and I watched him surf for a while, but I was dejected: *he was doing turns, for goodness sake.* But I didn't see a single barrel that session. Later, I paddled out with another local, Andy Bain, who I'd later discover was the legendary steward of Thurso East — a man who knew the nuances of this wave better than anyone. We had an enjoyable session, but I couldn't stop wondering if it was all a hoax.

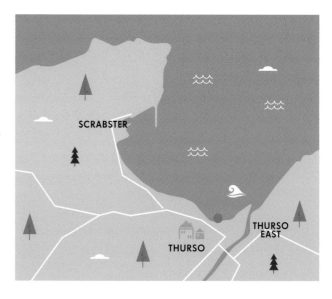

Eventually, I just asked Andy why it wasn't barrelling. I explained I'd come all this way on the basis of what appeared to be a myth. A prouder, less tolerant local might've told me to get stuffed, but Andy just chuckled and said I needed to come back on another swell. He outlined certain conditions to look out for: days when solid northwest swells align with rare southeast winds.

A year or two later, I made the drive once again. This time things were markedly different. The first thing I noticed was that the bay was dead calm, like a millpond. I thought I'd been hoaxed once again. Then I noticed a bloke unsheathing a 7ft pintail made for riding big tubes, and another bloke waxing up a semi-gun. A mate of mine that I'd met in the Scottish islands was with me and we looked at each other quizzically. Then it all made sense.

The water at Holborn Head, the point behind Thurso where swells pass before arriving at the reef, turned dark. Soon there were lines discernible inside the bay. Then, an immaculately groomed set arrived, thick and moving at formidable speed. Each swell hit the reef and thundered down the line with incredible precision and ferocity. It was double overhead and, yes, barrelling all the way with thick, serrated lips.

A river usually runs into the lineup, carrying tannins from the peat that results in chocolate-coloured tubes. But that swell coincided with a sustained dry period, turning the water deep blue. You could see the reef flashing underneath while riding in the barrel.

I was transfixed. I had never seen waves do that in all my years of surfing around the UK. But as fast as they had arrived, they

VIKING HARBOUR

Thurso is the northernmost town on the British mainland and was prime Viking territory – the name roughly translates as 'the place of Thor's river' in Norse. Like surfers today, the fearsome Norsemen were attracted to Thurso's geography, albeit for markedly different reasons: the deep bay made a perfect natural harbour and the area became a strategic Norse port until the 11th century, when the Viking expansion into Britain came to a bloody end.

Clockwise from top left: afternoon on the Scottish coast; taking flight at Thurso East; competition time at Thurso's world-class wave. Previous page: British pro Chris Noble surfs his home wave

"I may have already been on a trajectory toward melding my two greatest passions – waves and photography – but it was the perfection I witnessed at Thurso East that sealed the deal"

vanished again – the energy dissipated and the bay returned to a state of total calm. I'd never seen that either. It was 20 minutes between sets and there was nothing in between. No smaller ones, no inside double-ups. Nothing.

That set and the ensuing two days of swell changed the course of my life. I may have already been on a trajectory toward melding my two greatest passions – waves and photography – but it was the perfection I witnessed at Thurso East that sealed the deal.

I would return again and again, winter after winter – sometimes for months at a time, sleeping in my car, tent, barns, camper vans and eventually at mates' houses. Andy Bain ultimately became one of my greatest friends and a brother to me, a bond forged through many icy sessions at Thurso. While other surfers I knew were going to Australia, Hawaii and Indo, I spent my winters around Scotland's mainland and islands, with thick rubber and sparse crowds. It was years before I ever surfed a tropical wave, and it felt weird surfing without a wettie.

I've surfed Thurso in excellent conditions many times, but it's never been quite like that day: the size, the power, the hollowness – even the clarity of the water.

I've made a living taking surf photos since then and have been fortunate to document many exotic destinations around the world. But, when I see those rare conditions align on the swell charts, there's no place I'd rather be than Thurso.

ORIENTATION

Type of wave // Right reef break.
Best conditions // Solid northwest swell and southeast wind. Too much west in the swell and it will struggle to wrap around the headland at Holborn Head. Too much north and the wave will fatten out. Mid tide is best.
Nearest town // Thurso.
Getting there // Easily accessed via the A9 major road from Glasgow or Edinburgh.
Where to stay // There are a range of options in and around town, from comfortable hotels and B&Bs to basic camping. Sandra's Backpackers, above the fish-and-chip shop, is a popular budget option.
Things to know // Surfing in Scotland has boomed in recent years, so don't expect to have its premiere wave all to yourself. However, there is a plethora of waves around, some of them completely devoid of crowds.

MORE LIKE THIS
SCOTLAND'S TOP SURF SPOTS

SEWER PIPE

Deeper inside Thurso Bay, Sewer Pipe (also known as Shit Pipe) is an A-frame reef break that offers good quality rights and punchy lefts – it's an excellent option for intermediate surfers if Thurso is too crowded or intimidating. It's usually smaller than Thurso but, on the flipside, it handles the predominant southwest wind better and can offer clean faces when Thurso is cross-shore. The wave forms between two peaks and is easily accessed from the car park in front of the harbour, or by paddling out in the river that runs out and around the back of the break. At its best it can deliver zippy, walling waves that are loads of fun on any craft. Oh, and don't be too put off by the name: Sewer Pipe is so-called for the peat-stained water that flows out of the river mouth and gives the waves in the bay their trademark brown hue.

Nearest town // Thurso

BRIMMS NESS

Five miles (8km) west of Thurso on a rugged outcrop, Brimms Ness is home to three waves of varying intensity – a long left point that is a relatively easier prospect than The Cove and The Bowl, which are both short but demanding right-handers breaking over shallow reef. Like Thurso East, the point at Brimms Ness needs a specific northwest swell direction and a mid to low tide to work, but when it all comes together, it can offer excellent long rides with hollow sections. The Cove is the more manageable of the two reef breaks, while The Bowl has become infamous for its severe drop and wide-open tubes. Both are for advanced surfers only. Brimms Ness Bowl will pick up any swell that's around but the wind is often a problem, with the predominant westerly to southwesterly winds blowing onshore, so light or easterly winds are best.

Nearest town // Thurso

SKIRZA

When huge winter swells bombard Caithness, head over to Skirza on the east coast and you may luck into one of Scotland's most legendary waves. The long, powerful lefthander is located near Skirza Harbour and breaks over a boulder-lined point that can serve up barrelling lefts running for hundreds of feet at a time. Sitting inside a protected bay on the northern end of Scotland's east coast, Skirza is offshore in the strong westerly winds that often blow Thurso out in winter, but it needs a massive northerly swell or a good deal of east wind to get into the bay, making it a fickle prospect at best. If Skirza isn't breaking (and it probably won't be), continue for another 7 miles (11km) down the A9 to Sinclair's Bay, a beach break that is more exposed to swell and offers good quality lefts and rights.

Nearest town // Skirza

UNSTAD BAY

Some surfers seek out bigger swell to test themselves. Surf photographer Chris Burkard preferred to journey beyond the Arctic Circle to the north of Norway.

The snowy offshores stung my eyeballs and plunged my body into a hypothermic state. I was treading water in a 6mm hooded wetsuit and 7mm booties. My eyes, lips, and cheeks – the only flesh exposed – turned purple. The ocean itself felt balmy at around 40°F (4.5°C). But the 30mph (48km/h) winds whipping across Unstad Bay made everything feel much colder. The air was -10°F (-23°C). Even more concerning, my motor skills were slipping away and my camera trigger-finger simply stopped working. I decided it was time to start swimming back toward shore. The offshores here are what make this wave, yet they also present the biggest challenge.

After a few strokes, I realised I was actually paddling out to sea. The snow swirled in every direction, making it hard to tell up from down. Blinded by the squall, I had lost my sense of direction. A bolt of energy surged through me, propelling me toward the large slippery boulders on shore. Despite my legs feeling like pirate peg-legs, I smiled even as I navigated my way over the precarious snow and seaweed-covered rocks. Just then, Dane Gudauskas – one of the surfers I was photographing – reached out to help guide me in. But the worst was yet to come.

My body screamed in pain as hot water from the shower rained down on me. I was trying desperately to get the feeling back in my hands. I later learned that re-warming is a slow process, and trying to speed that up can cause serious nerve damage. It is perhaps the most valuable thing I learned on that first trip – I have been back here three times since, and am almost always on the verge of frostbite when I visit.

The images I have taken away from Unstad Bay, above the Arctic Circle in Norway, have been some of the most important

in my career. I have never given so much of myself for a photo. I've been a photographer for over 19 years now. Growing up in central California, without ever having a passport, it was my trips to the national parks that first gave me a thirst for adventure. But I actually got my start shooting surfers. I'd thought I'd made it when I began booking magazine assignments that took me to places like Bali and Australia. It was my dream job – or so I thought. It was actually really unfulfilling. It felt like commercialism at its worst, wi-fi everywhere, a bunch of BS, really. I'd done some cold-water surfing in Canada, Iceland and Alaska and was drawn to it. I knew Unstad Bay had a great

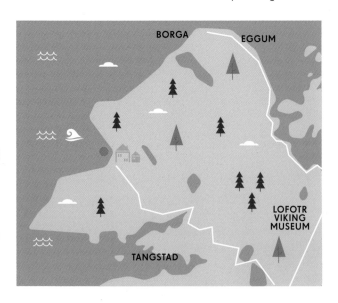

SURFIN' SAFARI

Norway's first surfers, Thor Frantzen and Hans Egil Krane made their living by working on ships around the world; having seen Australian surfers during a trip to Sydney in the early 1960s, they wanted to have a go back home. As they didn't have any boards, they fashioned their own based on those pictured on the cover of the 1962 Beach Boys album *Surfin' Safari,* and took them onto the waters of Unstad Bay. Their original boards are displayed in Unstad.

"I have been back here three times since, and am almost always on the verge of frostbite when I visit"

wave, and I wanted to go and put my stamp on it. It felt like a big surfing challenge – like going to the North Shore, but the opposite. That first trip to the Lofoten was in the spring of 2012.

The Lofoten archipelago is around 100 miles (160km) north of the Arctic Circle in Norway. Whether you make the final leg by ferry or get a connecting flight to one of the bigger towns nearby, it's a solid 36-hour journey from the US. The Lofoten Wall, as it's known, is a menacing fortress of tall peaks and mountains that rise out of the sea. It's a complex system of bays, bridges and tunnels that eventually deliver you to Unstad Bay, which surfers have long called the 'North Shore' of the area.

From above, Unstad Bay is shaped like a catcher's mitt – no wonder it draws every ounce of swell off the North Atlantic. These massive swells travel across the open ocean, before smashing into the Lofoten Wall. But every so often, the winds switch and howl offshore. When this happens, the winter swells become calm, marching in like corduroy. And these are the moments you savour – because they are so rare.

This is when the left point works in ruler-edge perfection, running down the cobblestones, producing dredging Mundaka-esque tubes. Some have said that if the Norse gods were to design a surf spot, he would have made it like Unstad: a hollow peeling left point, with a wide sweeping beach break in the

centre, and a deep-water dredging righthander further out to sea on the far north end.

No sharks, no razor-sharp reef. The risk is actually relative, and is something that has diminished for me over the years. The ice-cream headache I got the first time I touched that water screamed at me to head back to shore. Now, I know what to expect. While we were filming *Under the Arctic Sky*, we got pummelled by a 50-year storm. I found the isolation freeing. It feels real – adventure as it should be.

My first couple of trips to Unstad were for magazine assignments. I've since been back to finish two passion projects, a film and a photography book, then later to shoot a commercial for Lufthansa and to host a photography workshop. Every time I've visited Unstad Bay I've travelled with some incredible surfers. On the first trip it was Dan Gudauskas and Keith Malloy; since then it's been everyone from Brett Barley to Peter Mendia. And, yes, I've also been with a couple of great surfers who simply didn't last long in that water at all. It's not for everyone.

Ironically, I never really do all that much surfing when I'm in Unstad Bay. My passion is photography, so I usually spend all my energy treading water chasing the perfect shot. Maybe on a day when the waves are less than perfect, I'll grab a board and catch a few.

From left: Unstad Bay local Nils Nilsen; the Lofoten deliver waves and wild Northern Lights; Mick Fanning launches off Norway's frigid swell. Previous page: Chris Burkard's Unstad Bay photos number among the world's most iconic surf images

Sitting out in the water there, I feel a deep sensation of just how small I am within nature. There's so much beauty in the Lofotens, but there's also mystery. These old rocks with their tiny, craggy bays, the complex fjords and idyllic towns have hidden and protected some of the world's hardiest men, women and children for the last couple of thousand years.

Unstad Bay has now become a sort of rite of passage for surfers seeking out this same cold-water adventure. When we first visited, we literally camped in someone's backyard. These days, there are a few cabins to stay in, at least one surf camp and a new restaurant or two. But it hasn't really changed much – especially the view from the water. The locals have worked really hard to keep it the way it was.

I've urged countless friends and surfers I've met to make the trip, to put in the effort to go and experience it for themselves. It's a place that teaches patience, whether it's waiting for great waves or waiting to get the shot. Just getting there will test your will – and your bank account – but I've seen this place convert even the most diehard tropical surfer. As with a photo, a wave that requires so much of you leaves an impression like no other.

Here, a 6mm wetsuit isn't much different than Viking battle armour. Because, let's be honest, when you enter that water in Unstad Bay, you are going to war.

ORIENTATION

Type of wave // Beach break, left and right point break.
Best conditions // June to August for smaller waves, September to May for bigger waves.
Nearest town // Leknes is 15 miles (24km) south.
Getting there // Fly from Oslo to Bodø; take a boat to Stamsund (4 hours), then a short car transfer to Unstad.
Where to stay // Unstad Arctic Surf resort can sleep up to 55, and also has cabins, beach houses and apartments for rent (www.unstadarcticsurf.com).
Things to know // The average water temperature is around 12°F (-11°C) toward the end of summer, and 6F (-14°C) in April. You'll need a thick hooded wetsuit, boots and gloves (a 6/5mm in April). Between November and February there is little daylight, but between mid-April and August you can surf almost 24/7.

Opposite: Basque pro surfer Indar Unanue heads for the nearest hot tub after a session in the Faroe Islands

MORE LIKE THIS
COLD-WATER CLASSICS

KLITMØLLER, DENMARK

Denmark may be more famous for its cycle-friendly streets than its surfable waves, but that hasn't stopped the stretch of coast around the quaint fishing village of Klitmøller from earning a low-key reputation as a 'cold Hawaii'. This is on account of it being a surfers' paradise rather than for its tropical vibes, of course, but it's also dependent on the wind dropping; when it's too blowy the coastline becomes a magnet for windsurfers and stand-up paddleboarders. Located in North Jutland in the northwest of the country, Klitmøller has a mussel-covered reef break that can be ridden left and right. Other good waves to look out for nearby include Bunkers, Inside Reef and Vorupør Bay.

Nearest town // Klitmøller

FAROE ISLANDS

Located between Iceland and Scotland, not far from the Arctic Circle, the Faroe Islands got their name from Viking settlers in reference to the many sheep here (Føroyar translates as 'Sheep Isles'). Buffeted by huge Atlantic swells, the Faroes first came to the attention of most waveriders when Chris Burkard made a surf travel documentary here in 2015. Since then, plenty of pros (and their photographer entourages) have ventured here to ride waves amid the dramatic cliffscapes, green-swathed mountains and often brutally cold weather conditions. Local surfers and surf tourists are thin on the ground but growing in number each year, though breaks can be dangerous and hard to access so it's advisable to use a local guide. The waves are best during spring and autumn swells and are suited to good intermediates and experts.

Nearest town // Tórshavn

REYKJANES PENINSULA, ICELAND

Chris Burkard also catapulted Icelandic breaks into global surfing consciousness with the film *Under an Arctic Sky* in 2017, though the sport has more than its fair share of hardcore locals who are adept at reading the constantly shifting weather charts. The best and most consistent region to surf is the Reykjanes Peninsula, in the southwest of the country, just 30 minutes from Reykjavík. The Reykjanes Peninsula is the only place in the world where the mid-Atlantic ridge is visible above sea level, and it's also a Unesco Global Geopark – think geothermal pools, ethereal backdrops and volcanic wonder. Reykjanes has some beginner spots, such as Sandvík and Thorli, but as the seabed is mostly lava reef and basalt rock, it's more suited to intermediate and expert surfers. It makes sense to use a local surf-guide company as conditions are often changeable, frequently wild, and always cold.

Nearest town // Grindavík

LA GRAVIÈRE

Brendan Buckley visited Biarritz in France for crepes and café au lait. But after sampling Hossegor's famous pounding beach break, he decided to move there for good.

'I think I'm almost there', my friend told me over the phone. 'The next station is Pay-o.'

'Maybe Bayonne?' I replied, because it made more sense, geographically, and, well, there is no such place as Payo in France. I assumed he was just trying to repeat what he'd heard over the train's loudspeaker.

'P-A-U', he spelled out.

'Oh, Pau!', I replied. 'Get off at the next stop – you're on the wrong train.'

I'd moved from the US to Biarritz three years earlier and was just beginning to get the hang of the language. My best friend, however, was visiting France for the first time. But he wasn't exactly here for a French lesson. He had recently embarked on a landlocked year of studying in Italy, and four months in he needed to break the longest dry spell of his surfing life. It was his singular ambition for the visit. As he put it: 'I just need to get barrelled.' He came to the right place.

Hossegor is the epicentre of wave riding on the European continent, hosting the entire spectrum of surfers: long-haired longboarders with groovy vans; performance-obsessed shortboarders, who do jumping jacks in spring suits; old men who shred; little girls who shred. While Biarritz – the larger, more famous city, some 40 minutes to the south – also has some great surf, it doesn't get the world-class waves of Hossegor.

All kinds of surfers make a pilgrimage to La Gravière, either to paddle out and take on the notoriously fast, barrelling beach break, or just to stare out at the bombs as they detonate so close to the sand it's hard to imagine getting a few turns in. You've probably heard so much about 'La Grav' that you feel like you've seen it or surfed it even if you've never been to France. It's a wave that surfers gravitate toward, regardless of what the reports tell them.

The odds were in our favour, however, as it was late October. In autumn, the town shuts down and the waves turn on. The calendar says winter doesn't begin for another two months here, but it actually begins right after the annual WSL contest in mid-October. Straight after this there's an exodus: parking lots empty and windows are shuttered. Nightlife hotspots like L'Escargot shut down and even Dick's Sand Bar turns the volume on the stereo down a little.

Instead of driving straight to La Grav, we did something a little more French: we stopped for a glass of Bordeaux at a bar outside

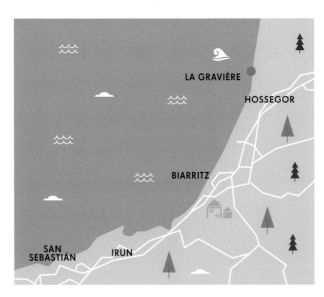

Les Halles. This, I explained to my friend, was one of the ways in which France changes you – especially if you're an American expat with overly romantic notions about the French lifestyle. I fell in love with Hossegor on my very first trip, in which I indulged in just about every cliché available to me. I used terribly broken French every chance I could; I had picnics on the beach while the sun slipped into the Atlantic; I drank wine in romantic cafés and almost convinced myself I enjoyed oysters; and I fell more deeply in love with my partner here. I also caught really, really good waves.

My friend and I headed to La Gravière the following morning as the sun was rising. We ran across the dunes until the ocean revealed itself. The waves looked fun – but although my friend was bursting with excitement, I told him that we could do better. He seemed annoyed to be passing up perfectly good waves, but Hossegor holds a long stretch of great breaks and I happened to know that when La Grav isn't really cooking, hunting for another good sandbar almost always pays off. Plus, La Grav wasn't going anywhere.

Hossegor is on the southern end of a long and straight stretch of coastline that is forever at the mercy of the moody North Atlantic. As we drive, the crowds thin. The towns eventually surrender to a forest of pine trees, and beach accesses become fewer and further between – as do the surfers. As predicted, we found a fun left bowling into to the beach with just two people out. We suited up.

A few hours later, sore, sunburnt and ravenous, we hit Creperie Cloarec in Seignosse; a crepe here is basically the French version of an energy bar. The beach just in front of the creperie, Les Estagnots, happens to hold another fun, but tricky, wave. We paddled out again and I watched as my pal struggled hilariously to figure out the currents and awkward bowls.

Afterward, we grabbed a beer at Café du Paris, a typical French brasserie (albeit covered in surf posters and stickers). After that we hit Chez Minus to scarf down some mussels. Diversions like these are part of the rhythm of surfing life here. Hossegor was always a popular beach destination for the French, but as surfing grew in popularity, it became intertwined with French culture in a way that feels unique and uncontrived: this is a place where you can buy wax at a boulangerie. Eating, drinking, and people-watching are a way of life here.

The following day, winter arrived in earnest: heavy rain, oversized swell, troublesome wind. And we still hadn't surfed La Gravière. We found a few waves at nearby La Centrale, but the weather simply wouldn't let up. In fact, it was looking like my friend's trip might end before I could show him the area's best wave; and this might be my fault, since I had steered us away from it a couple days earlier.

My friend's flight back to Italy departed from Bordeaux, a two-hour drive away. The day before he was set to leave, he decided to rent a car just in case he would need to hit La Grav and then head straight to the airport from there.

We woke at dawn on his final day and drove separately to Hossegor. We didn't even bother to check the waves this time – we were surfing La Grav no matter what. When we arrived, however, we could see it was big. Almost too big.

THE PIT OF LA GRAVIÈRE

When La Gravière is being pounded by double-overhead sets, a break just south, in front of the village of Capbreton, often has a mellow, waist-high wave. The reason for this is a giant trench just offshore, the Pit of Capbreton. Waves that hit Capbreton come out of the deepest part of the trench's channel, whereas those that hit La Grav come off the shallower side.

We paddled out anyway and proceeded to spend most of our time dodging the bombing closeouts, picking off a few decent corners here and there. Eventually, I had to head to work. We said our goodbyes and I left him in the lineup.

Four hours later, my phone rings. It's a local who I surf with occasionally. But when I answer, it's my best friend on the line. Turns out, he had taken the key fob of his rental car into the ocean with him. He couldn't start his car when he got out – so he simply paddled out again. Indeed, he surfed for another three hours, missing his flight completely. Apparently, the tide came in, the swell dropped a bit – and the waves turned on. It was good, he told me.

'How good?' I ask.

'Like, *classic* La Grav', he answered.

ORIENTATION

Type of wave // Barrelling beach break with rights and lefts.
Best conditions // Proper La Gravière needs a high tide;
ideal size is 4–10ft. September and October offer the most
consistent swell, wind and weather conditions.
Nearest town // Hossegor.
Getting there // Biarritz is 40 minutes away and has the
closest airport and train station. However, Bordeaux and
Bilbao are both a little less than two hours away and often
have cheaper flights. A car will make your life easier here.
Where to stay // Jo&Joe Open House is in Hossegor.
Airbnbs are plentiful and van camping is also quite easy.
Things to know // There's a cliché about the waves in
France: if you check the surf and it's firing, you're already too
late. And it's true. Tides are massive here and they can turn
a wave on and off within an hour. Keep your options open
and never be too stubborn to paddle down the beach.

*Clockwise from top: searching for classic La Grav peaks as the tide shifts; the
Hossegor waves draw the best of Europe and beyond; the villages here are a
beguiling mix of old and new. Previous page: Australian pro Julian Wilson
competes in one of the many international contests staged at La Gravière*

Clockwise from top left: British pro Ellie Turner during the buzzing Lacanau surf festival; Parlementia goes off in winter; the former whaling port of Guéthary, best base for catching the Parlementia wave

MORE LIKE THIS
FRANCE'S TOP SURF SPOTS

CÔTE DES BASQUES

If it wasn't for La Gravière and the beach breaks of Hossegor, this is probably what most people would picture when they envision surfing in France: a fun wave, nestled beneath a castle, offering a perfect view of the Pyrenees. It's located on the southern end of Biarritz and has lefts and rights that usually like a lower tide. As a matter of fact, the beach doesn't even exist at high tide, but you can still scurry across some rocks and get a few waves if there's enough swell. There's a dedicated longboard crowd here, as well as a bunch of surf schools. As you paddle further south, it gets less crowded and more powerful, with plenty of fun peaks for shortboards. Don't expect to beat the crowds, though. Just embrace them and be sure not to miss a sunset drink at Etxola Bibi after.

Nearest town // Biarritz

LACANAU

Lacanau is similar to Hossegor, though more mellow in every way. It's a similar setup – a big, open beach break with sandbanks that turn on and off with the tide – but it doesn't have anything quite as memorable as La Gravière. In a way, that works in Lacanau's favour. It still gets plenty of great waves, but compared to Hossegor it has remained relatively removed from the international scene, despite having hosted many professional contests – this is a place where you can often beat the crowds. Don't be afraid to drive north or south of the town, and especially don't be afraid to spend some time trekking down to the beaches from the many coastal car parks. If you do, you can often set up shop and spend a day in near solitude, scoring different peaks as they turn on with the tide.

Nearest town // Bordeaux

PARLEMENTIA

When a large swell hits western France, Parlementia is the region's go-to big wave. It's located off the small Basque town of Guéthary and has a small, hip scene of surfers who adore it. Parlementia is a reef break that features a long and sometimes soft, sometimes steep right, and a left that will allow you a turn or two. It breaks on pretty much any swell and is usually best around mid tide. But here's the thing: it can hold almost anything that the Atlantic throws at it. While it's fun nearly every day, you're unlikely to see it in full form if you visit in September or October. However, every winter features a few lucky days of big swell, good wind and an accompanying pack of chargers capitalizing on that combination. Other than Belharra, which requires a Jet Ski to access, and La Nord, which can be hit-or-miss, Parlementia is the area's primo big wave.

Nearest town // Guéthary

STAITHES

Alf Alderson likes the fact that England's best reef break is a little too far north for the masses. But as one of the UK's greatest hits, most surfers eventually make the trip.

The first time I surfed Staithes I was quickly disabused of the notion that I'd simply be pulling up to the harbour and paddling out. Staithes is tucked away under high, crumbling sea cliffs beneath the rolling North York Moors, and the lanes that lead down to the village are so steep and narrow that only locals are allowed to drive past the pastel-painted cottages, with their characteristic red-tiled roofs. Staithes' residents are hemmed in by cliffs on one side and wild seas on the other, effectively trapped on two sides by the natural landscape. Pirates never lived here, but they should have – I can't think of a seaside scene better suited to Long John Silver than Staithes, where he'd sit outside a pub with a parrot on his shoulder.

It was late May, the sun was shining warm in a clear blue sky. And yet I tramped down to the harbour from the visitor car park above the village in winter wetsuit, boots and gloves because, yes, even in summer you need a good coverage of neoprene when surfing off the Yorkshire coast. And boots are also essential for tippy-toeing your way out over the reef.

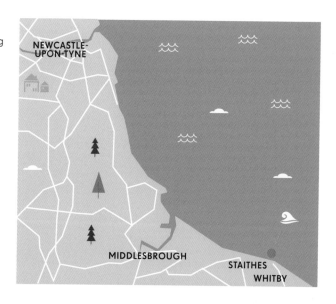

HISTORIC PORT

Whitby, just south of Staithes, is where Dracula supposedly landed when he reached British shores. This former whaling port is overlooked by the remains of an 13th-century Gothic abbey; the original 7th-century building was destroyed by Viking invaders. A magnet for Goth types, Whitby is home to the Captain Cook Memorial Museum, and is also famed for serving up the UK's best fish and chips – perfect after a hard sesh at The Cove.

It's somewhat ironic that the man who 'discovered' the Hawaiian islands should have spent his teenage years gazing out at some of the finest reef breaks in England. Captain James Cook, born a few miles inland from Staithes in 1728, lived briefly in this picturesque village on the Yorkshire coast before going on to sail up and down the North Sea, and eventually across the world.

These days, surfers come from all over the UK for the three fast, powerful reef breaks that rear up here from the murky waters of the North Sea. Northerly groundswells that may well have travelled all the way from the Arctic grind ashore in Staithes after being funnelled down and diverted shorewards. Occasionally, those waves then encounter prevailing offshore winds. And, presto, Staithes starts firing.

As the Southwest Peninsula – England's traditional surfing heartland – faces southwest, most of the area's better spots are bedevilled by prevailing onshore winds. Not so on Yorkshire's easterly facing coastline, where these same winds are offshore. On the other hand, this rugged coastline, some 30 miles (48km) south of Newcastle, lacks the sixty years of surf culture and associated hype found in places like Newquay – there's no surf shop in Staithes and the nearest is a very down-home affair just up the coast in Saltburn. The local surf community here is relatively small and, well, local. Few surfers up sticks and move to Yorkshire for their regular wave fix.

And on that first trip, it was immediately apparent that this isn't a spot for tyros; as I picked my way through the shallows over submerged rocky slabs, with kelp fronds snaking around my shins, a steely grey lefthander reeled along the horizon. I felt like I was a long way from the sandy, blue-green beach breaks of my home in west Wales. I was reminded of friends such as Saltburn local Gary Rogers and Newcastle big-wave charger Gabe Davies, who have told me scary tales of taking on heavy, pounding Staithes at triple overhead and coming off second best (when it gets like that, you'll find me sitting in the Cod & Lobster pub above the bay with a pint).

Most of my trips here unfold under a backdrop of sea and sky, blended in a grey-brown wash, an atmosphere where the thrill of anticipation is tempered by the sombre scenery and the chilly waters. Regardless of the weather, something funny happens when a great wave comes along. Taking off on one of the bowly lefts that mark The Cove, feeling that weightless drop before hooning along the face and seeing the lip of a barrel unfurl in front of me, I feel like I could be in Portugal.

As well as The Cove, there are three distinct breaks to choose from at Staithes, depending on swell and wind directions: The Point, a hollow left which can also provide a short, very shallow right; and The Harbour, a bowly left-hand peak breaking in front of the harbour wall. It's a goofy-foot paradise. Being a natural footer isn't the only reason Staithes can be intimidating.

From left: Staithes' reef throws up one of the UK's best and most serious waves; the village harbour is hemmed in by high cliffs and open sea; reaching the break here is part of the adventure. Previous page: dawn patrol above Staithes village

"Staithes is hemmed in by cliffs on one side and wild seas on the other – pirates never lived here, but they should have"

The cold, shallow water and hard-charging locals give it an edge. On top of that, sitting in the lineup at Staithes can feel jarring if you're used to a more traditional surf experience.

It doesn't matter how sunny it is, and no matter how often I surf here, it's always the cold that gets the better of me. I actually got lucky with the weather during my first trip, but I remember the chill beginning to penetrate my thick neoprene cladding. And so began the torturous process of waiting for *one last wave* into shore. Afterwards, I scrambled out of the sea, up the hill to the car, and embarked on the frustrating, numb-fingered wrestling match with my suit. Finally, cocooned in a warm fleece and thick jacket, I did what I've done after every one of my sessions since, whether I've come with friends or on a solo mission: headed right back down the hill to the Cod & Lobster for a pint of Yorkshire ale in a warm, surfer-friendly pub (they even post the surf report on their website), whilst watching the waves crack off across the reefs.

I can't help but wonder what Captain Cook would have made of it all.

ORIENTATION

Type of wave // Left-hand reef breaks on shallow reefs.
Best conditions // Low to mid tide on northerly swell and southwesterly winds, best between September and April.
Nearest town // Staithes.
Getting there // The nearest airport is Teesside, 35 miles (56km) west. Car hire is available there, but there's no visitor parking in Staithes – you need to park above the town in Bank Top car park (fee) or Crowbar Lane (free).
Where to stay // There are plenty of B&Bs and campsites.
Things to know // The ideal equipment is a high-performance shortboard, or a semi-gun for bigger days. Minimum 5/4 mm wetsuit, or thicker for winter, is recommended, as are booties and a hood.

*Opposite from top: surfing
Porthleven, Cornwall; Porthleven
produces a reef break that can test
the UK's best*

MORE LIKE THIS
BEST OF THE BRITISH ISLES

PAMPA POINT, IRELAND

A freight-train left if ever there was one, Pampa is southwest of Bundoran, Ireland's surf city, itself a great starting point for journeys into the mountainous wilds of Donegal. But surfers mainly come for the hollow and powerful waves. With a steep takeoff, Pampa takes no prisoners: you've got to hold your line and maintain as much speed as possible to have any chance of making the tube. Rides of up to 500ft are possible, and on big days Pampa will hold 8ft–10ft waves. Pampa is named after a prominent PMPA insurance sign that once stood nearby, and was featured in 1995 surf film *Litmus*, with Joel Fitzgerald and Tom Curren (the latter surfing to a soundtrack of his own guitar sounds). Too heavy? No problem. Rossnowlagh beach, some 5 miles (8km) south of Bundoran, is a surf paradise for beginners.

Nearest town // Bundoran

LYNMOUTH, ENGLAND

Cream teas and scones? Check. Rolling green hills? Check. Rugged moorland and country pubs so quaint you have to pinch yourself? Check, and check again. Devon is England's very own Riviera and many regard Lynmouth as the country's best left-hand point break. And while Devon spawned a maritime tradition as rich as any – Sir Francis Drake, Sir Walter Raleigh and Sir Francis Chichester were all Devonians – today the reliable north-coast swell here has generated a robust surf scene, which includes big-wave surfer and Nazaré vet Andrew Cotton. Not as fast as Pampa or Staithes, but a classic all the same, Lynmouth in north Devon fires up when a large westerly swell hits southwest England and the wind is southerly or southeasterly. It works anywhere between 3ft and 10ft, and serves up very long rides.

Nearest town // Lynmouth

PORTHLEVEN, ENGLAND

Facing southwest, Porthleven – or 'Levvie' – is a working port exposed to everything that the prevailing southwesterly Atlantic gales can throw at it. And here in the far west of Cornwall, that is a lot. Testimony to the violence of winter storms here is a 30ft sea wall on the main beach; even so, waves will crash over it onto Loe Bar Road. There's no escaping the raw, elemental nature of Porthleven. The sea permeates every aspect of life and people are tough here: England's first-ever heavyweight boxing champion, Bob Fitzsimmons, came from nearby Helston. First surfed in the mid-60s, Porthleven, along with Thurso East in Scotland, is the UK's iconic wave. If you like fast, hollow, board-snapping rights, this is the place. Oh, and crowds, too. Porthleven is jam-packed any time it works. Best not to paddle out if you lack experience in heavy reef setups.

Nearest town // Porthleven

NAZARÉ

The sea has provided for the people of Nazaré, Portugal, for centuries, and the tradition continues with Big Wave tourism. Portuguese photographer Ricardo Bravo has witnessed this evolution.

The first time I went to Nazaré looking for waves, it was flat. We were on a road trip scouring the coastline for something to ride and somebody suggested the beach of Praia do Norte, where a headland juts out into the Atlantic Ocean just north of the Nazaré village.

I'd been to Nazaré before when I was younger. It was a place I went with my parents on lazy weekend family trips. I remembered cobbled streets thronged with old ladies wearing layered traditional skirts; fisherfolk drying their catch close to the road; and the funicular that goes to the top of the promontory overlooking the village. I remembered all of these things, but not waves.

We ended up surfing another beach further north and I forgot about Nazaré again – until two years later, on a day that would change the course of history for this small Portuguese village.

It was November 2001 and I had been invited to photograph a European bodyboarding contest at Praia do Norte. When I returned to the lookout on top of the cliffs, I was greeted by carnage on the beach below. A group of bodyboarders were fighting for their lives, getting stuck in the monstrous shore break with a relentless current dragging them down the beach; another handful of riders were out at the back dropping into huge triangles of water. Everybody was shocked at what the wave was capable of.

A year later, another bodyboarding contest was organised. In general, the beaches around here are considered to be best avoided. Most families from Nazaré make their living from fishing, and many have lost someone to these wild seas. Nazaré's main village beach, Praia da Vila, was already considered extremely dangerous. Further north, Praia do Norte, where the swell often triples in size and power, seemed like a piece of hell on earth.

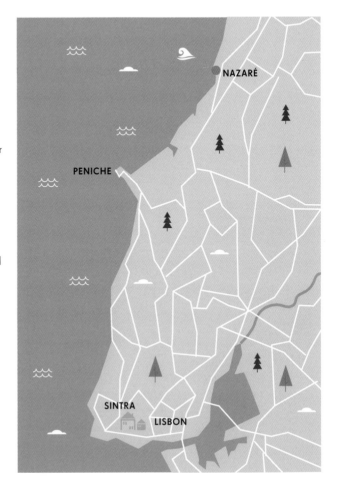

None of this deterred local bodyboarder Dino Casimiro, however. Born and raised in Nazaré, Dino always knew the strange wave that formed off the cliffs was something special, but only later did he learn that the reason behind this phenomenon was Nazaré's submarine canyon. This underwater ravine is the longest in coastal Europe, rising from a depth of almost 16,400ft (5000m) to a mere 164ft (50m) just southwest of Sítio da Nazaré, the old village to the south.

A passionate photographer, Dino had a Kodak photo album filled with evidence of how big and perfect the waves in front of his village got. Not big as in 25ft, but big, as in 50ft-plus. The problem was finding someone to ride them.

Dino was the driving force behind those first contests, and I recall the mayor proudly telling me in an interview afterwards: 'Praia do Norte was dead, nobody wanted to come here. Now we have found a way to make it reborn!'

Despite this, the wave remained the preserve of a few crazy bodyboarders, and went unridden on the bigger days. It was hard to imagine that anyone would be able to surf the massive peaks, let alone survive the pure chaos that separated the beach from the backline when those winter swells rolled in.

Then, in 2005, José Gregório, Paulo do Bairro and Tiago Pires gave it a go by towing in, scoring a mix of unforgettable rides and thorough beatings while showing it was possible. But Dino knew this was only the beginning. He believed that the biggest waves in the world could be surfed at Nazaré, so he started sending out messages to the best international big-wave riders, showing them photos of the huge, perfect peaks and begging them to come ride them. Months would go by and he'd hear nothing back. He'd try again, and still nothing. Then Dino sent a message to Garret McNamara. Garret replied immediately.

PORTUGAL'S SWELL MAGNET

Nazaré is the only beach break in the world that gets swells this big. The reason is its geography: there's a dropoff to deep water just offshore and the beach is v-shaped, which funnels Atlantic swells into the bay before they unload on the sandbars; waves here top 40ft with surprising regularity This is also why, when the rest of Portugal is flat, Nazaré is still a solid 4ft or 5ft. And, believe it or not, it's known to produce some pretty incredible small waves, too.

Clockwise from top left: Carlos Burle drops in; Grant 'Twiggy' Baker with his weapon of choice; rugged coastline carved by massive swell; a sculptural homage to surf culture. Previous page: French pro Justine Dupont takes on the Nazaré wave

*"It was hard to imagine
that anyone could surf
these massive peaks"*

It took five years before McNamara eventually made it over to Nazaré, but when he did, the evidence of him riding waves that seemed to swallow the entire cliff rippled out across the world.

Today, Nazaré is a household name, visited by surfers and by thousands of tourists who come from all over the world to watch the spectacle. On the biggest swells there are drones, cinema cameras and famous journalists registering every breaking wave that's ridden. There's a whole new economy floating the village, based entirely on the once-forbidden waves of Praia do Norte.

But as the big-wave elite push harder and harder to try and ride that mythical 100ft wave, there have also been a number of terrifying moments documented here – these leave me with the sobering realisation that it's not a question of if Nazaré will claim more lives, but when.

And as much as I admire those who come to ride Praia do Norte, it's the ocean and its magnificent shapes that leave me awestruck every time I witness it break. In my years of travelling the world, I've never seen anything remotely similar to the waves of Nazaré: they are powerful, raw, unpredictable and frightening. Even if surfers manage to ride them for brief moments of glory, these giants will always be indomitable.

ORIENTATION

Type of wave // Right- and left-hand beach break, anything from 3ft to 50ft-plus.
Best conditions // Big swell hits from September to March.
Nearest town // Nazaré.
Getting there // Nazaré village is a 1½ hour drive north of Lisbon.
Where to stay // Nazaré has a range of accomodation, from luxury hotels and Airbnbs to reasonably priced hostels.
Things to know // Nazaré has become one of the most famous big-wave surf spots in the world, and the best one for spectators. Even if you'll never surf it, watching the show from the headland affords a rare view of big-wave surfing, and it's worth the trip for spectating alone.

Opposite: South Africa's formidable
Dungeons begins to break at about
10ft, but regularly tops 40ft

MORE LIKE THIS
THE NEW BREED OF BIG WAVES

MULLAGHMORE, IRELAND

Mullaghmore is a tiny village perched on the ruggedly beautiful west coast of Ireland, just a short way west of Irish surf mecca Bundoran. Before the discovery of this big wave in the '90s, Mullaghmore was most (in)famous for being the place where English earl Lord Manbatten (and his 14-year-old grandson) were killed by an IRA bomb in 1979. However, thanks to big-wave charger Richie Fitzgerald, images of Mullaghmore's heaving, freezing 40ft slabs of Atlantic Ocean (that only a tiny percentage of the surfing population would want anything to do with) are now seared in the surfing consciousness. But like many of the big-wave locations around the world, the simple spectacle of a big day is worth travelling for, and the headland where 'Mully' breaks is a great spot to pitch up and watch the carnage.
Nearest town // Bundoran

DUNGEONS, SOUTH AFRICA

Located near Hout Bay – a pleasant suburb 12 miles (19km) from Cape Town – Dungeons was first surfed in the 1980s and is perhaps the one big wave in the world with a name that truly warns of its danger. This spot has all the characteristics that make a wave truly terrifying: cold water, huge kelp beds, great white sharks and a swell that, on its day, can get as huge and hollow as just about any big wave in the world. It doesn't break often, and only when the perfect conditions conspire, as storms peel off the Roaring Forties winds. Dungeons is situated a full mile (1.6km) offshore, right next to a seal colony, in some of the sharkiest waters on the planet.
Nearest town // Hout Bay

PUNTA GALEA, SPAIN

Punta Galea doesn't have near the name recognition of other big-wave spots around the world, but most surfers will recognise footage of the Spanish marvel doing its thing, especially after it became the location of the WSL's inaugural Big Wave World Tour competition in 2014. Situated 20 minutes from the Basque port of Bilbao, the wave is a unique setup: it breaks on one side of the Bilbao harbour, and comes to life during big swells that roll in all the way across the Atlantic. Whilst Punta Galea's cast is usually a who's who of underground Basque chargers, it was given the ultimate validation when it became one of only six locations around the world for chosen the BWWT event, which was won here by Californian Nic Lamb.
Nearest town // Bilbao

THE PEAK

Ireland's entire coastline is rich with rideable waves. Alf Alderson heads to Bundoran, where an unlikely but iconic surf town has sprung up beside some of the best swell in Europe.

I was getting snaked by my heroes. Not just once or twice, but during the entire session. I was sitting in the lineup for The Peak at Bundoran in Ireland. My mates and I are rarely the best surfers in the water, but we were even further from that here. For bobbing around beside us in the steel-grey Atlantic was a who's who of faded superstars from the 1970s and 1980s: Mark Richards, Gary Elkerton, Martin Potter. They may have been past it, but all were former world champions.

Perhaps I was just intimidated. I had posters of these guys on the wall of my student accommodation, growing up in England. So I was feeling an uncomfortable combination of awe and contempt. Like us, they had come for the Quiksilver Masters World Surfing Championships. Though unlike us, they were competing. So, here we were catching waves alongside surfing royalty. Or, I should say, getting snaked by surfing royalty.

Oddly, Ireland is one of those spots that seems to be on every surfer's bucket list, no matter their ability. Yet, it doesn't have

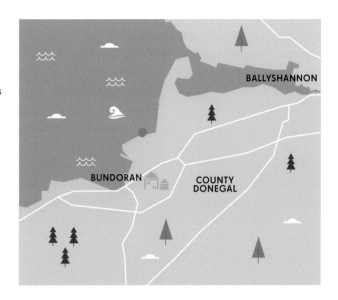

AN UNLIKELY CONTEST VENUE

The waves around Bundoran were not surfed until the late '60s, and the area only became a household name in the surf world when it hosted the European Surf Championships in 1985. But the waves are so good here – not to mention the craic – that the town hosted the ESC again in 1997 and 2011. Bundoran was also the location for the Billabong Monster Tow-in Surf Session in 2011, when the world's best big-wave surfers descended to take on nearby Mullaghmore.

the history of most surfing meccas. Wave-riding took a while to take root here. A handful of local pioneers – such as Kevin Cavey in the south of the country and Englishman Andy Hill in the Bundoran area – kicked things off in the 1960s. It was around this time that people realised consistent, high-quality beach, reef and point breaks existed along every stretch of coastline facing south, west and north – even the east coast of Ireland gets decent waves from time to time.

The lineup at spots like Easkey in County Sligo had become a United Nations of adventurous surfers by the 1970s, and with the added bonus of quintessentially Irish bars, live trad music and Guinness from the source, the trickle of visitors carrying board-bags gradually increased. Soon, the secret was out: Ireland has world class surf.

High profile surfers such as the Malloy brothers began to explore the country of their ancestors in the noughties (Kelly Slater once visited, but immediately branded it 'too cold'). By the time Bundoran boy Richie Fitzgerald and English pro Gabe Davies successfully took on the huge, gnarly left at Mullaghmore Head, Ireland was fully established alongside big hitters like Hawaii and Indo as a serious surf destination.

It helps that Ireland itself has long been considered a destination that has something for everyone. Every time I surf in Ireland, and Bundoran in particular, it's about far more than simply riding waves. The area's wild, romantic landscape and rich culture are almost the polar opposite of the backdrop we're used to on surf trips. My own visits to Bundoran also tend to include a trudge up the lower slopes of the 1500ft Benbulbin, which rises like a fantastical monolith above the town. Looking around, it's easy to see how the strange, melancholy atmosphere here has fuelled the country's artists and poets over centuries.

From atop the hill, I stared out at the coastline of Sligo and Donegal, once again daydreaming about all the surf here. Ireland's outline twists and turns like a scalded snake, and any surfer can immediately see how the country has some of the best and most varied waves in Europe. Flat days are rare here. I've always managed to find a wave, every visit, whether mellow rollers beyond the golden sands of Tullan Strand or challenging, head-high A-frames at my favourite spot, The Peak.

What happens after a session here is always as memorable as the surf itself. I gravitate toward the infamous Bridge Bar, which lies smack in front of The Peak. Here, my mates and I plan

"In the Bridge Bar, my mates and I plan dawnies, only to jettison those plans after a few pints of creamy stout"

dawnies, only to jettison these plans after a few pints of creamy stout. I have a feeling that more dawn sessions are abandoned in Ireland than at any other surf destination in the world. Who wants to wake up early in the cold rain, anyway?

The next morning, looking for redemption after getting skunked the day before, I eventually make the long paddle out to The Peak again. My hangover washes away slowly. The journey and effort always allow for some anticipation to build. Eventually I can see the racing left clearly. Of course, the rights are going off here, too.

As if picking up where we left off in the pub the night before, the banter begins. We all know that when the conversation dies, it's time to look to the horizon, where a set is rolling shorewards. Finally, without any world champions to compete with, I snag a clean head-high left. The power of the swell requires only a couple of easy strokes to get into it. Then, it's a smooth drop down the grey face and a race with the lip before kicking out.

And in Ireland, there is almost always someone there to congratulate you on your ride, whether you know them or not. Chances are, though, if you don't know them, you will recognise them again the next time you're out. Because no surfer visits Bundoran just once.

ORIENTATION

Type of wave // Left-hand reef break.
Best conditions // Low tide, through autumn and winter.
Nearest town // Bundoran.
Getting there // Belfast International and George Best Belfast City are 2½ hours' drive away; Dublin International is a 3-hour drive.
Where to stay // There is plenty of surfer-friendly accommodation, including Bundoran Surf Co Lodge (www.bundoransurfco.com) and Turfnsurf Lodge (www.turfnsurftours.com).
Things to know // A car is essential to make the most of the range of breaks here. Bring equipment for cold-water waves that range in size from knee-high to triple overhead.

Opposite, clockwise from top left:
Lahinch is one of Ireland's best
places to learn; Inch is a favourite
among longboarders; Portrush is
Northern Ireland's top surf spot

MORE LIKE THIS
GEMS OF THE EMERALD ISLE

PORTRUSH, COUNTY ANTRIM

Portrush is Northern Ireland's answer to England's Newquay, a popular tourist destination, always crowded in summer when there's a bit of swell. Once the holiday season is over, however, things become less hectic. There's a fine selection of breaks either side of Portrush; Portballintrae is consistent and often biggest. Portrush itself offers two options, West Strand (usually bigger) and East Strand, and like the rest of the breaks along this coastline they're oriented in a generally northerly direction, which means the region's prevailing winds are offshore. For those looking to lose themselves amongst some of Europe's wildest waves and coastline, simply head west into Donegal, where you'll find more consistent waves and a consistent lack of crowds.
Nearest town // Portrush

LAHINCH, COUNTY CLARE

Lahinch, a short distance south of Galway on Ireland's west coast, has become particularly popular with beginners, which means that it can look more crowded at the main breaks (called Beach and Left) than it actually is. But on any decent swell, many of those in the water will be lucky if they can get to their feet. That's not to say there isn't a solid cadre of local talent ready to rip it apart – and with two additional and more challenging Lahinch waves (Cornish Left, a fast, barrelling left; and Shit Creek, a challenging reef break), alongside renowned nearby breaks such as Crab Island and the intimidating big-wave Aileen's to the north, it's no surprise that that this area is one of Ireland's surfing heartlands.
Nearest town // Lahinch

INCH, COUNTY KERRY

In the far southwest of Ireland, Inch is blessed with two distinct breaks along with stunningly beautiful scenery and a wealth of wildlife (this is one of the few places in Europe where you might see dolphins, seals and sea otters in the same stretch of water). You may have seen the 3 mile (5km) stretch of Inch Strand at the movies, its mellow beach breaks peeling in the background of scenes from *Playboy of the Western World* (1962) and *Ryan's Daughter* (1970). It's a favourite with longboarders and beginners. Just to the north is Inch Reef which, a few times a year, produces a fantastic 1000ft right. Of course, given the quality of the wave it can be busy, despite the difficult access down a low cliff-face. Plus, staying in the lineup isn't easy due to a strong rip, but it's worth the effort when it's firing.
Nearest town // Inch

MUNDAKA

Some say Mundaka is Basque for 'fickle'. After years of visiting northern Spain, hoping for conditions to cooperate, Jake Howard finally scored.

I actually had a board specially shaped for Mundaka. It was a 6'4" pintail, designed for a swell I'd been chasing for years. This time I planned on being there for a full three weeks while I covered a world tour contest in the area. But it was still impossible to know if I'd be able to use my board. Scoring at Mundaka is never a given.

My trip began with an autumn deluge. October fury in the North Atlantic had spun off into the Bay of Biscay and parked itself above the region. It was wet and cold. I sat in my hotel room, fighting off a flu bug I'd picked up from all the travelling. All I could do was stare out the window and watch the harbour below.

Mundaka is a town that feels like it has just emerged from the Middle Ages. The better-known tourist town of San Sebastián – which also has some fun beach breaks – is about 1½ hours' drive to the east. Spain's fourth largest city, Bilbao, is only about 30 minutes southwest. The imposing church overlooking Mundaka's lineup, the Iglesia de Santa María, dates back to the 10th century and the town still has a very medieval vibe. Fishing still drives

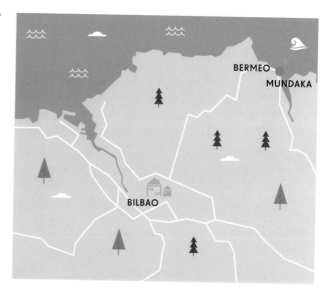

"During the two-week window of the world tour event here, they were often stymied, and usually moved it up the coast to the more consistent break at Bakio"

the local economy and the Basque people have a long, storied relationship with the sea. The Basque surf scene is made up of very strong watermen and women.

From my hotel room, I looked out over the harbour, where snugly moored fishing boats bobbed up and down just yards from the surf break. The wind whipped at the waters outside the ancient harbour walls. There was nothing I could do but wait – wait for the weather to break. Wait for my fever to break. Wait for the swell to fill in. Wait for the capricious Basque conditions to finally cooperate.

For three years I'd been chasing Mundaka, and I still hadn't had a proper surf here. Coming to town to cover the Billabong Pro, several times, I had yet to see the wave do its thing. Sure, a lot of world-class breaks are fickle – and that's what makes many of them so magical – but Mundaka is beyond unpredictable. Because of the way it's protected from the raw energy of the Atlantic, it requires a very specific swell angle. And that is precisely why so many surfers chase it. When it turns on, it's a freight-train, top-to-bottom left-hand barrel that requires commitment. However, before any of that, the wave simply requires patience.

It wasn't until the early '80s that Mundaka appeared on the international surf map. Later, in the early 2000s, surfing's pro world

tour was held here several times; it was in Mundaka that 11-time world champ Kelly Slater clinched his ninth title. However, during the two-week waiting period of the contests, the action was often stymied, and the venue usually ended up being moved up the coast to the more consistent beach break at Bakio.

But when it does turn on, Mundaka remains one of the best waves in Europe. As I paced my hotel room, there was definitely some fear mixed in with the anticipation and cold medicine. My happy place is in a playful, chest-high beach break wedge. Mundaka has teeth. Basque pro-surfer Kepa Acero broke his neck and nearly drowned here on a big day. It is possible to catch Mundaka on a smaller swell, but that can be even trickier than when it's in full form.

Then, after four full days of rain, the clouds finally thinned and my fever broke. The northwest swell that had been looming in the forecast marched in past Izaro Island, as predicted. I kept looking over at my new board in the corner of the room.

Mundaka is situated at the mouth of the Oka River, and the sand flowing out of the river's estuary sets up its bank. When the sand is good, the odds of scoring rise exponentially. But this part of the world sees massive tide swings, and the tides are too high more often than not. This time, however, it was all coming together.

LEARN THE LANGUAGE

Though Mundaka is in northern Spain, you'd be better off speaking English than Spanish. The Basque people tend to identify more strongly with their regional roots than mainstream Spanish culture, and the language spoken here is Euskara, an old tongue unrelated to any other in Europe. It can be tricky to get a handle on, but knowing a few key phrases will go a long way in the lineup – and in the bar after your session.

From left: Mundaka village; American surf instructor Mike Dobos in front of his local surf school; Mundaka's barrel is rare but divine. Previous page: Portuguese pro Vasco Ribeiro locks into Spain's best left

ORIENTATION

Type of wave // Left-hand, sand-bottom point break.
Best conditions // Low tide going high, on a strong northwest groundswell, during the North Atlantic autumn.
Nearest town // Mundaka for the best access (though French surf towns like Biarritz, Anglet and Hossegor are only a couple of hours away).
Getting there // Fly in and out of Bilbao, which is a 30-minute drive away.
Where to stay // Hotel Kurutziaga Jauregia provides the closest accommodations to the surf; it's cosy and right in the heart of town. The Mundaka Hostel & Sports Café is a little further away, but still within walking distance.
Things to know // Staying in position in the lineup is challenging. Enter through the harbour to insert yourself directly into the lineup. Once in unprotected waters, it's like stepping onto an aquatic treadmill.

I woke up before daybreak, climbed into my wetsuit and waxed my new board. Nobody else was stirring, except of course the fisherfolk in the harbour below. I was mentally prepared for a heavy session, as I'd heard that stiff offshores can make it even harder to get down the face.

After walking down the cobbled streets to the harbour, I carefully picked my way down a set of slippery, moss-covered steps until I reached the water's edge. I jumped in, paddled a couple of hundred feet and I was sitting in the lineup. The water was cool but pleasant – like Santa Cruz back in my home state of California. I took another look at the ancient church looming over us. The outgoing tide carried me effortlessly into the takeoff zone.

I was only in the water a few minutes before a large, rolling set came steaming through in the early dawn light. A few silhouetted figures splashed around me like jumping fish. I dodged the first two waves, perhaps not quite ready. But the third wave that came my way was the one.

I was up. Anxiety washed away, replaced by the thrill of flying down the line. The waves were indeed serious, and the session required my full attention. But Mundaka had finally let me in.

*Opposite: Spain's Playa de Somo,
near Santander, has a beautiful
beach, consistent waves and a cool
vibe*

MORE LIKE THIS
NORTH COAST SPAIN'S BEST

SOPELANA, SPAIN

There's a little something for everyone at
Sopelana, which is just 40 minutes' west
of Mundaka. Its user-friendly surf zone
hosts everyone from surf-school students
to pros (especially during the frequent
contests). And the break is set along a
beautiful stretch of coastline, where a
rock reef at the west corner of the beach
offers a consistent, dependable peak at
high tide. Once the tide turns around and
drains, the beach break is still an option.
Predictably, this area can get crowded, but
it can be less intimidating than other waves
in the region. The ideal time to surf here is
between October and April.
Nearest town // Sopelana

PLAYA DE SOMO, SPAIN

Playa de Somo is perhaps the most
consistent wave in all of Spain. A
1½-hour drive west of Mundaka, it is
a surf-tripper's dream. Over the years,
the local community has been built up
largely around serving visiting surfers,
with great surf shops, hostels, bars and
restaurants, as well as ample camping
options. The break itself is a dependable,
quality beach break that can hold surf up
to about the 6ft range. But the smaller
days are ideal for beginners. The great
thing here is that as the swell builds, the
surf gets hollower and more suited to
high-performance rides. Like everywhere in
this area, the autumn and winter months
are your best bet, and north to northwest
swells are most promising.
Nearest town // Santander

ZURRIOLA BEACH, SPAIN

Zurriola's wave may not the best in the
Spanish Basque country – within an hour's
drive of San Sebastián you can score at
Mundaka or Hossegor – but what it lacks
in surf quality, it makes up for spectacularly
in cultural cred. 'Zurri' is the only real
surf beach in a city of nearly 200,000
people, and in the 1970s it became the
first spot in the Bay of Biscay where surfing
took a stronghold. Just foosteps from
San Sebastián's pedestrianised cobbled
streets, with their world famous wine halls,
pintxos (tapas) bars and Michelin-starred
restaurants, the beach injects a vibrant
surf vibe into one of Europe's great cultural
hubs. Consistent, but crowded – and
with the quality dependent on the ever-
changing sandbanks – Zurri is nonetheless
one of the world's best city surf breaks.
Nearest town // San Sebastián

SENNEN COVE

In the UK's far west, Alex Wade found a home in a place where the landscape is raw and you never know who – or what – you might encounter in the lineup.

'm sitting in a lineup at the far western edge of the British Isles. These waves were never on my doorstep growing up, but now they're home. It's late September and the waters of Sennen Cove are a balmy 66°F (19°C). The sun is still warm. There are just a few of us surfing, trading lefts in the middle of the beach. All around there is raw, rugged beauty – from the weathered granite cliffs at the far end of the bay to the Brisons, two islets that, from a certain vantage point, resemble a horizontal Charles de Gaulle. The sea is crystal clear. It always is here in the far west.

I've just paddled back out. I'm sitting on my board, waiting, when suddenly there's an almighty splash. A dolphin has breached, almost close enough to touch. Airborne for an instant, it's underwater again, surging rhythmically away. Seconds later, there's another. We whoop and shout and crane our necks, trying to anticipate where they'll next appear. But when they break the surface, they're far away. And our eyes are now drawn to a set on the horizon.

A 3ft green-blue wall heads straight for me. I take off, and just as I look along the face, there's an explosive burst of grey, blue and silver, angling down the wave. It's a dolphin, surfing the same wave. I trim to the left, standing, watching the dolphin ahead of me, letting the wave carry us both and wishing that this moment would last forever.

In 35 years of surfing, the best oceanic experiences of my life have happened in easy reach of my home in Cornwall. Sennen Cove is the mainland UK's most westerly beach, a wild and magical place, pummelled by swell all year and with a setup that's perfect for all types of surfers: longboarders, pro surfers like Sam Bleakley and James Parry, and shortboard rippers like ex-pro boxer

Sam Smart. Sennen Cove, 290 miles (467km) from London, is a broad church. The beach faces northwest and stretches in an arc, from the village houses near the harbour breakwater on the left to the northern end, the less accessible area known as Gwenver. To follow this trajectory is to go from beginner-grade waves to serious surf of excellent quality. Gwenver itself – or Spot G, as it was known for many years, even after it had been outed – is one of the best beach breaks in Europe, let alone the UK.

Putting down surf roots here involved following a well-worn route through many of Southwest England's surf hubs. My teens were spent surfing north Devon's waves, before trips to Cornwall took

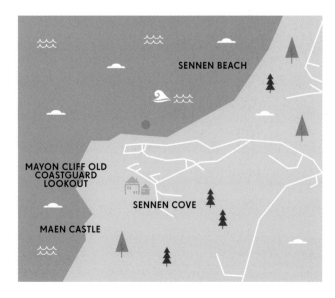

over. Inevitably, that meant a lot of sessions at England's surf city, Newquay. Fun, hectic, packed, competitive – Newquay is where surfing in the UK began. I loved my visits there; in Newquay, there's surf culture at every turn. But the far west was calling. There was something in me that instinctively responded to the remoteness of the UK's weatherbeaten southwest tip.

I was always in search of the empty lineup. I first came to Sennen in my early 20s and felt, at once, that it was home. It wasn't just the glistening white sand and exposure to swell (the old saying is right – if there's no swell at Sennen and Gwenver, there's none anywhere). It was the landscape: secluded coves, high moors dotted with holy wells and stone circles, windswept cliff walks, abandoned tin mines and, everywhere, the sea.

In Sennen, there is also a strong sense of history intermingled with the wildness. DH Lawrence lived nearby, Virginia Woolf spent summer holidays at Talland House in nearby St Ives; artists and sculptors such as Terry and Anthony Frost, Patrick Heron, Roger Hilton, Barbara Hepworth and Peter Lanyon are but a few of a long list who have lived and worked in the area.

The wild west was also the setting for the UK's first (and only) surfing village. Chris Tyler, an ex-architect, ex-trawlerman and surfer, set up the Skewjack Surf Village in 1971 as a surf camp and focal point for surfers in the southwest. A short way inland from Sennen Cove, its heyday was in the mid-1970s, with the BBC turning up to film an episode of *Holiday '76* there. Though it closed in 1986, Skewjack's legacy of bonhomie is alive and well. This is a place where surfing is chilled and localism is frowned upon.

"The far west was the place I surfed with my sons, whose favourite move was to drop in on me"

It took time for me to relocate – some 15 years, in fact. Finally, when I was 40, I settled in the village of Porthcurno, just along the coast from Sennen Cove. With my sons, I've surfed every swell going. We'd paddle out in thick pea-soup winter fog, we'd paddle out on bright summer evenings; sometimes we'd paddle out when there was barely a ripple. The point was to be in the sea. Surprisingly often, we'd find an empty lineup.

Sure, Porthleven – England's best right-hand reef break – is a 30-minute drive away. Yes, there are still secret reefs and points, even in Cornwall. I've ridden bigger, more consistent (and warmer) waves in Portugal, Australia and Costa Rica. But the far west became the place that I surfed time and again with my sons, whose favourite move was to drop in on me.

It was actually at Gwenver that I felt I'd found the meaning of surfing (if there is one). It was a summer's evening and, for some reason, no one was surfing. Some basking sharks were out to sea, families were playing on the sand. There are 500 steps from the car park above Gwenver to the beach; from the top, I could see the beginnings of a swell. I made it down the steps in record time.

Once on the shore I realised I didn't have the beautifully shaped, 3ft waves to myself: a woman was just about to reach the lineup. Turned out I knew her, a little. We spent that evening taking turns, riding perfect peeling left after perfect peeling left. We didn't say much. The next time I saw her was two full years later. And we both remembered that evening with complete clarity, as the best surf we'd ever had. This surf session had created a special shared experience between people who barely knew each other.

Clockwise from left: Sennen's small-wave days are great for beginners; the Cornwall coast is the surf capital of the UK; quality waves roll in past Cape Cornwall. Previous page: British pro George Carpenter surfs Sennen Cove

ORIENTATION

Type of wave // Beach break.
Best conditions // September and October are prime months, when the sea is at its warmest, and there's swell.
Nearest town // The tiny town of St Just is a 15-minute drive north.
Getting there // Sennen Cove is at the end of the line – it's a 5½-hour drive west from London (or, an hour further from the capital than Newquay).
Where to stay // Sennen's Old Success pub has rooms, good food, and waves on its doorstep. Above Gwenver beach there's camping Trevedra Farm campsite.
Things to know // As with all beach breaks, the rips will be strong on big days. Don't try and park in the cove in the summer – it'll be rammed. Instead, park in the field above the cove and walk down to the beach.

Opposite, clockwise from top left:
Newquay's surfers turn Santa for
the Run and Surf event at Fistral
Beach; Croyde Bay has a wilder
feel; the waves roll in at Fistral Bay

MORE LIKE THIS
ENGLAND'S MOST ICONIC

SCARBOROUGH, YORKSHIRE

Scarborough is one northern England's surfing hubs. The town touts itself as the oldest seaside resort in the country, and people have been taking to the waters here since the 17th century – although surfing only arrived in the late 1960s and didn't really take off until the '80s. It's no wonder Scarborough has the widest selection of surf shops on the UK's North Sea coast: North Bay is the most consistent of the town's two bays, picking up northerly swells and big southeasterly swells, which break beneath Scarborough Castle. South Bay has beach breaks and a fast, right-hand reef at its south end and, like its northerly cousin, is best from low to mid tide. If you want the traditional English seaside experience after your sesh, check out the eclectic mix of donkey rides, blaring amusement arcades, and the elegant Grand Hotel (once the largest in Europe) above the beach.

Nearest town // Scarborough

FISTRAL BAY, CORNWALL

The UK's best-known surf spot may be a bit of a zoo, but that's because everyone and their brother now knows it has consistent, quality surf all year round – so much so that it attracts the WSL Boardmasters Festival every August. However, you'll share the surf with everyone from some of the best surfers in the country to screaming kids on boogie boards and grandparents on wooden belly boards. Surfing in the UK actually began in Newquay: to judge from old holiday advertisements, people have been riding belly boards here since the 1930s, and Malibu boards were introduced by Aussie lifeguards in the early '60s. There are now such close ties between the Newquay and Australian surf scenes that some say the local surfers are developing a slight Aussie twang in their warm Cornish lilt.

Nearest town // Newquay

CROYDE BAY, DEVON

As the nearest quality wave to London, as well as the other main cities of southern England, Croyde Bay is invariably crowded. But Croyde and the surrounding villages are classic old England – thatched-roof cottages, sunken lanes, high hedgerows and rolling hills – and surfing seems to fit in very nicely here. Indeed, Croyde and the nearby towns of Braunton and Woolacombe rely heavily on the sport for their income, with a wide selection of surf shops, surf schools and board and wetsuit manufacturers. Croyde has a range of breaks, from punchy low tide beach breaks (it's reputedly the fastest low tide wave in England) to more mellow waves as the tide rises. There are also a couple of challenging reef breaks and, close by, Saunton Sands, one of the most popular longboard waves in the UK.

Nearest town // Croyde

SUPERTUBOS

Portugal's heavy and unforgiving beach break is not the place to make mistakes. Stuart Butler found out the hard way.

The first time I surfed Supertubos, the wave snapped my leash. Twice in the same session. I think the name may be Portuguese for unforgiving.

It's a wave with a small margin for error. Of course, the technical tubes require focus, but the lineup also requires a certain brand of confidence. Weakness can be sensed and, somehow, seems to affect your entire session. Breaking my leash was not exactly helping.

As I paddled toward the lineup, there was already a thick crowd of wave-hungry locals. The elite crews have become masters at ensuring they get all the choice tubes. Supertubos is a place where the slightest hesitation or mistake will be noted by the others in the lineup, and likely bump you to the back of the wave waiting list, no matter how long you've been out there.

But the waves here also break close to shore so, if you time it right, it can be an easy paddle to get into position. I, however, didn't time it right. A 6ft set thundered in out of the Atlantic before I'd made it out back, and detonated right on top of me. I was

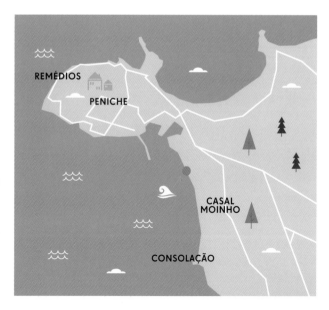

pushed hard toward the seabed, then washed right back up onto the beach I'd come from. My leash had snapped as easily as a pasta noodle.

Humiliated, I trudged back to the car, hopeful I had packed a spare. There wasn't one. I peeled off my wetsuit and raced into nearby Peniche, a small fishing town with ancient whitewashed buildings, a 16th-century fortress and, thankfully, a lot of surf shops. I bolted into the first one I found, bought another leash and floored it back to the beach. At this point, I was hungry for redemption.

Not all waves deserve this sort of single-minded determination. But Supertubos is something special. This world-class beach break near Peniche, about 1½ hours north of Lisbon, is a heavy wave that breaks remarkably close to shore, with a ferocity felt even by those standing on the sand. Supertubos is highly sandbar-dependent and it often closes out. But those who are skilled enough to snag the right one – and patient enough to earn a spot in the pecking order – are rewarded with a heaving cavern of water that spits you out in bliss.

Central Portugal is also known for its versatility, with a wave always worth surfing somewhere. On small-swell summer days with light winds, the beaches on the northern side of the peninsula – such as Praia do Baleal – gather plenty of swell drifting in from the North Atlantic. A meatier swell favours the southern side of the peninsula, where Supertubos is located.

I witnessed this myself when I first came to Peniche. Arriving at the beaches on the northern side of the peninsula, I had to cower behind the lip of a sand dune to shelter from a harsh north wind, which was churning the ocean into an angry, boiling mass of slate-grey waves. But to improve my situation I simply had to scoot over to the southern side of Peniche's small hammer-shaped peninsula, where that same north wind was funnelling straight offshore, catching the lip of each approaching wave and holding it up just right into a beautiful, spinning, hollow lefthander.

There's no shortage of local ocean knowledge in this part of Portugal. This former fishing town is made up of salty seafarers and their offspring, who have graciously welcomed an onslaught of surfers in the last couple of decades. In fact, surfing now drives most of Peniche's tourism. Post-session, locals and tourists alike mix around the central square: children kick footballs around and adults drift from bar to bar, snacking on freshly barbecued sardines.

Surfers flock here not just for Supertubos, but for a string of coastline offering several different experiences. Ericeira, 40 miles (64km) south of Peniche, is a charming town, piled high onto cliffs overlooking its beautiful coves. Legendry spots like the long, hollow right point of Coxos and the slab of left-hand reef at Pedra Branca (White Rock) are easily two of the country's most famous breaks.

Back at Supertubos with my new leash, I slipped back into my cold and sandy wetsuit. I began the paddle, paying more attention

LATE BLOOMER

Portugal's first recorded surfer was Pedro Martins de Lima, who used a board he'd bought in France to paddle out at Estoril, near Lisbon, in 1959; he was still surfing aged 80-plus! Portuguese surfing spread slowly, though, and didn't reach Peniche until 1964. But by the early '70s, foreign surfers – often travelling in VW Kombis – started turning up. The first major surf competition was held at Peniche in 1977; since then, the area's surf industry has exploded.

Clockwise from right: Studying the setup at Peniche; Brazilian pro Italo Ferreira takes the top prize at the Rip Curl Pro; a classic Iberian sunset. Previous spread from left: Brazilian surfer Gabriel Medina competes in the quarter finals of the Rip Curl Pro Portugal at Supertubos; shortboards are the preferred equipment on Portugal's most technical tube

to the incoming sets, and made it outside without incident. As if on cue, another peak even started to work slightly down the beach, which dispersed the crowds a little.

A set approached, but a local surfer slid into the first silky wave and tucked straight into a barrel. The next wave was a little larger and angled slightly more to the north – it was heading straight for me. I turned, made two or three easy paddle-strokes until I felt the wave pick me up. I dropped in and made one easy bottom turn as the wave stood tall. In front of me, the lip pitched – a rare invitation into the tube.

Once on it, it was a surprisingly simple wave to ride. I don't remember having to do anything but lean into it and enjoy the moment. Eventually, I was blasted cleanly out onto the shoulder. A smile wrapped around my face.

But as I turned to paddle back out, Supertubos was there to collect on what it had just given me. A new set came crashing down on top of me, ripping the board out of my hands. Then, I felt the familiar tug on my ankle. I had, once again, snapped my leash. No wonder the surf shops in Peniche are thriving.

"Those skilled enough to snag the right wave are rewarded with a heaving cavern of water that spits you out in bliss"

ORIENTATION

Type of wave // Beach break, where the lefts tend to be better than the rights.
Best conditions // 6ft-plus, swell from the southwest with northeast winds.
Nearest town // Peniche.
Getting there // Peniche is 60 miles (96km) north of Lisbon.
Where to stay // There are numerous surf camps, campsites and hotels. Baleal Surf Camp (balealsurfcamp .com) has a prime location overlooking the mellow waves of Baleal Beach.
Things to know // Supertubos might be a beach break, but don't underestimate how heavy it can get. Perfect conditions are not that common; closeouts are. Bring spare leashes. When it's good, expect heavy crowds – and a talented local crew, who ensure they get the pick of the waves.

Opposite: Sagres in southwest Portugal is famous for sun, spectacular coastal views and serious surf

MORE LIKE THIS
THE BEST OF PORTUGAL

COSTA DA CAPARICA

The Portuguese capital, Lisbon, might not seem like an obvious surfers' paradise, but this is a city with saltwater coursing through its veins. Stretching both south and west of the city are dozens of beaches, headlands and coves, facing all directions and working in almost all conditions. Take the regular ferries over to the southern side of the Tejo River, along which Lisbon is built, and you'll come to the beaches of the Costa da Caparica. Divided from each other by small jetties, each of the beaches can get swell. Head west of the city, though, and things become even more interesting as small seaside suburbs have beach, reef and point breaks, each with their own devoted local crew. The best-known is Carcavelos, a thick-lipped shore break that can get epic in decent west or southwest swell. Further west is Praia do Guincho, a beach break which makes the most of small summer swells.
Nearest town // Lisbon

TONEL

On the southwest tip of Portugal, in an area where many Portuguese take their holidays, the small town of Sagres is home to some superb waves, which break in a huge variety of conditions. Tonel is the most consistent. It's a quality beach break with a huge rock in the centre of the sand. On bigger swells the wedgy beach break peaks of Beliche will start to work. Very popular with bodyboarders, this is probably the best of the more consistent spots. There are many other semi-secret beaches, points and reefs in the vicinity, with something for almost all wind, swell and tide conditions.
Nearest town // Sagres

MOLEDO DO MINHO

There aren't many parts of Western Europe that could really be considered unexplored in terms of surfing. However, the Minho region in the far northwest of Portugal, abutting the Spanish region of Galicia, still feels pretty darn out there. There are no standout, world-renowned spots here, but with dramatic, forested hills tumbling down to a rugged and jutting coastline, there is plenty of spicy variety. Highlights include Moledo do Minho and Vila Praia de Âncora. These are spots where you will find yourself wondering if the wave just around the next corner could be a perfect, empty point break. Just make sure you pack a good wetsuit (the water is cold even in high summer), and give yourself plenty of time. It's a great area to explore in a camper van.
Nearest town // Porto

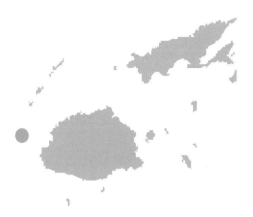

CLOUDBREAK

William Finnegan surveyed a lifetime of incredible surf adventures in his Pulitzer prize-winning memoir, Barbarian Days. Here, he reveals the wave that haunts him most.

I sulked for decades, basically, before I broke down and returned to Tavarua, a tiny island in western Fiji that gets some of the best waves in the world. I first washed up there in 1978 with my friend Bryan Di Salvatore. We had been bushwhacking through the South Pacific, searching for rideable waves, for months. We first saw Tavarua from a mountainside maybe 5 miles (8km) away. The island, a little sand-ringed patch of forest, was uninhabited, and the waves wrapping around its western shore were a surfer's fever dream come to life. We got village fisherfolk to ferry us out there. We camped, resupplied with fresh water each week by our mystified friends the fisherfolk, who had never seen a surfboard before. To my knowledge,

only two people had surfed Tavarua before we did. Bryan and I rode it in all conditions, big and small, rough-edged and immaculate. It was a long, fast, shallow and virtually flawless left. On good days, it was the best wave either of us had ever seen.

So we felt a certain protectiveness, in the painfully overcrowded world of surfing, toward this precious secret. We never told a soul where it was. We used a generic nickname even when we talked about it with one another. And we were therefore disappointed, to put it mildly, five years later when we found Tavarua splashed across the cover of a surf magazine. It seemed that American entrepreneurs had built a hotel, catering to surfers, on the island. They had also

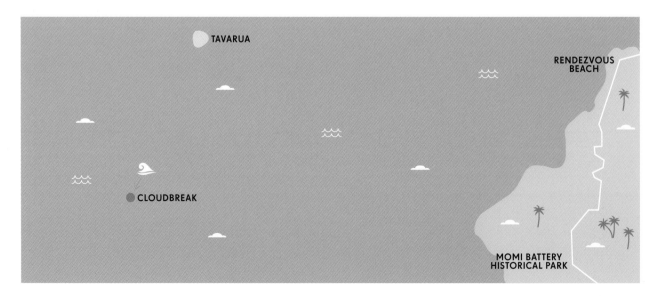

discovered a second great wave, on an offshore reef, which they called Cloudbreak. (They called the island wave, of all things, Restaurants.) The resort's pitch was something new in the world of surfing: paying guests would have exclusive access to the waves. An enforcement deal with local government ensured that anyone else who appeared at either spot would be driven away.

This was appalling on so many levels. I visited the resort once as a journalist, but ended up publishing nothing. It's a modest, low-impact establishment, yet it was deeply jarring to be there. A gift shop sold branded hats, T-shirts, coffee cups. Workers stayed in huts back in the jungle, in a semi-traditional village setup. The Fijians who remembered me laughed at me – I was the American who had failed to build a hotel. They all had jobs there now.

But my principled objections to the privatisation of Tavarua's waves weakened over time. It was politically indefensible, yes, but... life is short. The video clips of Cloudbreak were amazing. It was bigger and heavier than the island wave's reeling perfection, and now, in middle age, I could actually afford to spend a week there. I finally swallowed my pride and ethical objections and in 2002 I went, as a paying guest, to Tavarua. And I went again the next year, and the next, and the next, always in the heart of the southern winter swell-season. Bryan was magnanimous. He wanted detailed reports.

So, Cloudbreak. You need a boat to get out there. It's roughly 2 miles (3km) south of Tavarua (people are surprised to hear that we never noticed it back in the day, but we weren't even close). It's another long, fast left, with another unforgiving coral reef waiting just under the surface on the inside sections. Cloudbreak is not, however, simply bigger and more powerful than the island wave. It's fundamentally different. The reef, known locally as Naikuru Kuru Mailangi (Thundercloud Reef), is vast, and sits in a far more exposed position than Tavarua, receiving open-ocean swells from the south and the west and everywhere in between, unobstructed. This means that Cloudbreak is far more consistent than the island – there's almost always something breaking out there – and that it's often being hit by multiple swells generated by different faraway storms. The lineup, as a result, can be exceedingly complex.

I mentioned the mesmerising video clips, which virtually anyone interested in surfing has etched on the YouTube part of their brain. Those clips are misleading, simply because they're all shot either on super-clean days or giant days – or, most misleadingly, on super-clean giant days, which are extremely rare. Those days may happen only a few times per decade. In truth, Cloudbreak is usually kind of funky. You never know what you're going to find out there, which is one of the things I love about it. In photos and videos, it's always fierce and groomed. But it's often not fierce, nor groomed.

This disparity, between the stunning representations and the day-to-day reality of a great surf spot, is standard, of course. Still, it's unusually stark at Cloudbreak. That's because the spot is so consistent, and so exposed, and its finer iterations are so sublime. I've had sublime sessions there myself – some of the most exhilarating waves of a long surfing life, even though it's on my

"The island was unhinhabited and the waves wrapping around its western shore were a surfer's fever dream"

backhand. I've also had great sessions when it was crossed up, shifty, shouldering, closing out, and yet I somehow found magnificent waves tucked in among the dross. The place has more moods, more aspects, than any other surf spot I know. It can go, in a couple of hours, from mellow to scary, from junky to supreme, as a swell fills in and the wind clocks offshore.

There are constants. The reef, naturally, whose contours you can learn. The lineup markers – meaning, primarily, a dilapidated old judges' tower built for contests on the inside reef, and the mountains of Viti Levu, Fiji's main island, 5 miles (8km) to the east. (Those are the mountains from which Bryan and I first beheld Tavarua.) At extreme low tides, parts of the reef emerge and village women suddenly appear, walking on the exposed coral, collecting octopus, shellfish, and sea cucumber. They live in Momi and Nabila, on Viti Levu, and they're here for the long haul.

But the real constant, for a surfer, is surprise. Cloudbreak has so many faces, so many moods, that nearly every session is memorable, nearly always in a different way.

One large thing has changed. The government ended its surf exclusivity agreement with the Tavarua resort in 2010. Now anyone who can get out there can surf Cloudbreak or the island wave. Fijians can at last surf their own waves freely.

I've been back just once since the reefs were opened to the public. On good days, the crowds were pretty bad. It felt like other hotspots – the Mentawais come to mind – where outmanoeuvring the mobs becomes the main focus of a trip all too easily. Sadly, I swore off Tavarua again. Friends keep going, though, and they often come back raving about great sessions. I really miss Cloudbreak. So now, I must admit, I'm on the verge of returning. When you know a spot, you can always pick off waves, even in a crowd.

Clockwise from top left: Tavarua Island Resort is hallowed ground for surf travellers; Australian pro Laura Enever at the 2016 Fiji Women's Pro; better under the wave than caught inside. Previous page: Patagonia Surf Ambassador Dan Ross makes it look easy at Cloudbreak

ORIENTATION

Type of wave // Left-hand reef break.
Best conditions // South-southeasterly swell, east-southeasterly trade winds. Breaks at all tides, all seasons, but best at low tide and between February and October.
Nearest town // Nadi, on the Fijian main island.
Getting there // Visiting surfers will land at Nadi International Airport; there are regular bus and ferry transfers to islands in the Mamanuca chain (including Tavarua itself). The wave is best accessed by boat.
Where to stay // The islands surrounding Tavarua – Malolo, in particular – are full of affordable and insanely expensive options. That said, staying on Tavarua itself is still considered a bucket-list surf experience.
Things to know // It's often said that Cloudbreak works whether it's 3ft or 20ft, which is why most Cloudbreak veterens suggest bringing no fewer than three boards.

*Opposite: Swimming Pools on
Namotu Island is considered one
of Fiji's more accessible breaks.
Previous spread: Hawaiian big-wave
master Kai Lenny sits back and
enjoys the ride at Cloudbreak*

MORE LIKE THIS
FIJI'S LESS FEARSOME SURF

SWIMMING POOLS, NAMOTU ISLAND

Tavarua is part of the Mamanuca archipelago, off the western coast of Fiji's main island, Viti Levu. Just northwest of Tavarua, the much smaller Namotu island is home to several of the country's most iconic waves, including Swimming Pools and Wilkes. Swimming Pools, off the southern tip of Namotu, is often referred to as one of the best beginner reef breaks in the Mamanuca chain – even family friendly – with an ideal swell size between 3ft and 6ft. Conditions need to be just right for it to light up – northwest-westerly winds at mid tide – but when it does, it offers some of the thrill without quite as much consequence. There is not much on the island itself – like Tavarua, the Namotu Island resort once held exclusive rights to the waves – but the reef surrounding the island is now a popular destination for boat charters.

Nearest town // Nadi

NAMOTU LEFT, NAMOTU ISLAND

Considered by many to the best longboard wave in Fiji, this reef break off the northwest tip of Namotu is far more forgiving than Cloudbreak or Restaurants, thanks to deeper water and less exposure to the razor-sharp reef. It's a spot where you are as likely to run into stand-up paddleboarders as you are shortboarders, and everything in between. At its best between 3ft and 5ft, Namotu Left hits prime conditions on an incoming low tide, south-southwest swell, and east-northeast winds. But don't be fooled: the rip at low and high tide is no joke and, like most reef breaks in the Mamanucas, it's a different beast altogether in bigger swell.

Nearest town // Nadi

SIGATOKA, CORAL COAST

You don't need to be immortal to surf Fiji, but you do need to know where to find manageable swell. The Coral Coast along southern Viti Levu is home to some of Fiji's only beach breaks. This means it's also home to some of the country's most accessible waves and surf schools. Sigatoka is most consistent, with long lefts *and* rights. Just like all waves in this part of the South Pacific, waves in the area can also get pretty heavy, providing plenty of challenge for shortboarders. Best during low tide, small swells and light winds, the area around Sigatoka is surrounded by fun breaks. Meanwhile, the entire southern coast is lined with brilliant white-sand beaches, secluded bays, and affordable resorts. Much of the island's non-surf tourism is centred here and there are a lot of non-surf adventures on the menu, such as snorkelling, scuba diving and Sigatoka River safaris.

Nearest town // Sigatoka

NOOSA

When Janna Irons landed in this cool corner of Australia's Sunshine Coast, she discovered the surf trifecta: a laid-back town, neighbouring a national park, with world-class waves.

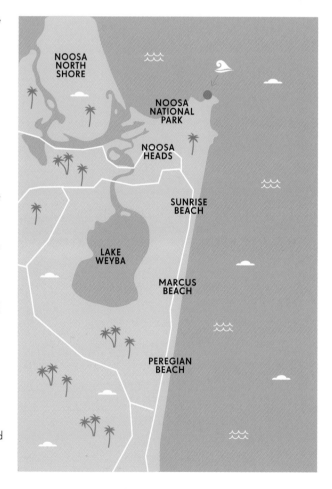

It was only my first wave, but by the time I'd paddled back to the lineup, I had already mentally composed the email to my boss explaining that I wasn't returning to work the following week. That's all it took – just one single wave at Tea Tree, in Noosa National Park on Australia's Sunshine Coast. I'd calculated that I could scrape together just enough money from writing at night to rent an apartment in town and then just surf here forever.

Of course, I wasn't the first to see the light. Australian shaper Bob McTavish once said that 'surfing Tea Tree Bay is like having a cup of tea with god.' After riding that very first wave, I understood exactly what he was talking about: its racy takeoff slowed at just the right moment, allowing for a perfectly timed arcing turn, before sloping to the ideal angle for the noseride of your life.

Tea Tree is just one of a half-dozen right-hand point breaks along this stretch of coastline. Located 90 miles (145km) north of Brisbane, Noosa is known for its pristine beaches, warm temperatures and near-perfect surf. Where Australia's Gold Coast is a magnet for pros, aggressive shortboarders and nightclubbers, this area feels decidedly relaxed, with its laid-back surf towns, farmers markets and station wagons with longboards strapped to the roof.

When I arrived, I parked in the shady lot where the road deadends into a thick forest. Out front, at a break called Nationals, jade-coloured head-high waves peeled across a sandy bottom. I stared in awe as I hastily slathered on sunscreen and untied boards from the roof of my car. 'Come on', my friend said. 'Tea Tree will be even better.'

We raced down the eucalyptus-lined path, my heavy longboard tucked under my arm, sweat threatening my tenuous grip on the rail, my bare feet burning on the hot black asphalt. As I rounded

the bend, I caught a glimpse of the point, a replica of doodles I'd made in the margin of my high school notebooks. A small group of tourists gathered at the lookout, but their eyes were trained away from the waves. I followed their gaze to the low branches of a gum tree, where a koala snuggled into its bough, uninterested. To see wildlife this close, while on the way to surf, hardly seemed like real life.

The Noosa point breaks are a short stroll from the town of Noosa Heads, in the coastal section of the dense, 15-sq-mile (40 sq km) Noosa National Park. This is Australia's most popular park, attracting more than a million visitors each year, who come to hike, spot rare Australian birds and marsupials, and try to catch a glimpse of migrating humpback whales. From each of Noosa's breaks, you can stare into this lush, carefully preserved wilderness.

A favourite for shortboarders is Granite, a 15-minute walk beyond Tea Tree. Little Cove, Johnsons and Nationals are closer to town, each spot producing world-class peelers. First Point, just a stone's throw from Noosa Heads' main street, is easiest to reach from town and, therefore, usually the most crowded. It's one of the best longboard waves in the world, with the perfect speed and slope for endless noserides.

It was during this trip that I also discovered what some would argue is Australia's finest contribution to surfing: après. After a long, early afternoon session in the water, I followed my friends to a wide, two-storey building at the edge of the sand. The Noosa Heads Surf Lifesaving Club, like all surf clubs in Australia, offers cold beers, good food and, most importantly, prime viewing of the lineup from a massive covered deck (I'm still waiting for this to arrive in the US; it's something our skiers discovered long ago). Here, friends relive their session over a few pints, watch conditions evolve, and decide whether they've had one too many to go back out.

Just behind Noosa's Surf Club, running parallel to Main Beach, is Hastings Street. This once quirky surf enclave is now a quaint yet classy downtown full of shops, high-end boutiques, cafés, gourmet restaurants and a few upscale hotels. It's become a destination not only for surfers but also for Australian tourists from the south escaping the cold. These days, kids lap at ice-cream cones and hipsters sip fair-trade coffee. One often assumes that living so close to great surf requires compromise, but Noosa's nearby nature, mellow nightlife and artsy, cosmopolitan feel made me think otherwise.

We, of course, couldn't afford the pricey lodgings that line the beach, or even the condo rentals that fill Little Cove, so we opted to stay at Halse Lodge, a historic guesthouse built in the 1880s that was converted into a youth hostel a hundred years later. Halse offered a shared room for $25 a night (a rate that rarely goes up), allowing surfers to share a room with wave-obsessed backpackers from all over the world, who will no doubt party late and snore loudly. But with First Point so close at hand, I would have paid $25 for a cardboard box.

SAVING OUR SURF

Every February, longboarders from around the world travel to Noosa to compete in the Noosa Festival of Surfing, the biggest contest in the world in terms of number of competitors. Noosa's status as one of the world's premier longboard waves helped solidify it as one of only 11 World Surfing Reserves, a designation that recognizes surf spots for their outstanding waves and surrounding environments, and seeks to protect them for future generations.

Clockwise from top left: the Noosa area has breaks for every type of surfer; koalas are a common sight in Noosa National Park; Noosa Heads is the sort of surf town you want to move to. Previous page: Noosa's protected coastline

"In the gum tree, a koala snuggled into its bough. To see wildlife this close, while on the way to surf, hardly felt like real life"

Each morning, we'd wake up, check the tide, and carefully arrange our surf sessions to maximise our time in the water: an early surf as the tide came in, lunch and naps mid-day (just long enough to forget about our rashed knees and bruised ribs), before another marathon session as the tide went out. At night, we'd watch a surf rock band with bad haircuts play at the Surf Club and dance until they kicked us out, all of us still salty and smelling of zinc and Sex Wax.

There are those surf spots, scattered around the globe, that are so perfect you're willing to do nearly anything to surf them – endure stifling heat or cold, embark on long treks down washed-out dirt roads, stay in sketchy accommodation. More often than not, there is nothing to do in a great surf spot but, well, surf. That's certainly not a bad thing, but when you find a place that lives up to your surf dreams *and* your non-surf dreams – all next door to a national park, no less – you start to wonder if there's really a reason to compromise ever again.

ORIENTATION

Type of wave // Right point break.
Best conditions // January through March; east-northeast swells, on a medium tide.
Nearest town // Noosa Heads.
Getting there // Brisbane International airport is 85 miles (135km) to the south of Noosa.
Where to stay // Halse Lodge is an affordable option; there are also hotels and condo rentals on Hastings Street.
Things to know // Noosa can get very crowded with very experienced longboarders. If First Point is flat, keep walking. As you follow the boardwalk toward the national park, the surf gets progressively larger as you approach Granite Bay. Beyond Granite is Alexandria Bay, a protected cove that can pick up swell when other spots are flat.

Noosa

Opposite: Shi Shi Beach in Washington state's Olympic National Park promises surf and solitude – but you'll need to hike in to find it

MORE LIKE THIS
NATIONAL PARK SURF SPOTS

SHI SHI BEACH, OLYMPIC NATIONAL PARK, WASHINGTON

A little less than a five hour drive from Seattle, Washington, at the northwest tip of the US, is a rugged and remote headland that sits just across the Salish Sea from Canada. This is also the northwestern tip of Olympic National Park, where the Shi Shi (pronounced 'shy-shy') Beach trailhead leads to one of America's wildest surf settings. After leaving the Makah Indian Reservation, it's a pleasant 2-mile (3km) walk through rainforest to reach a bluff overlooking the Pacific Ocean, and an isolated beach break. You'll need a permit if you plan on camping – it's a lengthy day-trip – but even a short session here is worthwhile, as it's very likely you'll have the surf all to yourself. It's unpredictable, but you can stack the odds in your favour by going on a northwest swell. Pack a 4-5mm wetsuit, with hood, booties and gloves to stave off the perennial cold, and enjoy the solitude.
Nearest town // Neah Bay

GARIE BEACH, ROYAL NATIONAL PARK, AUSTRALIA

Just an hour southwest of the Sydney Opera House, Garie Beach lies within the boundary of Royal National Park, one of the oldest national parks in the world. The Royal is replete with stunning coastline, from steep, rugged cliffs to 11 gorgeous beaches – all of which can get busy, due to their proximity to Sydney. A popular surf destination, Garie Beach has both reef and beach breaks, which deliver in most swell directions. Plus, Garie works year-round, offering a variety of punchy lefts and rights.
Nearest town // Sydney

BURLEIGH HEADS NATIONAL PARK, AUSTRALIA

Somewhat overshadowed by the recent creation of a 'superbank' man-made reef break, some 7 miles (11km) to the north, Queensland's Burleigh remains one of Australia's real surfing jewels. In fact, the 'Burleigh Barrel' – typically a transparent blue-green cylinder that grinds for 500ft at hyper-speed over hard-packed sand – was seen as one of surfing's greatest prizes throughout the '70s, '80s and '90s. It was also here that pro surfing exploded when the 1977 Stubbies Pro attracted an estimated crowd of 30,000. The bikini- and boardshort-clad fans that clambered on the boulders and under the Pandanus Palms lining the point proved that pro surfing had a future. It's also often overlooked that Burleigh's wave sits off a stunning headland of rainforest and eucalyptus groves, full of walking trails and prime whale-watching vistas.
Nearest town // Burleigh Heads

RED BLUFF

On a remote and magical stretch of coastline in Western Australia,
Ben Mondy discovers a wave he'll return to for the rest of his life.

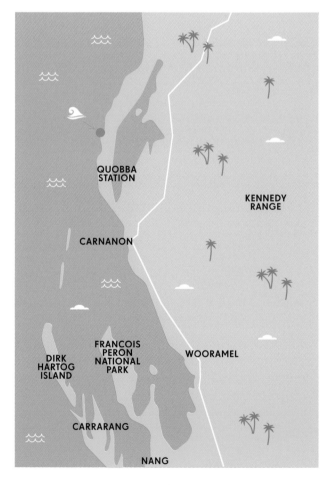

The journey ahead was already long, but suddenly it became much longer. Only 100 miles (160km) into our 850-mile (1368km) pilgrimage from Margaret River to Red Bluff, the cassette deck (Google it, kids) in my Ford XF Panel Van had decided to spool the magnetic tape into ribbons rather than play it.

The AM/FM radio had died many moons before – this was disastrous. The thought of the next 12 hours being sustained only by conversation with my two mates, the three of us wedged into the bench seat, was unbearable. Pablo, however, had a solution. He brought out his battered copy of *The Old Man and the Sea* and started reading aloud. Every three hours we would stop and shuffle the driver, reader and navigator roles.

Though there isn't much need for a navigator on this journey. After Perth, there is a 700 mile (1126km) stretch on Highway 1 that is ruler-straight and endless. The surf writer Kirk Owers recalled: 'You plant your foot on the gas, crank the stereo, and steer one-handed. Nothing happens along the way. You might see a dead kangaroo, a pack of dusty sheep, or a peripheral hallucination. Other than that, it's sand-plain and sky, sand-plain and sky.'

Except we couldn't crank the stereo. It was only in the last two hours, just as the sharks were killing Santiago's dreams in the book, that reading became impossible. From the town of Carnarvon to the working Quobba sheep station, the tarmac was replaced by a deeply corrugated dirt road, which threatened to dislodge our 10 surfboards, jerry cans of petrol, tubs of water and spare tyres on the roof.

If all this sounds extremely arduous, well, it was. However, for any surfer based in Margaret River, the pilgrimage is both annual and necessary. The Margaret River area is rightfully a world-class

Map labels: QUOBBA STATION, KENNEDY RANGE, CARNANON, FRANCOIS PERON NATIONAL PARK, WOORAMEL, DIRK HARTOG ISLAND, CARRARANG, NANG

surfing destination (the Main Break hosts an annual professional Championship Tour event). But within a short drive of that well-known wave, there are (arguably) more quality waves per square mile than any other coastal corridor on the planet.

But in winter, Margaret River transforms from a beautiful – albeit sometimes terrifying – swan into a very ugly duckling. Huge storms sweep in from the Indian Ocean, unleashing torrents of rain and persistent lashings of onshore wind that tear the giant waves into unrideable masses of untouchable fury. I've had weeks of my life soundtracked by the persistent drum of rain on a tin roof and the high-pitched roar of onshore gales ripping through the ancient Karri forests. Surfing isn't an option. Often, checking the surf isn't an option.

Yet, in Red Bluff, these same storms tee up perfection. After driving the better part of 1000 miles (1600km), when we rounded the corner into the sweeping bay, the grind of the southern winter and the gruelling journey immediately disappeared. The swell lines from the same storms that batter Margaret River had been transformed into clean, uniform sets. These lines were groomed by the predominant offshore breeze and basked under blue skies and a warm, but not hot, sun. It would be our home for the next four weeks.

Even though it always feels like it, we obviously weren't the first to make the trip. In the early 1970s, Margaret River surfers had heard reports of a perfect lefthander that corkscrewed off a huge red granite bluff way up north. The early pioneers initially camped in the caves that line the break, but as word got out and more and more surfers arrived for the winter, Quobba sheep station provided rudimentary facilities in exchange for a small fee. Their campsites were carved into the hill that slopes down to the white-sand beach; each site had a view of the bluff and the finger of rock that pokes out into the ocean, from which a perfect wave peels off.

The wave itself starts breaking at 4ft and holds up to a solid 10ft. A relatively easy drop leads into a 1000ft stretch of reef, most of which unfolds in the tube. The power of the Indian Ocean swells and the urchin covered reef means this is a challenging wave. Yet, the sheer perfection and predictability, where every wave behaves as the one that preceded it, widens the margin of error.

Halfway through our four-week stay on that first trip I saw Lars, who had first learned to surf on his gap-year trip to Australia, ride an eight-second barrel. His shriek of amazement at the end was recognition that he had achieved a feat that would ordinarily have been the preserve of expert surfers only.

Then, as of now, the camp remains without power or water. The toilets haven't changed, either; the holes dug deep in the ground are no place for the squeamish. We soon discovered careful rationing was needed. Having under-catered, the five-hour round-trip back over the rutted dirt track to Carnarvon was the longest beer and baked bean run I've ever done.

Luckily, it is the ocean that becomes your supermarket, as fresh fish becomes the staple of a very local diet. One evening, fishing

WHALE WATCHING

Each year, thousands of humpback whales migrate up and down the Western Australian coast via the so-called Humpback Highway. The whales often head to the Ningaloo Marine Park, located just 60 miles (96km) to the north of Red Bluff, and join the manta rays, giant turtles, elusive whale sharks and 500 species of tropical fish that reside there. The world's largest fringing reef, and a Unesco World Heritage Site, the park is a worthy diversion when the swell goes flat at Red Bluff.

Clockwise from top left: off-grid adventure; Red Bluff wave; motor out to the Humpback Highway. Previous page: an empty lineup awaits at Red Bluff

"The unrideable swell lines from the same storms that batter Margaret River have transformed here into clean, uniform sets"

off the rocks right near the wave, I hauled in a 30lb (14kg) cobia, only to have a group of reef sharks chase my catch almost on to the rocks. That night, we cooked the thick steaks over an open fire and fed 10 hungry surfers; knowing that they had almost been stolen by the ocean's apex predator made them taste even better.

Around 20 years ago, Monica and Reid Durrant, with the help of their eight kids, opened a small shop here. But while Mon's mango smoothies are good enough to almost justify the 10-hour car journey alone, and the Saturday pizza parties are legendary, the Red Bluff experience is still a unique, wild and raw one.

On that first trip, our gang of three eventually ran out of surfboards, fishing tackle, beans and money. It had been a month of epic waves, solid friendships and off-the-grid living. Yet, we knew that by now, Margaret River would have weathered the winter storms and returned to its natural surfing pleasure-dome status. The increasing desire to use a real toilet and drink cold beer was also a powerful motivator. So we packed up what was left of our provisions, wedged ourselves into the bench seat, and pointed the Panel Van south.

As soon as we made the transition from dirt track to smooth bitumen, Pablo cleared his throat and began: 'He was an old man who fished alone in the Gulf Stream and he had gone eighty-four days now without taking a fish...'

It was going to be an even longer trip back.

ORIENTATION

Type of wave // A 1000ft lefthander that tubes its entire length.

Best conditions // Southern Hemisphere winter (June to September).

Nearest town // Red Bluff is a 100 mile (160km) drive north of the town of Carnarvon, of which two-thirds is on a rough dirt road. Carnarvon is 600 miles (956km) north of Perth.

Getting there // Either fly into Perth and drive 10 hours north to Red Bluff, or fly into Carnarvon, from where it's a two-hour drive. A 4WD is preferable, but not essential.

Where to stay // There are unpowered and powered campsites, bungalows and shacks, all with views.

Things to know // The entry point to the wave is known as The Keyhole. On bigger swells, getting in and out can be a tricky negotiation.

*Opposite: just outside Kalbarri,
Jake's Point hosts a lot of local
talent*

MORE LIKE THIS
WAVES OF WESTERN AUSTRALIA

GNARALOO

Pronounced 'nar-loo', this is another wave located within the borders of Quobba Station, about 20 miles (32km) north of Red Bluff. While the landscape, abundant marine life and no-frills camping setup is identical to that at Red Bluff, the wave is a very different beast. Gnaraloo is a longer, warbling, more challenging mix of power, perfection and adrenalin that requires a high tide to cover the sharp coral reef that lies beneath. The wave comes out of deep water before unleashing on a shallow ledge and rifling down the line for 1500ft. Every few hundred feet or so the swell will shallow out again, with big steps in the wave signalling another very hollow section, which may not always be makeable. Not for the faint of heart (or intermediate surfer), Gnaraloo does however produce one of the most thrilling experiences of any wave in the world, in one of the most dramatic environments.

Nearest town // Carnarvon

JAKE'S POINT

Jake's Point is another perfect lefthander located on the remote northwest coast of Western Australia. While still 500 miles (805km) north of Perth, it is far less isolated than Red Bluff and Gnaraloo. The wave breaks at the end of a rocky platform located just outside the fishing town and tourist honeypot of Kalbarri. Its most famous surfing resident is pro Ry Craike, who, like most of Kalbarri's permanent residents, also makes a living from the crayfish industry and the abundant marine life that surrounds the wave. Short, powerful and perfect, the very small takeoff zone and the keen, hardened and talented locals can make this wave a difficult nut to crack for visitors. However, during the winter months (from June to September), the consistency of the large Indian Ocean swells means plenty of waves can be picked off from the pack. And with five-second tubes followed by a series of turn sections, one wave is all that's needed to keep you coming back for more.

Nearest town // Kalbarri

ROTTNEST ISLAND

For Perth surfers, Rottnest Island is a double-edged sword. For while it's only a 20 mile (32km) ferry ride from the Western Australian capital, and offers a wide range of quality waves in a pristine, untouched environment, it is Rottnest that blocks most of the Indian Ocean from reaching Perth in the first place. Nonetheless, 'Rotty', as it's known, provides a unique surfing experience. The protected nature reserve is home to the quokka, a small wallaby-like marsupial; it also has an array of white-sand beaches and a brace of quality reef breaks that pound into the island's secluded coves. The best of these are centred around Strickland Bay and Radar Reef, off Rottnest's far western tip.

Nearest town // Perth

BELLS BEACH

*When Chas Smith was barred from surfing one of his favourite waves in Australia,
it made him love it even more. It's also how he discovered something called Winkipop.*

When most people think of a surf town, they think of a place that is warm, palm-fringed, laid-back and perpetually sunbathed. And, yet, one of the most iconic surf towns on earth is none of the above. In fact, it actually challenges Detroit, Cleveland and England's Manchester for sheer blue-collar grit. It's a place where clouds hover low most days, bitter cold winds pierce in the winter, and hard-working men and women rise early and head off to factory jobs. Only in this town, those factories produce rubber wetsuits, shearling boots, T-shirts, trucker hats, board shorts, wristwatches that decipher the tides, and sandals that can open beer bottles.

Torquay, in Victoria, Australia, is the home of the once-mighty surf industry. Brands like Quiksilver, Rip Curl and Piping Hot were founded here. But, it's important to note, this was not by accident. It wasn't because Torquay is a population centre or a transportation hub. No, Torquay has gloomy weather, very few people, and only one way in and one way out. It was because Torquay has Bells Beach and one of the best waves in the whole wide world.

Now, I am not a blue-collar man, myself – and I'm not even Australian – but I have somehow woven myself into Torquay's fabric. You see, I had an unfortunate bust-up with an adored local pro that somehow made the news cycle, tying me, him, and this town together for as long as the internet exists. In fact, it caused Bells' most famous son, the Aboriginal surfboard shaper Maurice Cole, to call me a 'complete and total fuckwit'.

But my relationship with this wave itself transcends this incident. Despite it being a 17-hour flight from my home in Los Angeles, I have been fortunate to be able to surf Bells many times, as I would visit close friends who lived in Torquay as often as possible.

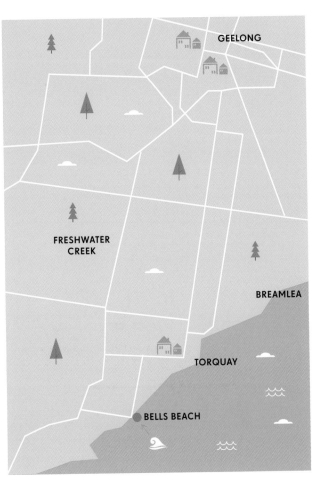

GEELONG

FRESHWATER
CREEK

BREAMLEA

TORQUAY

BELLS BEACH

I had navigated the strong wooden staircase that hugs the stark limestone cliff on many occasions, watching serious sets being pushed in by vicious Southern Ocean winter storms. Indeed, Bells works best when it's big, and it is regularly gifted 6ft to 8ft swells. It is not uncommon to see 15ft pulses. These are the days that separate the bold from the timid (or intelligent), when the timid (or intelligent) stand on the cliff, watching art meet carnage and wiggling their toes in their new shearling boots.

The wave isn't known for its barrel, and rarely does, but its racetrack face is wide, steep and strong. There are three main sections: Little Rincon, to the south; Outside Bells, which needs proper energy to break; and The Bowl, the most photographed and famous of the three. The Bowl hurtles toward the beach, begging for thigh-burning roundhouse cutbacks and rail-burying bottom turns.

While there is some debate as to where the wave got its name, certain historians claim it's after William Bell, a sailor who lived here in the 1840s; others insist it is named after John Calvert Bell, a rancher whose cattle grazed the headland. But there is no doubting its majesty. Standing on the cliffs and gazing out at it must be similar to visiting Jerusalem, Rome or Mecca for the faithful. It's a must-see, must-surf experience that will undoubtedly lead to some deep metaphysical understanding.

But the aforementioned bust-up actually led to a new discovery for me. I was in Torquay covering the Rip Curl Bells Beach Pro, which has taken place here every Easter weekend since 1962. At a party,

TRIBAL TRADITION

Bells Beach was once a meeting ground for the Aboriginal Wathaurong people, who would gather to trade supplies, fish the reef and hunt kangaroo. The Wathaurong are still a part of the Bells competition, as winners get their faces painted by elders in the traditional style. Bells also hosts the Australian Indigenous Surfing Titles every year – world-class surfers like Pipeline master Robbie Page have come up through its ranks.

I ran into a surf star who was furious with me because of a story I had written about him. He ended up saying a few things that he, hopefully, regrets. His main sponsor, Rip Curl, took notice.

The next morning, I drove the 4 miles (6km) from the centre of town toward Bells Beach, like I had so many times, just as the sun came up. I parked and gazed at the wave. I was just about to suit up and head down to surf when an event security guard told me to move along. The contest trials were set to begin soon and I wasn't even allowed to watch them, much less surf. I thought about walking the trail from Point Danger to Point Impossible. It's a gorgeous walk beside cypress trees, emerald grassy meadows, cackling magpies and nude Australians enjoying their lucky country's bounty. But I didn't feel like walking, so I returned to town for a drink and a reassessment.

Interestingly, my banning gave me a unique opportunity to explore the surrounding environs and to feel as close to the region's truth as a local. Many Bells old-timers are a nasty mess, those cold-climate grouchy types who mumble inaudibly in order to conserve energy. And make no doubt about it, Torquay is a very cold town, especially when Bells is working. Cold, grey and damp, but not without charm, the centre is cute in a classically Australian sort of way. Semi-modern with a main thoroughfare that turns into the Great Ocean Road, it's lined with cavernous Quiksilver, Rip Curl and Piping Hot stores alongside strip malls selling Ghanda and Super Duper.

The fact that the surf industry has been faltering for years, like the auto industry in Detroit, the train industry in Cleveland, and the cotton mills of Manchester, gives the town an extra poetic dash. It's got heart. Real heart and economic depression mixes with the pokies (slot machines), pubs, meat pies and pints of Victoria Bitter to create a tableau missing from the gilded tech metropolises of the future.

And getting banned from Bells is also how I discovered Winkipop. The great four-time world champion Mark Richards once called Bells a 'dud' and 'the most overrated wave in the world' – but he loved Winkipop. It may sound like one of the Teletubbies but Winkipop, just a short paddle east from Bells, is a hollow right that speeds along a section reef, and provides high-performance thrills as valuable, or important, as any. It doesn't hold the size that Bells can, but size ain't everything. I had my first session at Winkipop later that day.

But, still, all I could think about was Bells. It even made me wish I had brought two boards: the usual longer, more classically drawn thruster for Bells – the sort that Maurice Cole shaped for Tom Curren when he showed what was possible on that canvas – but also a high-performance shortboard for Winkipop.

I imagined I was Tom Curren on a Maurice Cole, anyhow, and wondered if Cole would ever forgive me for being a 'complete and total fuckwit', and shape me a board that would allow me to make art the next time I surfed Bells, too.

A boy can dream.

Clockwise from top left: Torquay is the long-time home of some iconic surf brands; Bells' stairway to heaven; the view from the cliffs is exhilarating; the Great Ocean Road's Memorial Archway. Previous page: it's not all grey at Bells Beach

"*Standing on the cliffs gazing out at Bells must be similar to visiting Jerusalem, Rome or Mecca for the faithful*"

ORIENTATION

Type of wave // Right-hand reef break.
Best conditions // April–September, when low-pressure Southern Ocean storms start churning. Works on all tides.
Nearest town // Torquay.
Getting there // Fly to Melbourne and hire a car; it's 60 miles (100km) from Melbourne to Torquay.
Where to stay // Torquay has a plethora of relatively low-cost hotels and motels.
Things to know // Bells is an iconic wave with hearty and skilled locals. As with most spots that have this sort of pedigree, respect is paramount. Bring a clean, classic board with traditional lines. A good thruster is a great fit for this wave.

Opposite: the Great Ocean Road's Twelve Apostles Marine National Park gives way to Port Campbell and the Easter Reef break

MORE LIKE THIS
AUSSIE COLD-WATER CLASSICS

EASTER REEF, VICTORIA

Easter Reef is one of Victoria's more rugged experts-only waves, but it's the perfect taste of true, beautiful, wild southern Australia. It is a cold-water reef break, a good 1500ft out to sea, that jacks to over 25ft during the Southern Hemisphere winter. It's dominated by a hearty local crew that put most surfers to shame. To get there, take the famous Great Ocean Road west from Torquay to Port Campbell (roughly 150 miles/250km). Driving the Great Ocean Road is a worthy adventure in itself. Easter Reef can be found just off the headlands outside Port Campbell, and is accessed either by a long paddle-out or by chartering a boat.
Nearest town // Port Campbell

WOOLAMAI, VICTORIA

Australia's surfing heritage is deep and pure, and some say it began right here at Cape Woolamai. Woolamai is a long, broad beach break that is part of Phillip Island's surfing reserve, and is a simple 1½-hour drive from Melbourne's St Kilda neighbourhood – a place famous for its smashed-avocado toast and flat whites. Adding to the accessiblilty, there is a car park, a wooden pathway leading to the beach and a relatively easy paddle-out to the shifting peaks that go left or right. It works best in Oz's winter, but also offers small, playful waves in the summer. Cape Woolamai's pink granite cliffs are also a highlight, and the beach is pristine.
Nearest town // Cape Woolamai, Phillip Island

MARTHA LAVINIA, TASMANIA

On a small island off Tasmania, the Martha Lavinia beach break – named after a ship that sank right out front – may not be in Victoria, but it's a popular spot for surfers from the southeast. Hovering halfway between Australia's mainland and the western edge of Tasmania, in the middle of the Bass Strait, King Island receives completely unfiltered Southern Ocean swell, and its waves are some of the most consistent in Tasmania. To get here, fly to the airport in Currie on King Island, then drive to its northernmost point (30 miles/48km). The wave is an epically fun peak, best in winter, and is uncrowded and pristine. There is parking near a lagoon, the paddle-out is easy, and the surfing is as exotic as it is fun. It's most consistent in the winter, but is windy and barren in the summer – bring a wetsuit.
Nearest town // Currie, King Island

BYRON BAY

When Alistair Klinkenberg discovered New South Wales' hippie surf utopia as a teenager, he thought he'd arrived home – and he's been coming back ever since.

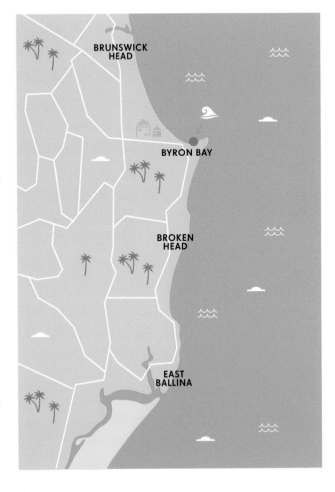

I was 14 the first time I surfed Byron Bay. It was 2004 and my family and I were on holiday from Southwest England. I had rolled into town in the back of my mum and stepdad's camper. At the time, I certainly looked the part: a thick mushroom cloud of sun-bleached hair, knitted brown sweater, worn jeans – basically, a country soul, 35 years too late. But even at that age, I felt like I'd been to Byron before. I'd read Nat Young's hedonistic autobiography about selling up in Sydney and moving here; and, when I was in Bali the previous year, I'd picked up a pirated copy of *Morning of the Earth*, which chronicled the Byron Bay surfers of the 1970s, escaping to off-grid tree houses, and living off pumpkins and endless right point breaks.

As I sat in the lineup as a teenager, my parents actually became concerned that I was spending too much time in the water. But then a crusty local leaned over and set them straight. 'Nah, he's not coming in', he told them. 'Why would he, he's having the time of his life.' My parents haven't said a bad word about surfing since.

Some 15 years have passed since that winter when we spent the month camping at the Broken Head campsite, but I've been coming here ever since. In fact, I've even spent months at a time here (especially once we moved to Sydney a few years later). In the meantime, Byron Bay – with a population that hovers just under 10,000 – has transformed into one of the most in-vogue holiday destinations in the world (Matt Damon has a house on the same road as Chris Hemsworth). It's certainly no longer a 'hidden' escape for those who prefer to chop their own firewood or grow their own food. Yet it's still, somehow, undeniably Byron, a place where I end up sitting cross-legged on the floor of a vegetarian restaurant at least once every time I visit.

The Northern Rivers, of which Byron is the headstone, is often referred to as the 'Rainbow Region' due to its hippie, activist roots. The Aquarius Festival (Australia's answer to Woodstock) is widely regarded as the spark that lit the fire in 1973, transforming the region from a conservative livestock area to the hessian blend it is today. But, while the hippies may have come for the socially conscious lifestyle, I would argue that it was the surfing that probably made them stay – it's certainly what helps the area stay true to its roots. For me, the blending of the activist and surf communities here is what defines this place. It's no surprise many notable surf activists, including David Rastovich, have put down roots here.

And while I'll always be drawn to the energy on shore, it was the surf that made me fall in love with Byron Bay. The right-hand point breaks produce long, tubing waves for a flotsam of local shredders, backpackers, fun boys and other floaters who blow into town with board bags. Broken Buckets – the wave made famous by Nat Young's iconic performance in *Morning of the Earth* – is highly sand-dependent but, when working, the peaks are perfect and consistent. Broken Head, just outside of Byron town, is every bit the Australian surfing dream: white sand fringed with gum trees; cool, quiet mornings punctuated by the unmistakable call of whipbirds; and electric blue A-frames up and down the entire beach.

That the points can get crowded is no surprise with such a bustling, surf-hungry town nearby. But the incredible beach breaks can be just as satisfying. The stretch from Tallows (just around the bend from Byron's famous lighthouse) to Broken Head is a treasure: 6 miles (10km) of peaks that spread the crowds and handle reasonable size. This was my haven during my month-long tenure at the Broken Head campsite as a teenager.

SAVE THE WHALES

When most Australians think of Byron, they think hippies. And while the 1973 Aquarius Festival set a flower-power tone, the town also had a short-lived flirtation with whaling. From 1954, Byron Bay's whaling company was permitted to take 150 whales per season. Declining catches had shut down local whaling by 1963, but humpbacks still pass offshore of Byron mid-year on their way to give birth in the more temperate Queensland waters, and provide primo whale-watching opportunities.

Clockwise from top left: Byron serves up some easy evening surf; Cape Byron lighthouse stands sentry over the coast; bustling Byron Bay is now an in-vogue holiday spot. Previous page: the coastline here is a surfers' paradise

The surf breaks at Lennox Head, a short way south of the Broken Head campsite, were yet another highlight along this stretch of shoreline. This was my Eden – days spent surfing and tripping over my feet at the sight of beautiful French backpackers frolicking in the shore-break. I'll never forget rounding the bend and getting a glimpse of it in full cry for the first time. The top-to-bottom tube can handle as big a cyclone as the Pacific can muster, and runs for over 300ft. It's closely guarded, though, lined with perilously slippery cobblestones (I've still got a barnacle scar on my ankle from getting pinballed through the rock garden trying to get in).

Years later, I actually ended up editing a newspaper for Byron's modern-day Aquarius, a music festival called Splendour in the Grass. In doing so, I began to see just how special Byron Bay's brand of surf bum really is. Although the bands of patchouli pioneers who moved to the area after the Aquarius Festival haven't entirely succeeded in keeping development out of the region, it remains a truly important hub for core activist surfers. In 2014, the Bentley Blockade prevented multinational gas corporation Metgasco from fracking an area just an hour inland from Byron Bay. More recently, Byron's surf-bum activists helped usher McDonalds and Club Med out of town.

Weirdly, despite soaring house prices and an increase in tourism every year, there's still an underlying vibe that feels as permanent as the reef itself. For one, Byron's protectors are tireless. But its history counts for a lot, too. Just as today's activists carry a torch lit back in the '70s, my own impressions of this place are heavily shaped by the very first time I visited. Every time I return to Byron, I'm transported back to that winter trip all those years ago.

"For me, the blending of the activist and surf communities are what defines Byron Bay"

ORIENTATION

Type of wave // Right-hand point breaks and beach breaks.
Best conditions // Austral autumn: March–May.
Nearest city // Brisbane.
Getting there // Fly to the Gold Coast (an hour from Byron) or Brisbane (two hours away) and rent a car. Brisbane has more connections.
Where to stay // Everything from five-star luxury to hostels are available in Byron Bay. If you want to splurge, stay at The Atlantic; for a more authentic experience, pitch a tent at the Broken Head campsite.
Things to know // The area around Byron Bay has waves to suit all boards, so bring whatever you like to ride the most. You're highly unlikely to need a step-up on the North Coast. The main hazard here is the crowds, and a lineup that welcomes unpredictable beginners. If the crowds get you down, emptier waves are never too far away here.

Opposite: Arugam Bay in Sri Lanka
has taken a sustainable approach to
both growth and surf tourism

MORE LIKE THIS
WAVE-RICH ECO-RETREATS

ARUGAM BAY, SRI LANKA

Arugam Bay is the most famous surf spot in Sri Lanka, and perhaps one of the best spots in all of Asia (it even holds an international comp). It was put on the map by European hippies in the '70s, but a new era was ushered in once the consistent right point in front of the village – and other quality setups in the area – were eventually discovered by surfers. The legacy of the original travellers remains strong here, though, in the form of multiple vegetarian restaurants and yoga studios, and an impressive level of environmental consciousness within the local community. To soak it all in, book a room at Surf N Sun, a beautiful, locally owned eco-lodge with onsite yoga and great food – ask the owner Saman to show you around the area in his vintage Land Rover.

Nearest town // Arugam Bay

BATU KARAS, INDONESIA

A few new pins have been dropped on the well-surfed Indonesian archipelago lately, and many are a reflection of the increasingly eco-conscious mindset of surf travellers. Whereas Indonesia was once all about the biggest, hollowest tubes, more and more visiting surfers are seeking out long, perfect, longboard-friendly right points, alongside sustainable living and local organic menus. Batu Karas has all of the above. This once sleepy village – a popular getaway for Javanese families that's pretty tough to get to – has long prioritised treading lightly on the environment, and this ethos has attracted more and more surfers over the years. Yet, it still has a stong vibe amongst locals, who come to hang on the black-sand beach and surf the fun beginner-friendly point.

Nearest town // Batu Karas

BELLINGEN, AUSTRALIA

Many say Bellingen is like Byron 30 years ago. And this cool town mid-way along the coast of New South Wales certainly shares many qualities with its cousin, four hours to the north. With a very unspoiled vibe, beautiful hinterland and powerful local activism, the only real difference is that, unlike Byron, Bellingen isn't actually on the coast. But that's not to say you can't score pumping surf here. After an easy 10-minute drive to the ocean, hook a left and take your pick: the empty beach at Bongil Bongil National Park; Sawtell's killer point break; or the dozens of spots around Coffs Harbour, including popular Diggers Beach and the legendary left point, Gallows.

Nearest town // Bellingen

SHIPSTERN BLUFF

Imagine if your home break happened to be a man-eating leviathan. Shaun Wallbank and a crew of fearless locals have somehow tamed Tasmania's most fearsome slab.

As surfers in Tasmania in the mid-1990s, we were the butt of many a joke to those who rode waves on the 'mainland' of Australia. We were teenagers at the time and cut our teeth surfing soft beach breaks around Frederick Henry Bay. Mainlanders made jibes about our weather, our water temperature, and our abundance of bad surf. In fact, one national surfing magazine even named one of our local beaches the worst surf spot on the continent.

But around the same time, we heard salty Tasmanian fisherfolk tell tales of a mythical wave at the bottom of the Tasman Peninsula, that supposedly reached 15ft or more. It broke under the shadow of Shipstern Bluff, an ancient outcrop of rock that has stood defiantly in the face of the Southern Ocean for 165 million years. To the fishers, this was a maritime hazard to be avoided at all costs, a wave that only those with a death wish would go near. But where they saw ugliness in the way this wave exploded at the base of these enormous cliffs, we pictured beauty.

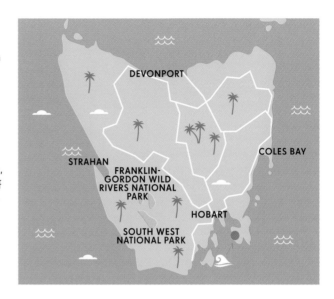

At first, discovering a 15ft reef break in known great white shark territory was like a cruel joke. Going from surfing average beach breaks to 'big waves' would be like competing in the Tour de France right after getting your training wheels off. And the power and size of the wave is remarkably apparent, even from shore. The noise of the sets sends vibrations through your chest and echoes off the cliffs.

The most defining feature of Shipstern's wave is the 'step': as long-period swell lines surge up from deep water and unload on the dolerite platforms, the waves mimic the shape of the rocky slabs below. Halfway through their short life, the waves trip on a final rise of rock and the infamous step folds and breaks mid-face. This is what sets it apart from all the other big waves in the world and makes surfing it much more difficult. It is also the reason why most surfers use straps on their boards.

When you enter the water, the energy is even more palpable. The first time I jumped off the ledge behind the break I felt glad just to have survived the leap. Paddling up behind the break, things start to get real. It often takes several sessions before a surfer dares even look over the precipice. But eventually, we all had to make a choice – to go or not to go. If we go, we have to commit – wholeheartedly commit. I remember finally making the drop, seeing a boil and a speed bump coming up. As I hit the step, I somehow hit it right, skating across the flats to line up the barrel.

A fall sends you to a place where seconds will feel like hours – you probably won't penetrate the water's surface until the wave sucks you up and you begin to feel weightless. Plunged under, your body gets ripped in every direction imaginable, all at once, as the hydraulic forces argue over who gets which limb. To this day, I'm amazed no one has died from the impact.

Shipstern is not a break you surf alone, and our crew became a tight-knit group after we decided to take it on. We were following in the footsteps of guys like Marti Paradisis – who is perhaps the first and only Tasmanian to make a career from surfing – and Andrew Campbell before him, a Tasmanian expat now living in Bali. Campbell was the first to be towed into it using a Jet Ski.

At the time, my friends and I were just finishing school, surfing as often as we could. By chance my father won a Jet Ski. Andrew began using it at Shipstern, and after that, it's all we thought about. We'd team up in pairs and meet at the Dunalley Bakery at 5am for breakfast and coffee. On one fateful morning, one of the gang (who will remain nameless) arrived at the boat ramp to launch his Jet Ski. As he jammed his pickup into reverse and looked over his shoulder, all he saw was an empty trailer. The Jet Ski lay in the bushes by the side of the highway, somewhere back near Eaglehawk.

Our crew pushed each other, competing for the biggest wave of the day, or the best barrel. When the Australian and Global Big Wave Awards finally took notice of Shipstern, we had even more incentive. As we tried to chase bigger and bigger swells the conditions we met would get worse and worse, the wind would be

Clockwise from top left: relaxing after a long day shooting the waves; Australian pro Lizzie Stokely takes on a Shipstern monster; South African pro Craig Anderson paddles out. Previous page: Australian pro Kipp Caddy at Shipstern Bluff

wrong, but we'd surf anyway – until more and more injuries crept in, some life threatening. We began to smarten up.

In the end, the excitement of surfing Shipstern Bluff was too much to keep secret, especially once the photos started getting out. Andy Irons came to town once, and surfed Shipstern with reckless abandon; it was a great inspiration to the younger chargers.

But for the most part, the nature of the wave and the weather in Tasmania have kept the masses away. Thus, relatively few people know what it's like to get barrelled at Shipstern Bluff. If you're lucky, you'll find yourself in the middle of a barrel big enough for a school bus, the view of the sea cliffs adding to the drama. Some of my greatest memories are from sessions late in the day – the 'Arvo Pulse', as we call it. These winter swells heave out of the Southern Ocean, the saltwater painfully cold and dark green, with the addition of fresh water from the surrounding estuaries. Before the sea goes from silver to black at sunset,

"The old fishermen saw ugliness in the way this wave exploded at the base of the enormous cliffs – we saw beauty"

ORIENTATION

Type of wave // Extremely dangerous right-hand slab.
Best conditions // Shipstern reaches its remarkable size in the Austral winter, and works in any tide.
Nearest town // Nubeena, though it's a small town with limited supplies. Hobart is a two-hour drive away.
Getting there // Fly into Hobart Airport, hire a car. It is a stunning 2.5 mile (4km) hike to reach the wave itself.
Where to stay // Stay in or near Hobart, where accommodation options are much more plentiful and you can easily re-supply.
Things to know // Shipstern Bluff is for advanced surfers only. Most people should be going to enjoy the view. But the hike to reach it is one of the best walks in Tasmania, along beautiful coastal cliffs, high above crashing surf. You will need to descend toward the water to get the best view of the wave.

there's a couple of hours when the waves are backlit by the setting sun, and they shine emerald green.

Recently, Shipstern Bluff was thrust into the spotlight in a way it had never been before, when Red Bull decided to hold its annual Cape Fear big-wave event here. In some ways, we felt this was antithetical to surf culture in Tasmania and the decision of whether or not to host the event was not taken lightly. We all agreed it would require a full consensus among our local crew. In the end, the idea of sharing it won out. Some of us even surfed in the event.

And while we didn't get the conditions we were ultimately hoping for, it was still a hugely positive experience. For me, personally, it was an honour to line up next to some of the best surfers in the world. Yet, for us, this wave will always be defined by the hundreds of anonymous sessions: friends pushing each other, looking out for one another, no cameras, no contests. With time, we came to tame the beast. Together, we taught ourselves to surf a wave once considered impossible.

Opposite: Eaglehawk Neck off
Pirates Bay is often firing when
Shipstern turns off – albeit with
mortal-friendly surf

MORE LIKE THIS
TASMANIA'S TOP SURF SPOTS

EAGLEHAWK NECK

Pirates Bay, an hour east of Hobart, is one of the most spectacular bays in Tasmania. Teeming with aquatic life, including frequent sightings of great white sharks, the area is renowned for its amazing fishing. While the waves are the polar opposite to those you'll find at Shipstern Bluff, the beach at Eaglehawk provides surf in opposite conditions, and in northeast weather patterns there are some nice gutter-style beach-break waves to be had, similar to those on much of the east coast of Australia. On your way for a surf grab a coffee at Cubed Espresso Bar – a renovated '50s-style caravan parked above the bay that makes one of the best coffees you'll find in the state. It's an unexpected spot for such a claim, but coupled with the ocean views from the tables, it lives up to the hype. The break is off Pirates Bay Drive before you get to Eaglehawk itself.
Nearest town // Hobart

WEDGE

As the name suggests, this break produces powerful A-frame peaks that lurch out of deep water and onto a shallow beach. Wedge works on the same conditions as Shipstern Bluff, so you'll have to make the choice of whether you want to surf or spectate. The wave is 40 minutes' drive south of downtown Hobart, so very accessible from Hobart Airport. Head down the South Arm peninsula to a large car park with a spectacular lookout, with vistas over Storm Bay and Betsey Island. As with all decent Tasmanian waves, waiting for the right conditions can be like watching paint dry, but the middle of winter presents a decent chance of success. Bring your 5mm wetsuit and head-to-toe rubber.
Nearest town // Hobart

REDBILL BEACH

Redbill is close to Bicheno, one of the prettiest towns on the east coast of Tasmania; there are signs to the beach as you get to the north end of the town. There is often a righthander off the southern end of the beach, but waves peak along the entire stretch. You'll need easterly swell and any winds from the west, but it breaks at all tides. Be wary of the rip at the southern end and, again, of great white sharks (the most recent attacks in Tasmanian waters have occurred off the east coast). Don't surf at dawn or dusk if there have been sightings. As an old whaling town, Bicheno has a rich maritime history and, as with many places in Tasmania, specialises in seafood. The area is also famous as the home of fairy penguins (look up Bicheno Penguin Tours). Wineglass Bay and the spectacular Freycinet Peninsula are also accessible from here, about 40 minutes south.
Nearest town // Bicheno

AWARUA FIORDLAND

For the settlers of a vast roadless area in New Zealand, the sea is sustenance.
Will Cockrell went in search of an adventure here, and stumbled onto surf.

My one and only truly adventurous surf trip wasn't supposed to be a surf trip at all. I was on the South Island of New Zealand, an area along the west coast known as Fiordland National Park. But the words 'national park' suggest happy hikers, interpretive signs and trails. I was in a place so remote and Jurassic-feeling it was hard to imagine any visitors, let alone surfers. There was roughly 5000 sq miles (12,950 sq km) of roadless bush between me and the nearest town, and the snowcapped Southern Alps create such a formidable barrier to the area that the best way in or out is by plane or helicopter.

I was in a large bay facing the Tasman Sea, where a wide and gentle river emerged from the forest and emptied into the salt water. It was the sort of melting pot where apex predators love to dine. The beach itself was an epically long stretch of fine sand – long enough, in fact, to land a small plane, as we had the evening before. At the far end of the beach, sand gave way to a garden of tide pools. Beyond the rock pools, I was told, there was a wave. But, as I said, this wasn't a surf trip.

I was travelling around the world with my non-surfing fiancée. Sure, I had rented a board and caught a few waves in places like Raglan and Bali's Bukit peninsula during our journey, but these sessions were more obligatory, a little bit like having a pint of Guinness in Dublin. In Fiordland, we were in search of a travel experience where a guidebook and our gadgets were useless. It was one of those ideas inspired by the most random of tips, about a place that you have to see to believe, that almost shouldn't exist in a world where the word undiscovered is an endangered species. However, the tip did come from a surfer – perhaps I should have known.

Fiordland is New Zealand's largest national park. Its claim to fame is Milford Sound, one of the country's most visited natural wonders. But beyond the well-worn tourist circuit is a rugged and vast landscape with little more than a few leftover settlers, many of whom moved into the area in the '50s and '60s in search of a new way of life. They built rustic hunting cabins and, with permission from the government, began living off the land. Anne and Mitch Mitchell did just that in the late '60s, and even went on to raise their three children here – Kelley, Grant and Warrick spent most of their childhood in Fiordland, learning to fish, hunt and dress a red deer by the time they were teenagers. Once the children had grown, the

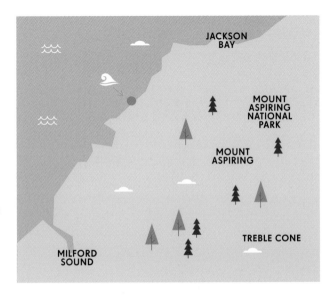

"It wasn't a lifetime of surfing that taught Warrick about the ocean, it was the ocean that taught him how to surf"

Mitchells stopped living in Fiordland full time, but returned often as stewards of the land. Warrick, in particular, made it his mission to carry on his family's legacy here, and eventually set up Awarua Guides – named for the river that flows right by the old hunting cabin. Hosting others here allows Warrick to essentially share the Fiordland lifestyle with anyone looking for a wild and immersive experience. This is exactly what my fiancée and I came for. Warrick had no idea he would eventually be specialising in surf trips.

After throwing our backpacks from the tiny plane, we jumped out onto the sand. At Warrick's suggestion, we immediately pulled nets over our heads to protect from the inevitable onslaught of midges. We had barely dropped our backpacks in the cabin when Warrick handed us wetsuits and weight belts. It was time to catch dinner. Standing chest deep in the ocean, my fiancée and I watched as Warrick plucked massive lobsters from their rocky hiding places.

The following morning, I was in a wetsuit again. Only this time, carrying a 7ft surfboard under my arm. I vaguely remember mentioning waves the night before, but more in a *'so, you get some good waves out here, eh?'* sort of way than in a *'let's go surfing'* way. Warrick, of course, heard the latter. And he didn't seem at all concerned with my abilities – we were going surfing.

Never missing an opportunity to stock the fridge, Warrick whipped a fishing rod into the river as we walked toward the point. As I hopped from rock to rock, I looked out to sea, nervously, trying to get a sense of the size. Then, with eyes back on the rocks, I stopped in my tracks. Two penguins waddled slowly past me.

Wading out through the kelp, I finally had a clear view of a shockingly good A-frame about 150ft in front of me. It was head high, but the water was glassy and the takeoff looked gentle. Beyond the kelp, we began to paddle out. Within minutes, Warrick had popped up on a righthander. After the drop, all I could see from behind the wave was the spray of his cutbacks at the lip, one after another.

Warrick is one of those rare watermen for whom it wasn't a lifetime of surfing that taught him about the ocean; it was the ocean that taught him how to surf. From a young age, he could read tides and currents well enough to harvest whatever bounty his family needed from the sea. He fished, went diving and played in the ocean constantly, sometimes riding waves in his canoe. He didn't even own an actual surfboard until he was a teenager. But the minute he took it out onto the waves, he and the board were one. His infectious enthusiasm and confidence eventually coaxed me onto a wave of my own. After making the drop, I prematurely bailed for fear of riding into the rocks.

The waves we were surfing were impressively fun. But, according to Warrick, they were often world-class here. Apparently, the deep-water A-frame where we sat keeps its shape all the way up to 15–20ft, occasionally barrelling in either direction; he also said that the river-mouth sandbar offers a completely different setup; the beach break right in front of the cabin serves up fun and accessible waves; and more river-mouth sandbars are a short helicopter ride away.

Warrick later told me how a surf guidebook called *The South Seas* described Fiordland as the 'the last frontier' – an undiscovered region that surfers don't know anything about. This, of course, amused Warrick, as he'd been surfing waves up and down the Fiordland coast for a decade.

After our session, my return trip to the cabin felt somehow different than the walk out. As time passes in Fiordland, perspective shifts dramatically. The initial rawness – the overwhelming onslaught of creatures, biting and buzzing, slimy and odd-looking, underfoot, underwater, and flying overhead – made us a little edgy. But then we began to see sustenance and harvest, and settled into the rhythm of living off the land. Hopping from slimy rock to slimy rock, I thought about which seaweeds were edible. Within 24 hours, my fiancée and I had truly settled into the magic of Fiordland, snacking on mussels we caught ourselves, feasting on lobster and venison harvested within a mile of the table we sat at, happily drinking our cans of Speights through the mesh of our head-nets.

Two years after we visited Awarua Fiordland, Red Bull dropped pro surfers Cooper Chapman, Jackson Coffey and Jordy Lawler off on Warrick's doorstep and, with his help, they captured several killer sessions in video clips titled *Surfing's Middle Earth*. Warrick says he now hosts over a dozen groups of surfers a year, including quite a few pros, and teams such as O'Neill, Billabong and Yeti. The most recent edition of *The South Seas* not only includes the Awarua area, but several of Warrick's photos from these sessions.

Interestingly, most people who come here these days have the opposite experience I did – they come for the surf and end up immersed in a masterclass in extreme foraging. Awarua leaves an impression that has become lore in the surf world. Now I'm just dying to get back for an actual surf trip.

From left: Awarua holds a few different setups, for all levels of ability; most meals are caught in the sea. Previous page, from top: Awarua's little-known A-frame has attracted some of the world's best surfers; reaching the Awarua Guides' hunting cabin requires an all-day hike or a 15-minute helicopter ride

ORIENTATION

Type of wave // Deep-water A-frame reef break, with left- and righthanders.

Best conditions // The Austral autumn, into early winter, is most consistent; mid-winter is cold, but surprisingly good.

Nearest town // Queenstown is less than 50 miles (80km) away as the crow flies – or a 15-minute helicopter ride.

Getting there // The Awarua Guides hunting cabin is accessed via helicopter from Glenorchy, near Queenstown.

Where to stay // The best way to experience and surf this part of Fiordland is riding shotgun with Warrick Mitchell. An Awarua Guides adventure (awaruaguides.com) includes a flight from Glenorchy, delicious meals and a comfy bed, either in the hunting cabin or one of his surf safari tents.

Things to know // Warrick is as much a teacher as he is a host, inviting guests to go lunging for lobster and gut fish.

*Opposite from top: the Kaikoura
coastline promises a host of wild
surf spots; the Otago Coast's
Murderers break boasts fast
barrels when it turns on*

MORE LIKE THIS
SOUTH ISLAND SWELL

KAIKOURA

The stretch of coastline around Kaikoura
is perhaps what Fiordland would look
and feel like if it had roads and towns.
Some 2½ hours north of Christchurch, on
the South Island's east coast, it is by no
means remote. It is, however, extremely
raw, a place that's rich with sea life,
large untamed swell and massive ocean
mammals. South from the tiny town of
Kaikoura lie a dozen or so of the South
Island's best breaks. Perhaps the most
popular is the right-hand point break
north of town called Mangamaunu, which
fires often and at a manageable size,
breaking into a boulder beach framed by
lush mountains. A more serious swell can
be found just a few clicks south of town at
Kahutara. This is also a right-hand point
break, but a much heavier one that comes
into its own in the colder months, and is
well over head-high.
Nearest town // Kaikoura

OTAGO COAST

Dunedin is the second largest city on New
Zealand's South Island, with a university
that gives it a young and fun vibe. The
nearby surf, however, is a more serious
matter. Diehards flock to what is known
as the Otago coast for the massive south
swells that roll through in winter. Surfers
here share the breaks with yellow-eyed
penguins, sea lions and, of course,
great whites, but the variety makes it a
popular spot even in summer. Some 25
miles (45km) north of town is a heavy and
hollow right-hand point break, Karitane,
that sits right in front of mouth of the
Waikouaiti River. About halfway between
Karitane and Dunedin is Murderers. Don't
let the name scare you: the fast right-hand
barrel breaks at manageable size, but it
needs just the right conditions to turn on.
A Mavericks-esque big wave known as
Papatowai draws big-wave surfers from
all over.
Nearest town // Dunedin

GOLDEN BAY

For a truly wild, windswept experience
without the menace of huge cold waves,
make the stunning hike out to Wharariki
Beach on the very northern tip of the
South Island. The Golden Bay area
is a rural peninsula culminating in a
conservation area full of trails, wild
beaches and inlets. It requires a 20-minute
hike to reach Wharariki Beach, adding
to its remote feel, and a surfable swell is
far from guaranteed. Nonetheless, the
setting alone makes it a popular spot. The
trail winds over hills and dunes, before
delivering you to a massive beach with
dramatic rock formations jutting up out of
the sand and the sea. And if you're lucky,
one of the several peaks along this beach
break will have enough shape to ride a
few punchy, beginner-friendly waves.
Nearest town // Nelson

TEAHUPO'O

*This infamous wave paints a picture of carnage and ferocity. Ben Mondy
instead tunes into the calm and beauty that truly defines this part of Tahiti.*

Tevi gently pushed the boat away from the jetty, cranked the five-horsepower Evinrude, and sliced into the emerald waters of the calm lagoon in front of the Vaiani pension. In the distance, where the coral reef provided the border between the lagoon and the intensely deep blue of the Pacific, I could see Teahupo'o – tiny surfers dropped into waves, disappearing and then reappearing in a thunderclap haze of white mist. More often, however, the tiny surfers rode the swells, disappeared, and then stayed that way. Teahupo'o looks as though it dips below sea level, taking the surfer with it.

But instead of motoring out to the wave, Tevi turned the tiller to the left, put the wave to our backs, and chugged serenely away from the tumult. The inner conflict was visceral. It was my first trip to Tahiti. As a dedicated surfer, Teahupo'o had been front and centre in my consciousness for as long as I could remember, be it via footage from the annual pro surfing competition or the gut-churning wipeouts ridden during an infamous swell people called Code Red. I'd always dreamed of travelling to this part of the Pacific. Could I ever surf it? Would I ever surf it? These were questions I was still asking myself as the wave retreated over my left shoulder.

Tevi sensed my torment, but semi-comforted me by explaining that this particular swell was borderline too big for even the best locals or the most experienced pros. I'd get my chance, he promised. Twenty minutes later we pulled into a pristine white-sand beach on an outlying island, or *motu*, that came complete with picnic tables. It was so stunning, I'd almost forgotten about the wave.

In minutes Tevi had filleted a tuna he'd caught that morning, washed it in the sea and marinated it with fresh lime and sea salt. Like a magician – albeit a heavily tattooed French Polynesian one –

he passed milk from a freshly hacked coconut through a muslin sieve, onto the fish. As a final flourish to this traditional meal of *poisson cru* ('raw fish'), iced bottles of local Hinano beers were produced and plates dished out. Tevi then began twanging expertly on his ukulele, singing traditional Polynesian songs in his deep timbre. 'Teahupo'o can wait, the waves will keep coming', Tevi said between verses and swigs of beer. 'For now, let's enjoy the beauty of Tahiti.'

It was a mesmerising experience and, for an hour or two, actually took my mind off my fixation with Teahupo'o. That, however, couldn't last forever, so long as I was this close to it. On the way back from our lunch Tevi asked if I wanted to just check it out, from afar. He

motored into position just a stone's throw from the pack of waiting surfers as a massive slab darkened the horizon. It was huge. Every instinct told me to get the hell out of there, but I trusted Tevi and simply clenched my ass and white-knuckled the side of the boat.

Now, one thing that makes Teahupo'o unique is that its perfection gets increasingly compressed as the waves increase in size. First surfed in the late 1980s, it was a massive wave ridden by Laird Hamilton in 2000 – known as the Millennium Wave – that ushered in a new phase of big-wave surfing. Teahupo'o's primacy as the world's heaviest and most perfect wave has been unchallenged ever since.

On most big swells, and every August for the annual professional surfing competition, the best surfers from all over the planet fly in to surf here. The tiny village of Teahupo'o is transformed from a sleepy backwater to Waterworld, as surfing's elite comes in search of death or glory – there have been plenty of both. But, in many ways, this provides a distorted view of what the real Teahupo'o experience can be. It ignores the people and the culture, and their ocean-based lifestyle. Tevi became my North Star in tuning in to the real Tahiti, which is as carefree as the wave is heavy.

Teahupo'o – which translates as 'the end of the road' – is just over an hour south of the airport in Pape'ete. Many envision Tahiti as the place where honeymooners canoodle in glass-bottomed bungalows. I, however, was staying in a small pension, run by Tevi's family, which is the far more common experience here. Family homestays are in fact the best accommodation option in Teahupo'o, as the experience adds a massive dose of local culture. I had never been treated so well and I truly felt like I had been adopted into their clan.

A LIGHTER SIDE OF TEAHUPO'O

You wouldn't think a wave of this magnitude would lend itself to stupidity, but over the years Teahupo'o has hosted some of surfing's silliest stunts. In 2012, Bruce Irons surfed (and got barrelled) at Teahupo'o completely blindfolded. In 2015 Hawaiian surfer Jamie O'Brien rode it while on fire. That same year, Robbie Maddison modified his motorcyle wheels with small planes to keep him afloat and rode his dirt bike – successfully – in 10ft swell.

Clockwise from top left: at Teahupo'o, spectating is an extreme sport; it's all about the waves in this surfing town; Tahiti's serious swell matches its mountainous interior. Previous page: Australian big-wave surfer Mark Mathews sits deep at one of the most intimidating breaks in the world

Most days were simple: shared breakfasts of fresh fruit and croissants, before the kids took the boat to school; sunset beers whilst fishing on the wharf. Tevi's eldest boys, Manoa and Matahi, would guide me on hikes to the local waterfalls, or on spearfishing missions for giant mahi-mahi.

During these diving excursions, through gin-clear waters among hyper-coloured reefs, Tevi's sons explained how, over millions of years, the river waters tumbling from the steep mountains and into the ocean had gouged a huge channel into the coral reef. And how, just beyond the coral, was a reef wall and a 150ft (46m) drop. A third of a mile (500m) further out, the sea floor fell another 1000ft (300m), and one mile (1.6km) further offshore it was at least a mile (1.6km) deep. Both keen surfers, Manoa and Matahi explained that this is what creates the wave at Teahupo'o.

After a few days when the swell had dropped slightly, Matahi and Manoa took me out to finally surf the wave. One of my revelations here was how, at a small size, I was able to truly enjoy all the perfection with none of the danger. Taking off on a 4ft wave was relatively easy if you could just avoid the distractions of the rainbow-framed mountains or the fluoro coral underneath. Every wave offered the same open tube and a relatively high chance of being spat into the safety of the deep channel.

Despite the scores of perfect waves I surfed, it was still a single wave, experienced as a spectator, that remains the highlight of the trip. I watched a tiny, brave surfer paddle into a three-storey wall of water, disappear, and then emerge with a blast of thick spray that even engulfed our boat. We were so close that the still-prone surfer high-fived Tevi as he exited the shoulder and rode into the channel. Through the falling droplets I realised it was Matahi.

Tevi later said to me: 'You are in our family now, you will keep coming back, and one day you will catch a wave like that.' He was right about the first part – the latter remains a work in progress.

"Could I ever surf it? Would I ever surf it? These were questions I was still asking myself as the wave retreated over my left shoulder"

ORIENTATION

Type of wave // A world-class lefthander that starts breaking at 3ft, but holds shape as large as 50ft.

Best conditions // Peak season is May–October, when swell is most consistent. The Teahupo'o Pro is held each August.

Nearest town // Teahupo'o is a small village that has a couple of restaurants and a little shop.

Getting there // Fly to the capital of Pape'ete, from where it's a two-hour taxi transfer to Teahupo'o.

Where to stay // Most of the accommodation is in family run pensions, while surf lodges offer bungalows and self-catering options, all within a short walk of the coast.

Things to know // It's not all death and glory here: just 10 minutes by boat from Teahupo'o are the waves Big Pass and Little Pass, both great hotdogging waves suitable for all levels. And a 20-minute drive away is Papara, which offers super fun and consistent black-sand beach breaks.

Opposite: On the quiet side of Mo'orea, Ha'apiti offers up a popular left that breaks like Teahupo'o – minus the terror

MORE LIKE THIS
TAHITI'S TOP SURF SPOTS

VAIRA'O, ITI PENINSULA

Vaira'o is aother one of Tahiti's best waves, a perfect lefthander with a steep, hollow barrel at the takeoff that is followed by a long wall. Located on the western shore of the Iti Peninsula, just north of Teahupo'o, the flawless lefts roll into the Tapuehara Pass, about 1½ miles (2.5km) offshore (so it requires boat access). There isn't a whole lot of action in the village nearby, but the wild beauty, rugged cliffs, caves, waterfalls and beautiful beaches more than make up for a lack of nightlife. The wave's consistency means that it breaks almost every day, providing plenty to feed the relatively small crowd that comes to surf here. Whilst you do need to have a certain level of skill to surf Vaira'o, it's certainly not in the same league as Teahupo'o.

Nearest town // Vaira'o

HA'APITI, MO'OREA

Located on Tahiti's neighbouring island of Mo'orea, Ha'apiti is another reef-pass lefthander that comes without the terror of Teahupo'o. At head-high, it's an easy takeoff to a very long wall that hugs the curve of the coral reef – and at this size, even beginners and intermediates can get a first taste of Tahitian coral juice. Located on the quiet southwest coast of Mo'orea, away from the bigger hotels and resorts, Ha'apiti is a surf town where the local grocery store and bakery are the communal hubs, and surf camps are the most common accommodation options. Crowds will be an issue when the waves get good, but the vibe is friendly and there are usually enough waves to go around. Mornings are the best bet as the afternoon sea breezes can affect wave quality.

Nearest town // Ha'apiti

TEMA'E, MOOREA

Adjacent to the Mo'orea airport and Sofitel resort, Tema'e is a famous yet fickle righthander that, unlike many of Tahiti's premier waves, breaks close to shore. When there isn't any swell, the white-sand beaches and beautiful lagoon provide great swimming and snorkelling. However, when a big south swell makes it to this protected section of the reef, it bursts to life and provides some of the best and heaviest waves on the planet. A series of backdoor sections grow bigger and shallower as the wave wraps down the line, with huge tubes on offer. The wave is onshore in the prevailing trade winds, making it a rare jewel and one coveted by the local surfers who wait months for it to turn on. As with Teahupo'o, a level of expertise and courage is needed to surf Tema'e, but those that do count it as one of the most memorable experiences of their surfing life.

Nearest town // Tema'e

RAGLAN

When Will Bendix pulled up beside this famously long lefthander on New Zealand's
North Island, his Kiwi road trip came to a very sudden stop – a week-long stop.

When my partner Hannah and I set off on a circumnavigation of New Zealand's North Island, we packed a couple of boards *just in case*. But we had decided we didn't want our route to be dictated by swell charts, as was usually the case. We had hired a self-contained camper van and wanted to go wherever the road took us. Well, as it turned out, that was straight to Raglan.

Two hours south of Auckland, New Zealand's most iconic wave has drawn surfers to its perfectly manicured walls since the 1960s, after it first appeared in Bruce Brown's classic surf flick *The Endless Summer*. With 10,000 miles (16,000km) of coastline and constant exposure to swell from both the Tasman Sea and Pacific Ocean, it was inevitable that the country would harbour a world-class wave or two. And there it was, the goofy-foot answer to Bruce's Beauties.

Raglan is far from New Zealand's only world-class wave, however. Both coastlines are riddled with high-quality surf – you'll find everything from the fun beach breaks of the Coromandel Peninsula to the epic reefs of Gisborne and the endless points of Northland. But with its easy access and reliable conditions, Raglan remains the perfect place to orientate yourself.

New Zealand itself was created 100 million years ago when it broke away from the Gondwana supercontinent and drifted off

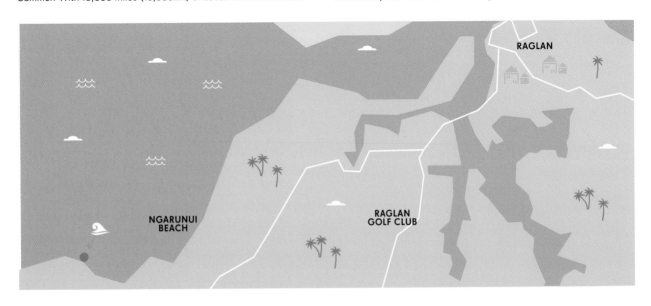

*Above, from left: Ngarunui Beach is one of many great surf spots between
the town and the famous lefthander; the endless lefts of Raglan; the wave is a
longboarder's dream. Previous page: all types of boards are welcome at Raglan*

like two pieces of an ancient jigsaw puzzle. In Māori mythology,
however, it was the demigod Māui who brought the North and
South Island into being. Māui caught a fish as big as an island,
which his older brothers helped haul to the surface. The brothers
were supposed to wait until the god of the sea had been appeased
before cutting up the gigantic fish, but they grew impatient and
began to carve out pieces for themselves. These became the
valleys, mountains, lakes and rocky coastlines of the North Island,
which is still known to the Māori as Te Ika a Māui, or Māui's fish.

The brothers must have scooped out a few extra bits around
State Highway 23, where our van lurched from side to side as we
traversed a series of twisting hairpin bends. After leaving the sprawl
of Auckland behind, the landscape shifted from rolling farmland to
the lush, forested hills of the Waikato District. Our van hugged a
steep cliff along the final stretch of road before a deep bay came
into view below us. The first thing we noticed were the lines of swell
piled up to the horizon.

The next thing we noticed was the line of campervans, piled up
along the rocky headland. Raglan is actually divided into three
bays that lie southwest of its small town: Indicators, furthest south;
Whale Bay; and finally Manu Bay, closest to town. Locals claim that
on legendary days, you can ride a wave all the way through – a
distance that made my knees quiver just looking at it.

We pulled into the car park where vintage kombis sat alongside
state-of-the-art behemoths. Kiwis and foreigners milled about
their vehicles, or lounged on the strip of grass separating the car

park from the rocky shore, chatting and watching the water. The
gently peeling 3ft waves were all the motivation we needed and we
scrambled for our boards.

While hastily screwing my fins in I heard someone ask 'what's
that you're riding there?' I turned around to see a man who looked
to be in his mid-50s with a mane of shoulder-length white hair. He
was holding a sleek fish with wooden-keel fins under his arm, which
explained why my stubby surf craft had caught his eye. I handed
my board over to him to have a look. He sized it up, giving an
approving nod. 'Looks like fun out there, should get even better on
the low', he said. 'See you in the water, mate.'

Despite the flotilla of shortboarders, loggers, Mal-riders and fish
aficionados, the atmosphere in the lineup was similarly amicable.
Parents called their kids into waves. Friends hooted each other
on during the sets. The biggest threat was the risk of getting run
over by an unwieldy novice, or entering or exiting the water via the
slippery boulders that line the shore. The standout was our new
acquaintance, who flowed effortlessly through the crowd as he
carved graceful lines on his twin-fin.

The following morning, when the surf pushed to 6ft, the wave took
on a different persona. The longer period heft in the swell kicked the
back ledge into gear, throwing up heaving barrels over a shallow
rock shelf that drained for 150ft at a time before opening up into a
high-performance wall. The pecking order also became more clearly
defined, with a solid contingent of local tube-hounds dominating the
sets on the outside. Not many waves went unridden.

"There are less crowded lineups, for sure. But it was an ideal place to feel the pulse of the New Zealand surfing experience"

Somehow, I found myself still out there at dusk in a rising swell. Unfamiliar with the lineup and afraid of getting obliterated by a set wave, I drifted deeper and deeper out to sea, until the impending dark forced me to suck it up and catch an uneventful wave in, along with a newfound respect for Manu Bay.

Our home for the following week became the basic Te Kopua Whanau campsite near town, where the sliding door of our van opened onto the back of a sprawling estuary. Days were measured by the rhythm of the waves, as we surfed, meandered around Raglan and decided on the best time to have our first sundowner (around 5.30pm, it turned out).

At night we'd alternately listen to rain pouring down on the roof of our camper van or the choir of insects. But the mornings were always the same: a light offshore wind funnelled down the valley, brushing the ocean into textured lines.

We looked at Whale Bay and Indicators many times, and yet always found ourselves drawn back to Manu Bay. The car park became the small world around which we orbited, meeting Kiwis and fellow travellers from around the world, revelling in the convivial atmosphere and user-friendly waves. There are far less crowded lineups, to be sure, but it was an ideal place to feel the pulse of the Kiwi surfing experience.

Finally, the swell went flat and we reluctantly pointed the nose of our van inland to continue our New Zealand adventure. This wasn't a surf trip, after all, and there was much of Māui's fish left to explore.

ORIENTATION

Type of wave // Rocky left-hand point break.
Best conditions // Raglan works through the tides, but Indicators and Manu Bay typically prefer the low tide. The famous left gets swell year-round, with March–May the most pleasant months for good waves.
Nearest town // Raglan, approximately 5 miles (8km) east.
Getting there // Raglan is a two-hour drive south of Auckland.
Where to stay // There are several backpacker places and high-end lodges close to the waves around Whale Bay and Manu Bay, but limited options for camper vans. There are two nearby campsites – Raglan Holiday Camp has fully serviced amenities, while Te Kopua Whanau is bare bones.
Things to know // If Raglan gets too crowded, head out onto the coastline south along State Highway 45. Littered with waves, it's not called the 'Surf Highway' for nothing.

Opposite: New Zealand pro
Mischa Davis surfs a Raglan-esque
lefthander at Shipwreck Bay

MORE LIKE THIS
NORTH ISLAND CLASSICS

SHIPWRECK BAY

Some 180 miles (290km) north of Auckland, near the township of Ahipara, lies Shipwreck Bay and a series of excellent sand-bottom left points that can deliver some of the longest waves in New Zealand on their day. Like Raglan, the wave is split into a series of breaks and features a mellower inside point called Wrecks, as well as a more challenging outside point known as The Peak. The Wreck is closest to town and easy to access, but you'll need a 4WD to get to The Peak, or be prepared for a long walk. Being further north, the water is typically warmer and the climate borders on sub-tropical, with endless sand dunes stretching up the 90-mile-long (145km) beach. The downside is Shipwreck Bay needs a pretty big swell to break and is a rare occurrence – Raglan will typically break more times in a week than Shipwreck Bay will in an entire month.

Nearest town // Ahipara

THE RAGLAN BAR

A series of shifting sandbanks make up the Raglan Bar, located at the entrance to Whaingaroa Harbour on the opposite side of Manu Bay. When the elements all align, the sandbanks link up to create an incredible righthander that spins off for ages with barrels galore. It's also far less crowded than its famous cousin across the bay. But the wave comes with a few caveats: it's fickle and breaks far out to sea with torrential rip currents, thanks to water moving in and out of the harbour mouth. Having a boat to get to and from the lineup is strongly advised, and you need to be aware of your surroundings and know what you're doing. The quality of the wave also depends on the tide, with incoming tides optimal. On the right conditions the Bar can hold up to 12ft, but is for intermediate to expert surfers only.

Nearest town // Manu Bay

MATAKANA ISLAND

Matakana Island is home to a series of world-class beach breaks that lie just off the tip of the Mt Maunganui peninsula on the North Island's east coast. To get there, you have to take your own boat or catch a ferry across from the mainland. Paddling across on a surfboard is strictly prohibited, but you are allowed to use a kayak. Matakana's glorious peaks come alive in a good northeast swell and have been ridden regularly since the 1970s, when legendary Kiwi surfer Kevin Jarrett transported himself and a couple of friends to the wave in his family's commercial fishing boat, where they revelled in the powerful lefts and rights. Even today, Matakana retains the feeling of a pristine paradise. There are only about 250 residents, no shops or restaurants, and thick pine forests cover the island from end to end.

Nearest town // Tauranga

VANIMO

In the far reaches of Papua New Guinea, rideable waves are not guaranteed. But Beau Flemister found a place where the swell is so good, an entire village has picked up surfing.

Maybe it was the bloodstains – the dozens of coagulated, Pollock-esque patterns spattered randomly about the dusty street. Or maybe it was the woman's facial clan tattoos. Perhaps it was the girl in line behind me at the market who stood in disbelief as she touched the sunbleached hairs on my arm, while staring at my face. I just kept asking myself: 'where the hell am I?'

I was in Vanimo, the only real town of the Sandaun Province in far northwest of Papua New Guinea. Our handler-host, Steve, intercepted us from the airstrip, swinging us by the market for a few bags of rice and other supplies. En route to the village, he gestured across the bay to a point. 'There's the left', he said. 'It's

breaking good today.' Even from so far away, I could see uniform lines of whitewater thundering into a wide open channel. 'Lido village is on a point', he continued, 'so, if it's not offshore on the left, it will be on the right.'

Through the car window, I watched women sitting in roadside lean-tos selling T-shirts and sarongs. Dozens of men milled around, as per the other listless Pacific outposts I'd visited before. Oh, and it turns out the 'blood' wasn't blood at all – it was betel-nut spit; chewing the nuts is a nationwide habit that quells hunger, offers a decent high and, frankly, turns the local smile into a horror show.

I was straight out of college and high on getting lost. I wanted to find surf somewhere where no one could tell me much about

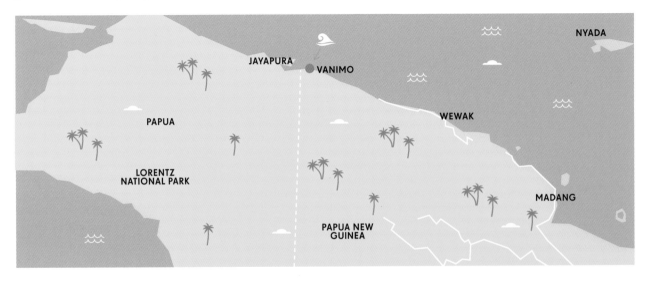

A PNG PORTRAIT

In 2010, filmmaker and surfer Adam Pesce visited and lived in Lido village near Vanimo while shooting the acclaimed documentary, *Splinters*, a poignant picture of indigenous surfing in Papua New Guinea. Focusing on various local surf stars in Lido, and the events leading up to the inaugural National Surfing Championships, *Splinters* – which was released in 2011 – examines gender, tradition, and the complex effect surfing has had on village life in Papua New Guinea.

"One local woman apparently had the gift of being able to call in big waves during storms (and cast spells on rival clans)"

it, where the coastline was ample and guidebooks slim. I wanted Melanesia: the deepest, most mysterious part of the South Pacific. For this sort of adventure, I felt like I needed an able and equally curious travel companion. With paws for hands from decades of swinging a hammer, my dad wasn't computer savvy, but would be far more useful than me doing just about anything else. He'd spent over half his life building houses and was a competent free diver and spear fisherman; I could find airfare deals on Kayak and calculate exchange rates. I thought we would make a good team.

Somehow, I'd found the contact for the 'President of the Surfing Association of Papua New Guinea'. Andy Abel, a local Papuan surfer who'd been educated in Australia, was spearheading surf clubs in various regions of the country in order to generate surf tourism. But unlike the normal Westerner-run models, he was trying to put the power in the local community's hands. No easy task as tribal differences, if not outright war, were still rife here.

We'd met Andy in Port Moresby the day before, and couldn't wait to leave the place. It seemed every shop, home and structure in the capital was barricaded in razor wire and broken glass to fend off the notorious 'raskols' – a relatively adorable term for armed thugs – that wreak havoc in the nation's larger towns. Andy was visiting Vanimo to discuss building a surf camp, so we rolled with him.

After landing in Vanimo two hours later, we were twisting down the sandy lanes of Lido village. The payoff to our journey would soon become apparent: Lido's incredible righthander, as well as the powerful left we'd watched peeling into the bay, would offer multiple sessions every day, certainly keeping us busy – if not exhausted – for the following couple of months.

Pops and I were prepared to camp in the yard during our stay, but Steve was gracious enough to rent my dad and me a room in his simple thatched-roof family home. We stayed long enough to settle into the rhythms of village life, but we were still way out of our comfort zone. In Lido, toddlers could wield a blade far more nimbly that we could, as well as gut and scale fish far faster, paddle the lagoons in dugout canoes, and even start a fire sans matches. We watched 5 year-olds climb coconut trees and deftly hack open the nut with a machete in less than five swipes. We watched adolescents craft slingshots from a tree branch and discarded tyre tube, hit a fruit bat out of a tree, then cook it on a spit and eat it.

While my dad could fish and do a little handiwork in the village homes, I managed to save a shred of dignity by surfing halfway decently, which in Lido actually gave you some clout. Thanks to Andy and the SAPNG, there was a hidden, hungry surf culture among locals who had two magnificent waves on their doorstep.

From left: aerials on the Lido wave; Vanimo has a rich cultural heritage; celebrations by the sea in Lido. Previous page: Lido's waves still inspire a sense of discovery

At times (usually after school or when folks came back from their gardens) it felt like the whole village was in the water. Over the years, returning Westerners left their surfboards, while Andy had also wrangled donated ones from his contacts in Australia and beyond.

Naked toddlers caught the end-section whitewater on broken yellowed boards, women in rashguards and boardshorts sat out on the inside peak. Local heavies like Eskelly and Angelus sat deep and outside, ruling the lefthander. They were also some of the few men in Lido that had travelled beyond PNG to surf contests like the Pacific Games, perhaps the ultimate reward in this far-flung scene – if you surfed well enough, you had the rare chance to travel outside of the region.

We stayed at Steve's home for almost two months. But just when I thought we were finally blending in, I noticed a small boy gathering up my toenail clippings and inspecting each one in wonder like a scientist. We got to talking with some of the elders, who told tales of people belly-surfing on sago-palm rafts around these parts hundreds of years ago, and that there was still a woman who apparently had the gift of being able to call in big waves during storms (and cast spells on rival clans). 'But these days', said the old man, very seriously, 'with no tribes fighting around here, the spells are just used during soccer games.'

ORIENTATION

Type of wave // Lido's Left is a consistent, often overhead left-hand reef break; Lido Right is a right-hand reef break.
Best conditions // Lido Left is best with offshore winds on a mid tide. Lido Right needs dead winds (common in February), a mid tide and a larger swell to break. November to April see the most swell.
Nearest town // Vanimo, the capital of the Sandaun Province, is a 15-minute drive from Lido.
Getting there // Fly into PNG's capital, Port Moresby, catch a domestic flight to Vanimo. Or, from Indonesia's Jayapura, take a taxi to the border (1½ hours), followed by another hour-long drive to Vanimo.
Where to stay // Vanimo Surf Lodge, a SAPNG-sanctioned accommodation.
Things to know // Leaving a surfboard here when you leave is a classy move.

Opposite from top: arriving in Santa Isabel, Solomon Islands; Surfing Association of Papua New Guinea president Andy Abel surfs Tupira

MORE LIKE THIS
REMOTE SOUTH PACIFIC SURF

KAVIENG, PAPUA NEW GUINEA

Far-flung and idyllic, in the remote province of New Ireland off the coast of mainland Papua New Guinea, the sleepy town of Kavieng has been hosting intrepid surfers looking to escape the crowds for the last 20 years. Specifically, at the Nusa Island Retreat, a pricier (compared to Vanimo) eco-lodge with a handful of overwater and beachfront bungalows that are just a short boat transfer from several reef breaks. While not quite as consistent as the swell-magnet coast of Vanimo, Kavieng still has hollow peaks like Nago Rights and Nago Lefts, as well as softer, user-friendly waves like the wally right known as Long Longs. With world-class fishing and diving, plus kayaking and village tours, Kavieng is adventure with a dash of accessibility.

Nearest town // Kavieng

TUPIRA, PAPUA NEW GUINEA

Who would've thought that you'd ever see a WSL-sanctioned event run in sleepy Papua New Guinea. But in 2017, thousands of local spectators around Madang watched just that during the inaugural Kumul PNG World Longboard Championships at Tupira Beach. Offering a fantastic, reef-bottomed, hollow righthander at Ulingan Bay in front of the village of Tupira, the peak is a short paddle from shore with no boats required. The wave (and lack of crowds) are sanctioned by the Surfing Association of Papua New Guinea – like Vanimo – and the Tupira Surf Club runs the basic surf camp closest to the break. With one of the longer paved roads (in the entire nation) running along the coast, it's relatively easy to explore in these parts, and to check other breaks and points should you get bored with the one right out front.

Nearest town // Tupira

SANTA ISABEL PROVINCE, SOLOMON ISLANDS

The infrastructure in Papua New Guinea may be pretty basic, but the neighbouring Solomon Islands has half as many paved roads. But perhaps that kind of remoteness is exactly what you're after. If so, the far safer and little visited Solomon Islands – specifically, Papatura Island in Isabel Province – has a surf retreat that's located a short boat ride from a handful of epic tropical reef breaks. Receiving swell from the north, most consistent from November through April, and breaking mostly over shallow coral reef, the spots around Santa Isabel aren't normally larger than 6ft and offer waves for a wide array of skill levels, from cruisey longboard waves like Donuts, to more hollow, intense waves like Anchovies. The major allure, of course, is surfing with only the crew you came with. That, and the utterly world-class fishing, snorkelling and, most unforgettably, the Solomon Islanders themselves.

Nearest town // Suavanao

INDEX

Epic Surf Breaks of the World
August 2020
Published by Lonely Planet Global Limited
CRN 554153
www.lonelyplanet.com
10 9 8 7 6 5 4 3 2 1

Printed in Malaysia
ISBN 978 17886 8650 1
© Lonely Planet 2020
© Photographers as indicated 2020

Managing Director, Publishing Piers Pickard
Associate Publisher Robin Barton
Commissioning Editor Will Cockrell
Art Director Daniel Di Paolo
Designer Kristina Juodenas
Picture Research Ceri James
Editors Polly Thomas, Clifton Wilkinson
Print Production Nigel Longuet

Lonely Planet Offices

Australia
The Malt Store, Level 3,
551 Swanston St, Carlton, Victoria 3053
T: 03 8379 8000

USA
Suite 208, 155 Filbert Street,
Oakland, CA 94607
T: 510 250 6400

Ireland
Digital Depot, Roe Lane (off Thomas St),
Digital Hub, Dublin 8,
D08 TCV4

Europe
240 Blackfriars Rd,
London SE1 8NW
T: 020 3771 5100

STAY IN TOUCH lonelyplanet.com/contact

Authors Al Mackinnon, Alan van Gysen (story first published in *White Horses* magazine: www.whitehorses.com.au), Alastair Klinkenberg,
Alex Wade, Alf Alderson, Andy Davis. Beau Flemister, Ben Mondy, Brendan Buckley, Chas Smith, Chris Burkhard, Chris Dixon, Chris Nelson,
Greg Long , Jade Bremner, Jaimal Yogis, Jake Howard, Jamie Brisick, Janna Irons, Kitt Doucette, Matt Pruett, Nicholai Lidow, Paul Evans,
Ricardo Bravo (story first published in *White Horses* magazine: www.whitehorses.com.au), Sam Haddad, Scott Hulet, Scott Yorko, Shaun
Wallbank, Stuart Butler, Will Cockrell, Will Bendix, William Finnegan. **Cover and illustrations** by Ross Murray (www.rossmurray.com).